to be real

Telling the Truth and
Changing the Face
of Feminism

ANCHOR BOOKS
NEW YORK   LONDON
TORONTO   SYDNEY   AUCKLAND

to be real

EDITED AND WITH AN INTRODUCTION BY

rebecca walker

An Anchor Book

Published by Doubleday
a division of Bantam Doubleday Dell
Publishing Group, Inc.
1540 Broadway, New York, New York
10036

Anchor Books, Doubleday, and the
portrayal of an anchor are trademarks of
Doubleday, a division of Bantam
Doubleday Dell Publishing Group, Inc.

Acknowledgments for individual essays
appear on pages 291–92

Book design by Jennifer Ann Daddio

Library of Congress
Cataloging-in-Publication Data

To be real : telling the truth and changing
the face of feminism / edited and with an
introduction by Rebecca Walker.
p.   cm.
1. Feminism—United States.   2. Feminist
theory.   3. Feminist psychology—United
States.   I. Walker, Rebecca.
HQ1426.T623   1995
305.42—dc20   95-14412
CIP

ISBN 0-385-47261-7
0-385-47262-5 (paperback)

First Anchor Books Edition:
November 1995

10   9   8   7   6

For all the aunts, keepers, and teachers who helped
to raise me up:

Mrs. Cornelius, Grandma Miriam,
Louisa Floyd "Patchogue,"
Mimi Hunt and Debbie Perez,
Auntie Ruth and Uncle Bobby, Judy,
Susan Howard, Cyntharee Powells,
Henri, Gene Mattingly, and
Ms. Spilken

and

for my father

Editor's Acknowledgments

The process of editing an anthology is perhaps the most arduous and painstaking process I have ever known, primarily because there are so many factors beyond the editor's control. Learning to have faith in that lack of control was perhaps the greatest gift this book could have given me. Accordingly, my gratitude goes first to the great Universe, who supports and guides, and never makes it harder than it needs to be. Martha Levin, who gave me the opportunity to share my thoughts with so many, and Wendy Weil, agent extraordinaire, also have my enduring gratitude. I extend the same and more to Gloria Steinem, bell hooks, and especially my mama, Alice Walker, for giving me the legs on which I stand.

Thanks, too, to Catherine McKinley for crucial sistahly support; Donna Minkowitz for sharing her affinity for the dangerous meld of good and evil; Gregoriah Tate for general uplift and all those long talks about the title; Bennett Singer for the late-night, to-the-wire, superb editing he provided on many of these pieces; Angela Davis, for taking the time to lend her thoughts and voice; and my dad, Mel Leventhal, for giving me an office in which to write the proposal.

Thanks are also due to my editor at Anchor Books, Arabella Meyer, who graciously buffered me from pressure while pushing me forward; to Cathy Arnwine, who typed and transcribed quickly and well; to Candida Alvarez, who visited and dreamed of the sea with me; and to Trajal Harrell, who helped me to transform fear into strength. Special shouts to the SPY Management posse for their excellent management of all things public and publicitous; the Women in Love congregation for the music and the dream; the Board of 3WAVE for much-needed patience and understanding; and Omar Wasow and New York Online for making technology work for me.

For the strength and courage they gave me, I thank the beautiful, strong, and inspirational young women and men on college campuses across the country who came out to hear and talk with me, and all of the writers who contributed to this book, those included and those not: thank you for sharing what was so hard to share, thank you for sharing your lives.

Finally, I thank my very own Angel, without whose love, insight, encouragement, and unbounded support this book might never have been born. Lovey, I am forever in your debt.

Contents

Foreword

gloria steinem

Here is a room with ten people in it: a white married couple, both lawyers in their twenties, wearing jeans and carrying briefcases. A tall black man in a suit who runs an urban antipoverty organization. A round ladylike executive in a print dress, her Irish face set off by pearls, and a still rounder black woman editor in a tunic. Three youngish women: a tall white one in fatigues and a T-shirt bearing a lesbian slogan, an elegant television director of Japanese ancestry, and an alabaster-skinned, titian-haired woman in a transparent blouse who looks as sexy as the surveys she conducts. Standing near a tableful of food, there is a white writer with long hair and a short skirt, and an energetic, thirtyish black woman in a maid's uniform complete with frilly apron.

The question is: *who is the feminist?* (Try to answer before looking at the next line.)

The answer: *all of them.* (Be honest. Which ones didn't fit your expectation?)

In my experience, feminists as human beings have always been contrary to popular expectation—and to most unpopular ones, too. I was the writer in the short skirt, and I remember this gathering of twenty-two years ago because Carolyn Reed, the woman in the maid's uniform, had brought some friends and activists together to work on household workers' rights, and she used our very diversity to instruct us in the tyranny of expectation. Just as outsiders might assume the only feminist in the room was the white woman in fatigues (she was Jill Johnston, an activist, art critic, columnist, and author of *Lesbian Nation*), or that the conventionally dressed woman in pearls couldn't be a feminist (though she was Patricia Carbine, the publisher of *Ms.* Magazine), Carolyn explained that household workers had also been stereotyped; in their case, as ashamed of their work, not skilled enough to deserve good pay, too divided to organize, probably victims, and definitely not feminists. Indeed, they were assumed to be exploited by feminists, since women working outside the home must be exploiting those in it; a sort of economic version of two-women-can't-get-along. (Interesting, isn't it, that capitalists are praised for creating jobs, but women who create jobs at home are not?) That's why Carolyn and her sister workers had founded the National Committee on Household Employment: to professionalize this work, press for good pay and conditions, reinvent uniforms as badges of honor, and solve what turned out to be the real problem with feminist employers. Because they felt guilty about hiring other women to do the tasks for which they themselves had been so devalued, they often refused to create jobs, or didn't include household employment issues in their organizing. This meeting was the beginning of a household workers' campaign to explain that child care and housekeeping were at least as rewarding as most of what goes on in offices and factories—providing they were well-paid and respected.

It was efforts like these that eventually got both employers and employees to sign a pledge—good pay and other rights on one hand, job responsibilities on the other—though even the minimum wage didn't then apply to household workers.[1] In the end, such efforts created a coalition that helped to get household workers covered by basic labor laws. Carolyn and her colleagues had built a bridge between employers and employees by explaining that child rearing and work in the home were valuable, whether done by homemakers *or* paid household workers; thus all women would benefit if its value were recognized. By using a feminist paradigm of *and* instead of the patriarchal *either/or*—which is rooted in the daddy of all polarized thinking, the division of human nature into "masculine" and "feminine"—this process became an early step in the international effort to attribute an economic value to all productive work, whether done by unpaid homemakers in overdeveloped countries, or unpaid women who grow food for their families in underdeveloped ones.[2]

But that meeting took place in the 1970s. By the 1980s, the stereotype of an unkempt, probably lesbian white feminist with no children had been joined by the equally limited image of an elegantly suited, well-kempt, professional white woman with a briefcase that sometimes turned into a child or a vacuum cleaner. Created by advertisers who assumed women were the only buyers of home products, but who added suits and briefcases to capture women who also worked outside the home (thus ignoring the fact that most women are in pink-collar professions with neither suits nor briefcases), this Super Woman image might have added one or two more to the number of perceived feminists in that early room. (For instance, Brenda Feigen a legislative activist who, though wearing jeans, at least had a briefcase.) But it still would have excluded the three women of color, even though they were feminist pioneers (editor Margaret Sloan-Hunter, a founder of the National Black Feminist Organization, and Joan Shigekawa, a filmmaker who produced "Woman Alive!" an early documentary series, not to mention Carolyn Reed). It definitely excluded men, no matter what they had done (lawyer Marc Fasteau was the author of *The Male Machine,* an early feminist case for humanizing the male role, and Franklin Thomas, a pioneer of gender equality in antipoverty programs, who later led the Ford Foundation to its major support of women's projects, here and internationally).

As for sexy women like the one in the transparent blouse (Shere Hite, author of *The Hite Report on Female Sexuality* and *The Hite Report on Men and Male Sexuality*), they became even less likely to be counted as feminists. Given labels like "puritanical" and "anti-sex" that the mainstream soon invented for women who wanted the right to be sexual without hurt or humiliation—who separated sexual harassment from mutual attraction, for instance, or pornography from erotica—the popular stereotype of a feminist gradually excluded any woman who enjoyed sex, or even looked sexual. (An asexual stereotype that is still powerful, as you can see from younger contributors here who may assume mutually contradictory things about earlier feminists—that they were "into power" or "into poverty," impossibly strong or victims—but who can't seem to imagine them being sexual at all.) The main reason was (and still is) clear: a male-dominant culture makes dominance so synonymous with sex that those who reject the first are seen as rejecting the second. In my experience, even wearing a short skirt was supposed to be odd, and elicited anti-feminist questions about this "contradiction." In fact, feminism has always stood for the right to bare, decorate, cover, enjoy, or do whatever we damn please with our bodies—and to do so in safety—yet the female body used to blame the rape victim ("Why was she dressed like that?") is also used to blame the feminist ("Why was she dressed like that?").

If anything, the idea that there is or ever was one "right" way to be a feminist has become more prevalent in the 1990s. For one thing, this movement against the sexual caste system has grown so large that its diversity can no longer be represented in one room, as it sometimes was in the 1970s, when there were only a few hundred "crazy feminists" in each town. (When a 1995 Harris poll asked Americans if they considered themselves "feminist" by the dictionary definition, seventy-one percent of women and sixty-one percent of men said yes.) As a result, people working on equality now are much more likely to come together around a particular issue, profession, or shared experience, and thus to be vulnerable to the idea that the mythical movement of "real" feminists is somewhere else. Though the media aren't the whole problem, as Rebecca Walker points out in her introduction, this specialization does make us more vulnerable to believing media stereotypes of others, from such ultra-right-wing images as "femi-Nazis" or "antifamily" to mainstream media labels like "white-middle-class," "there-are-no-young-feminists," and those mutually contradictory ideas, "victim feminism" and "power feminists." (In fact, most feminists are married with children, a 1986 poll showed "nonwhite" women to be three times more likely than white women to consider themselves "strong feminists," and women under thirty are more likely to call themselves feminists, according to that 1995 Harris poll, than are women over thirty.[3] As for wanting to be victims, women have always been praised more for singing the blues than songs of triumph, but that's among the gender problems feminism is trying to solve.)

To complicate all of the above, there is now a majority of feminists who didn't experience those rooms of the 1970s and 1980s. In my generation, we came to feminism as adults. Our revelations came from listening to one anothers' very different lives, discovering shared themes, realizing we were neither crazy nor alone, and evolving theories as peers. The result was a long and organic process that felt like rebirth, as if we were inventing ourselves and feminism. Most of the contributors to this book had a very different experience. They were born into a culture with many images of feminism, or they came to it young via the media and books, existing groups and women's studies, teachers, parents, and siblings. Metaphorically, it's as if each of the ten people in that original room had borne children, raised them in different parts of the world, watched them absorb different versions of events in the room from those who were and weren't in it, and now, this new generation is also responding to the need to invent itself both with the approval of the world and in the hope of changing it.

I give you this handy room-sized metaphor for the recent feminist past for several reasons. First, I hope it shows that the problem of perception this anthology addresses is long-standing: a narrow stereotype has always eliminated most of the people in the room. By putting names and faces on some of those who were obscured, even in one room in the prebacklash 1970s, I hope you will consider the tragic loss if the diversity in these pages is not also honored. Second, I want to remind readers who are younger or otherwise new to feminism that some tactical and theoretical wheels don't have to be reinvented. You may want to make them a different size or color, put them on a different wagon, use them to travel in a different direction, or otherwise make them your own—but many already exist. To find them, talk to people who were in those past rooms, preferably *before* doing your computer search into media sources of what did or did not happen there. Trust people over paper. Finally, I want to prepare longtime feminists, women and men, for the inspiration and anger, déjà vu and excitement, frustration and hope they will find mixed in these pages; all the things one should expect from a smart, fractious, loving, diverse, intimate, and very big family. After all, it will take a while before feminists succeed enough so that feminism is not perceived as a gigantic mother who is held responsible for almost everything, while the patriarchy receives terminal gratitude for the small favors it bestows. This is true not only because there is a double standard, but also because feminism inspires hope. And hope is a very unruly emotion.

In the middle of "Pushing Away the Plate," for instance, a wonderfully observed essay by Min Jin Lee about her life as a young lawyer, I found myself talking back to the page about her belief that having it all means *doing* it all, a thesis she assumes is feminist. "Ladies, did I miss your point?" she asks of her feminist elders, and I want to shout, "Yes!" What about the two or three decades of feminist demands (still ongoing, and with at least a few successes) for changed work patterns to accommodate *both* parents of young children? Whatever happened to protesting against the fact that this country is the only industrialized democracy in the world without a national system of child care? Or to the belief that men should be as responsible for raising children and doing housework as women are? I understand that women's double role is a clear marker of where we are right now: many women are becoming the men we wanted to marry, but few men are becoming the women *they* wanted to marry. Thus, middle-class women now have two jobs, just as poor women always did—which is why we should be able to do something about it. But change has to be envisioned before it can begin. Otherwise, we get stuck in the self-doubt that the status quo imposes, thus causing us to blame ourselves instead of it.

At least Super Woman was a creation of traditionalists, however, movement terms like *identity politics* have also acquired odd images in a generation of translation and backlash. Several writers here assume the goal of identity politics is division, as if doing away with adjectives would magically bring about integration and a shift in power. In fact, some degree of pride in identity has been necessary to the empowerment of every wave of immigrants: part of a process that eventually allows integration without re-creating hierarchy. It's interesting that such groups as Jews, Italians, and the American Medical Association are not said to be practicing *identity politics* when they self-identify and organize. Like *politically correct, identity politics* seems to be a term reserved for the less powerful— which is exactly why it is ridiculed and suspect. From Black Power to Gay Power, the goal is not to perpetuate difference, but to protest the invisibility, suppression, and political uses of difference. If biology were the basis of feminism, we wouldn't need the term *feminist* to indicate belief in equality among both women or men. As June Jordan wrote:

There is difference and there is power.
And who holds the power decides the meaning
of the difference.[4]

Some contributors also feel criticized by analyses of the inherited or chosen institutions in which they find themselves. Just as some homemakers were made to feel defensive when an earlier generation of feminists pointed to the lack of reward and respect for homemaking—a version of blaming the messenger—Veronica Webb must now resist feeling judged along with modeling by the interviewer in "How Does a Supermodel Do Feminism?"; Jeannine DeLombard makes a case that butch/femme roles are "lesbian-specific genders" rather than a way of "mimicking heterosexuality"; Naomi Wolf takes an insightful and witty look at the current reasons for an appeal of traditional weddings; Jason Schultz adapts an old-style bachelor party to a new-style purpose of persuading men to talk vulnerably about sex; and Eisa Davis attempts to redeem hip-hop lyrics by pointing out the racist double standard by which their misogyny is condemned but Aristotle's is not. Reading Donna Minkowitz's explanation of being sexually excited by accounts of prison attacks and the rape with a baseball bat of a retarded girl, as she describes in "Giving It Up," makes me as sorrowful as reading about a gay person, someone who is Jewish, or a person of color who finds homophobic, anti-Semitic, or racist violence to be a sexual turn-on. But I appreciate her honesty in tracing these feelings to childhood beatings that made pain a price of love, and her agony over the mere idea that this might go beyond fantasy and harm anyone. Her essay is a reminder of the power of socialization—given early abuse, children socialized as males tend to harm others while those socialized as females tend to harm themselves—and the clear linkage between a society's degree of child abuse and its sexual tradition of sadomasochism. More important, her essay warns us against making others feel criticized for conditions they didn't create. It's partly feeling personally judged that makes some women defend the institution of pornography, or equate free-speech protests against it with censorship.

I confess that there are moments in these pages when I—and perhaps other readers over thirty-five—feel like a sitting dog being told to sit. In Jennifer Allyn and David Allyn's honest and useful account of trying to find a feminist solution to the great name problem presented by marriage, Jennifer writes: "I felt part of a new generation of feminists. We wanted to make room for play in our lives—dyeing our hair, shaving our legs, dressing in ways that made us happy—without sacrificing a commitment to political activism." Okay, maybe not all past feminists felt that way—or any single way—but I suspect that a majority did. Her assumption makes me fear that the stereotype has completely subsumed reality. So does the idea that the ability to be both a Christian and a feminist is news (what about all those "Jesus Was a Feminist" buttons, not to mention Catholics for a Free Choice and other longtime groups of Christian feminists?); that having three male writers in these pages is daring (the National Organization for Women, the largest feminist organization in the world, has always had male members); that serving in the army is completely contrary to feminist precepts (feminists refused to oppose women in combat, even when doing so might have eased the passage of the Equal Rights Amendment); that to be antipornography is to be procensorship (contrary to much disinformation, I have yet to find a feminist group that supports the "prior restraint" by the state that constitutes censorship, regardless of their feeling about pornography); and that to worship the Goddess is some kind of feminist prerequisite (try telling a political or a socialist feminist that). In the title essay, "To Be Real," the stereotype of a "real mother" is seen as coming from the media, but somehow *Esquire*'s "Do-Me Feminism" is not. Most of all, there is the notion that a depolarized, full-circle world view, one that sees *and* instead of *either/or, linking* where there has been *ranking,* has not always been a feminist specialty. That was the style of thinking in that early gathering of ten feminists, and it has continued to flourish wherever traditional, linear thinking is not imposed.

Consider these words from Robin Morgan:

> If I had to name one quality as the genius of patriarchy, it would be compartmentalization, the capacity for institutionalizing disconnection. Intellect severed from emotion. Thought separated from action. Science split from art. The earth itself divided; national borders. Human beings categorized: by sex, age, race, ethnicity, sexual preference, height, weight, class, religion, physical ability, *ad nauseum.* The personal isolated from the political. Sex divorced from love. The material ruptured from the spiritual. The past parted from the present disjoined from the future. Law detached from justice. Vision dissociated from reality."[5]

It has always been feminism's task to put these back together again by creating a fully human paradigm of "masculine" and "feminine" together. Imagine how frustrating it is to be held responsible for some of the very divisions you've been fighting against, and you'll know how feminists of the 1980s and earlier may feel as they read some of these pages.

But just when I think my frustration is peaking, I begin to notice that these essays are talking to one another; a tribute to a well-thought-out anthology. Anna Bondoc's "Close, But No Banana," an account of the pain of being a "different" daughter, balances the pain of having a "different" mother in Danzy Senna's "To Be Real," and Amruta Slee's "Congratulations, It's a Girl." Taken together, these three voices, each coming from a place of overlap between two cultures, show us that new songs are most likely to come from the richness diversity creates.

By itself, Allison Abner's joyous "Motherhood" seems to celebrate her choice of motherhood while criticizing Adrienne Rich for writing about it as an institution (though Abner still doesn't even hint that men might also become equally responsible nurturers), but together with Elizabeth Mitchell's insightful "An Odd Break with the Human Heart," the importance of being able to choose or not choose motherhood becomes clear. Mitchell's fascinating riff on women guerrillas also adds depth to Veena Cabreros-Sud's wonderful flat-out essay, "Kicking Ass," a fierce tribute to the necessity of self-defense that every woman with ladylike delusions about violence should read. It's also proof of Margaret Mead's insight that women tend to be *more* fierce than men in self-defense or in defense of their children. Mitchell's exposé of the empathy sickness that an overemphasis on dolls can produce is the other half of Jeannine DeLombard's lament about being restricted to boys' toys only. Together, they create one more support for *and* instead of *either/or;* for the importance of giving each child all choices.

To measure the range of this anthology, consider two essays that offer very different ways to slide temporarily past the moorings of gender, race, sexuality, age, and ethnicity, and sail toward the unique self. For Lisa Jones in "She Came with the

Rodeo," performance art meets the need "to toss off the expectations laid by our genitals, our melanin count, and our college degrees." For mocha jean herrup in "Virtual Identity," this opportunity comes from living in cyberspace, a place where fantasy becomes virtual reality, and safe companions come from anywhere.

To measure a similar diversity in writing styles, start with "Missionary Position," in which Gina Dent critiques the feminist use of personal confession in such impersonal and intellectual language as "the academic inquiry into the production of women's agency." Then read Greg Tate's "Born to Dyke," in which he describes himself in very personal terms as someone who has chosen to live in the world of black lesbian feminists: "In this sense and several others like his inability to derive stimulation from pornography or fellatio, he believes he is truly the brother from another planet."

For a hint of a different future, see "Beauty Laid Bare" by bell hooks, one of the best arguments for beauty as a necessity, something as nourishing as bread, as our nineteenth-century sisters told us in "Bread and Roses." She explains that black families have been deprived by urban poverty of a beauty that even rural poverty allowed. In "Testimony of a Naked Woman," Jocelyn Taylor sheds light on why some other contributors may have experienced feminism and existing liberation movements as restricting. "Though I honestly believe that parents, grandparents, extended family, etc., want to teach us how to 'act' in order to survive in a Black-hostile, woman-hating environment," she explains, "the lessons are often transmitted in the form of policing . . . [I want to] learn how I can affect the future without compromise; without altering my political beliefs, my connection to my community or my physical self."

If I were to choose one common lesson taught by these many feminisms, it would be this: *The greatest gift we can give one another is the power to make a choice. The power to choose is even more important than the choices we make.* In our long journey toward freedom we must cherish one another's choices. After all, by the measure of the abolitionist/suffragist century that gained a legal and social *identity* for women of all races and men of color, our current struggle for legal and social *equality* has at least seventy years to go. There will probably be future waves before human lives are not restricted by sex, race, or any other single element of a unique and complex identity. Whether we are connected by intimacy and love over time, or simply by a shared need to search in different directions, the means we choose must reflect the ends we want to achieve.

Because I entered when feminism had to be chosen and even reinvented, I experienced almost everything about it as an unmitigated and joyful freedom—and I still do. So I'm glad this anthology includes the different but equally joyous freedom of a much younger woman who is both different and the same. Jocelyn Taylor's energetic, out-on-the-edge odyssey stretches from trying to insulate herself enough to survive as a stripper (which she can't) to becoming free enough to march barebreasted down Fifth Avenue in a gay pride parade (which she does). During this journey, she comes to understand what no one could have taught her, and what she couldn't have attempted without her mother's struggle against self-hatred: "There's so much pain in invisibility. It took me a while to learn that I don't have to be the one in front of a camera feeling uncomfortable and thinking that something is better than nothing. No one does."

"When I think about the worldwide prevalence of the fear of women and the fear of Blackness, and the subsequent frenzy to control these entities . . . I have fantasies about riding with an army of naked women on horseback . . . it's a strong and fearless image that says we do not believe that our bodies are inferior or ugly, or open to assault of any kind."

Who could resist this bravery? Not I. It's the same freedom I've always loved in this poem by Alice Walker:

> It is true—
> I've always loved
> the daring
> ones
> Like the black young
> man
> Who tried
> to crash
> All barriers
> at once,
> wanted to
> swim
> At a white
> beach (in Alabama)
> Nude.[6]

The pages you are about to read can increase this daring. In all of us.

1. "A Household Employment Pledge," *Ms.* Magazine, February 1973, p. 47. (The National Committee for Household Employment became the Household Technicians of Amer-

ica. This pledge was updated and reprinted in *Ms.*, October 1979.)

2. See Marilyn Waring, *If Women Counted: A New Feminist Economics.* New York: Harper & Row, 1988. For an overview of this effort to value "women's work" and the environment, see Gloria Steinem, "Revaluing Economics," *Moving Beyond Words* (New York: Simon & Schuster, 1994).

3. 1986 Gallup poll, *Newsweek*, March 1986. "Women's Equality Poll: 1995," design and analysis by Louis Harris, conducted by Peter Y. Harris Research Group, Inc., New York, N.Y., prepared for the Feminist Majority Foundation, April 1995.

4. June Jordan, *Technical Difficulties.* Boston: Beacon Press, 1994, p. 197.

5. Robin Morgan, *The Demon Lover: On the Sexuality of Terrorism.* New York: W. W. Norton, 1989, p. 51.

6. Alice Walker, "v," *Her Blue Body: Everything We Know.* New York: Harcourt Brace Jovanovich, 1991, p. 79.

Being Real:

an introduction

a year before i started this book, my life was like a feminist ghetto. Every decision I made, person I spent time with, word I uttered, had to measure up to an image I had in my mind of what was morally and politically right according to my vision of female empowerment. Everything had a gendered explanation, and what didn't fit into my concept of feminist was "bad, patriarchal, and problematic." I couldn't stay intimate with a male friend who called someone a "pussy" derogatorily and revealed an un-decolonized mind, I couldn't live with a partner because I would never be able to maintain my independence and artistic strength as a woman, I couldn't utter thoughts of dislike or jealousy for another woman because that would mean I was horribly unfeminist, and so, horribly bad.

My existence was an ongoing state of saying no to many elements of the universe, and picking and choosing to allow only what I thought should belong. The parts of myself that didn't fit into my ideal were hidden down deep, and when I faced them for fleeting moments they made me feel insecure and confused about my values and identity. Curiosity about pornography, attraction to a stable domestic partnership, a desire to start a business and pursue traditional individual power, interest in the world of S/M, a love for people who challenged and sometimes flatly opposed my feminist beliefs—these feelings in themselves were not terribly terrible, and I think that for most who consider them they seem terribly trivial, but for me and my sense of how to make feminist revolution, they represented contradictions that I had no idea how to reconcile.

Linked with my desire to be a good feminist was, of course, not just a desire to change my behavior to change the world, but a deep desire to be accepted, claimed, and loved by a feminist community that included my mother, godmother, aunts, and close friends. For all intents and purposes their beliefs were my own, and we mirrored each other in the most affirming of ways. As is common in familial relationships, I feared that our love was dependent upon that mirroring. Once I offered a face different from the one they expected, I thought the loyalty, the bond of our shared outlook and understanding, would be damaged forever.

The thought of exploring myself and the world and coming up with new questions and different answers was not half as terrifying as the thought of sharing these revelations with people I admired and loved. That moment of articulating my difference, when I imagined it in my mind, was not one of power, of me coming to voice about my own truths, it was one filled with the guilt of betrayal. If the Goddess didn't work for me, if I didn't think violence on TV translated into real-life violence, if I didn't believe in the essential goodness of women's culture, I thought I might be perceived as betraying "The Movement" rather than celebrating it. I feared that this betrayal, which was grounded in staying true to myself, could mean banishment from the community for questioning the status quo. Because feminism has always been so close to home, I worried that I might also be banished from there.

The ever-shifting but ever-present ideals of feminism can't help but leave young women and men struggling with the reality of who we are. Constantly measuring up to some cohesive fully down-for-the-feminist-cause identity without contradictions and messiness and lusts for power and luxury items is not a fun or easy task. As one woman said to me at a small Midwestern college where I was giving a lecture, "I feel I can't be a feminist because I am not strong enough, not good enough, not disciplined enough." At an all women's college in Virginia, another young woman expressed relief when I told the group that there was no one correct way to be a feminist, no seamless narrative to assume and fit into. This soft-spoken young woman told the group hesitantly, "I have always believed in equal rights and been involved in speaking up, but I didn't think I could call myself a feminist because I am also Christian." The concept of a strictly defined and all-encompassing feminist identity is so prevalent that when I read the section in my talk about all the different things you can do and still be a feminist, like shave your legs every day, get married, be a man, be in the army, whatever, audience members clap spontaneously. This simple reassurance paves the way for more openness and communication from young women and men than anything else I say.

Buried in these vibrant young women's words are a host of mystifications, imagistic idealizations, and ingrained social definitions of what it means to be a feminist. For each young woman there is a different set of qualifiers, a different image which embodies an ideal to measure up to, a far-reaching ideological position to uphold at any cost. Depending on which mythology she was exposed to, she believes that in order to be a feminist one must live in poverty, always critique, never marry, want to censor pornography and/or worship the Goddess. A feminist must never compromise herself, must never make concessions for money or for love, must always be devoted to the uplift of her gender, must only make an admirable and selfless livelihood, preferably working for a women's organization. She fears that if she wants to be spanked before sex, wants to own a BMW, is a Zen priest, wants to be treated "like a lady," prioritizes racial oppression over gender oppression, loves misogynist hip-hop music, still speaks to the father that abused her, gets married, wants to raise three kids on a farm in Montana, etc., that she can't be a feminist. That is, she can't join a community of women and men working for equality, and can't consider herself a part of a history of societal transformation on behalf of women.

From my experience talking with young women and being one myself, it has become clear to me that young women are struggling with the feminist label not only, as some prominent Second Wavers have asserted, because we lack a knowledge of women's history and have been alienated by the media's generally horrific characterization of feminists, and not only because it is tedious to always criticize world politics, popular culture, and the nuances of social interaction. Young women coming of age today wrestle with the term because we have a very different vantage point on the world than that of our foremothers. We shy from or modify the label in an attempt to begin to articulate our differences while simultaneously avoiding meaningful confrontation. For many of us it seems that to be a feminist in the way that we have seen or understood feminism is to conform to an identity and way of living that doesn't allow for individuality, complexity, or less than perfect personal histories. We fear that the identity will dictate and regulate our lives, instantaneously pitting us against someone, forcing us to choose inflexible and unchanging sides, female against male, black against white, oppressed against oppressor, good against bad.

This way of ordering the world is especially difficult for a generation that has grown up transgender, bisexual, interracial, and knowing and loving people who are racist, sexist, and otherwise afflicted. We have trouble formulating and perpetuating theories that compartmentalize and divide according to race and gender and all of the other signifiers. For us the lines between Us and Them are often blurred, and as a result we find ourselves seeking to create identities that accommodate ambiguity and our multiple positionalities: including more than excluding, exploring more than defining, searching more than arriving.

Whether the young women who refuse the label realize it or not, on some level they recognize that an ideal woman born of prevalent notions of how empowered women look, act, and think is simply another impossible contrivance of perfect womanhood, another scripted role to perform in the name of biology and virtue. But tragically, rather than struggling to locate themselves within some continuum of feminism, rather than upset the boat a little by reconciling the feminism they see and learn about with their own ideas and desires, many young women and men simply bow out altogether, avoiding the dreaded confrontation with some of the people who presently define and represent feminism, and with their own beliefs.

Neither myself nor the young women and men in this book have bowed out. Instead, the writers here have done the difficult work of being real (refusing to be bound by a feminist ideal not of their own making) and telling the truth (honoring the complexity and contradiction in their lives by adding their experiences to the feminist dialogue). They change the face of feminism as each new generation will, bringing a different set of experiences to draw from, an entirely different set of reference points, and a whole new set of questions.

Whether they are loving hip-hop music and the often misogynist artists who make it (Eisa Davis), refusing to understand the world in terms of the biological categories which fuel identity politics (Danzy Senna), or winding their way through the disillusionment that comes with the reality of corporate life (Min Jin Lee), these self-proclaimed feminist writers grapple with some of the assumptions about who they are supposed to be, as people who believe in equal access, equal pay, an end to gender violence, and the right to privacy, and how they are supposed to interact with and respond to the world. As they struggle to formulate a feminism they can call their own, they debunk the stereotype that there is one lifestyle or manifestation of feminist empowerment, and instead offer self-possession, self-determination, and an endless array of non-dichotomous possibilities.

By bringing their considerable intellectual power and commitment to social change to bear on their own life experiences, these writers, and many other young women and men who are not represented here, push at all of our notions of what is good and bad, correct and incorrect behavior and ideology for a feminist. By broadening our view of who and what constitutes "the feminist community," these thinkers stake out an inclusive terrain from which to actively seek the goals of societal equality and individual freedom they all share. At the same time, they continue to build upon a feminist legacy that challenges the status quo, finds common ground while honoring difference, and develops the self-esteem and confidence it takes to live and theorize one's own life.

My hope is that this book can help us to see how the people in the world who are facing and embracing their contradictions and complexities and creating something new and empowering from them are important voices leading us away from divisiveness and dualism. I hope that in accepting contradiction and ambiguity, in using *and* much more than we use *either/or,* these voices can help us continue to shape a political force more concerned with mandating and cultivating freedom than with policing morality. Rather than judging them as unevolved, unfeminist, or hopelessly duped by the patriarchy, I hope you will see these writers as yet another group of pioneers, outlaws who demand to exist whole and intact, without cutting or censoring parts of themselves: an instinct I consider to be the very best legacy of feminism.

These voices are important because if feminism is to continue to be radical and alive, it must avoid reordering the world in terms of any polarity, be it female/male, good/evil, or, that easy allegation of false consciousness which can so quickly and silently negate another's agency: evolved/unconscious. It must continue to be responsive to new situations, needs, and especially desires, ever expanding to incorporate and entertain all those who wrestle with and swear by it, including those who may not explicitly call its name.

When I began this book, I knew I wanted it to break down notions of what a feminist is, to show that there are an infinite number of moments and experiences that make up female empowerment. In order to get that kind of variety, I asked practically everyone I talked to who seemed to be plugged into their own growth and concerned with the world around them to write for the book. Accordingly, the group you will read here is an eclectic gathering of folks: a fundraiser for women's organizations, a lawyer, a videomaker, an actor, a cultural critic, a professor, a musician, a director of special projects for a film company, a student, a writer of children's books, and yes, among others, two men and a "supermodel."

When I initially met with contributors, I told them I was editing an anthology on feminism and female empowerment in the nineties and asked if they had been thinking about any topic or theme or experience that seemed appropriate. Generally people offered almost generic experiences of being a woman in a sexist society. When I explained further that I was looking for essays that explored contradiction and ambiguity, that explored female empowerment from the perspective of what in your life has been empowering for you—as opposed to what has been disempowering, and irrespective of what is *supposed* to be empowering—then the small voices, the quiet, never-said-this-out-loud-before voices, began to speak.

As they shared their stories, I gradually revealed more about the book I wanted to read. I wanted to explore the ways that choices or actions seemingly at odds with mainstream ideas of feminism push us to new definitions and understandings of female empowerment and social change. I wanted to know more about how people reconciled aspects of their lives that they felt ashamed of with politics they believed in. I especially wanted to hear experiences of people attempting to live their lives envisioning or experiencing identities beyond those inscribed on them by the surrounding culture. By this point, there was usually a vigorous nod, a murmur of surprise, and what felt like a release of the floodgates. Almost every single person I talked to began to tell me about some personal contradiction they "had been thinking about for months," or some piece that they wanted to write but weren't sure was "acceptable" or "right," or some experience they had that segued "exactly" into what I was talking about.

My requirement was that the pieces be personal, honest, and record a transformative journey taken. I prefer personal testimonies because they build empathy and compassion, are infinitely more accessible than more academic tracts, and because I believe that our lives are the best basis for feminist theory, and that by using the contradictions in our lives as what Zen practitioners have called the "razor's edge," we lay the groundwork for feminist theory that neither vilifies or deifies, but that accepts and respects difference.

It was extraordinarily difficult for writers to produce works for this book. I spent innumerable hours alternating between therapist and editor. Many pieces didn't make it because writers were afraid to expose themselves. The pieces that did make it are strong pieces which open doors of understanding and prioritize political commitment *and* self-acceptance. Whether it is Jocelyn Taylor writing on her quest for public eroticism as activism rather than as objectification, Jason Schultz on the conundrum of straight white male sexuality within feminist practice, Veena Cabreros-Sud on reclaiming violence within a movement that prizes nonviolence, or mocha jean herrup using the Internet as a facilitator of a politics of ambiguity, these essays provoke us and enlarge our view, challenging us to accept other patterns of thought. Other essays, like bell hooks's on the role beauty and material objects play in her sense of progressive struggle, and Jeannine DeLombard's on her insistence on being a *femme*nist, make a space for us to forge new meanings from our attraction to things that may be considered "anti-revolution." Some of the more shocking pieces, like Donna Minkowitz's courageous reckoning with her own eroticization of violence, are disturbing journeys that may leave some readers in agony from having their norms so questioned.

The process of making this book has been for me one of parrying stones and gaining courage. Every essay that speaks to a different way of approaching female empowerment has reinforced my own evolving feminism, and has allowed me to confront that childlike and almost irrational fear of being different and therefore unacceptable. In real life, this journey has facilitated real discussion where before there was only mute fear. As I tentatively shared more and more of the ideas for the book, I found them met by mentors, family, and friends alike with enthusiasm and openness, teaching me that the prison we create for ourselves is the most onerous of all. And I have learned the lesson that just might save the planet: people can disagree and still love one another deeply; people can have completely different perspectives and still be right.

This book is a testament to the realities that there is no betrayal in being yourself, home must be made within, and the best communities are those built on mutual respect. The complex, multi-issue nature of our lives, the instinct not to categorize and shut oneself off from others, and the enormous contradictions we embody are all fodder for making new theories of living and relating. This continuing legacy of feminism, which demands that we know and accept ourselves, jettisoning societal norms that don't allow for our experiences, is a politically powerful decision. For, in these days of conservative and exclusionary politics predicated upon notions of black and white, of who is entitled to resources and who is not, of who is good and who should be incarcerated, it is more important than ever to fight to be all of who we are. Rather than allowing ourselves and others to be put into boxes meant to categorize and dismiss, we can use the complexity of our lives to challenge the belief that any person or group is more righteous, more correct, more deserving of life than any other.

Even now, though, at the end of this project, I find myself worrying and feeling guilty about the book's introspective qualities. Am I being a bad feminist by making a book that isn't about welfare reform, environmental racism, and RU486? What about the politics? What about the activism that people need to hear about? What about the expectations that this book will be an embodiment of what I seem to represent to the outside world: young feminist activism and organizing? On some level, an internal voice is still saying: how dare you make a book that is about ideas and not about problems, how dare you be a feminist in this way and not that way?

This question came up early on when I found myself feeling internal pressure to make a book I really wasn't all that desperate to read. That book was filled with incisive critique of the patriarchy, plenty of young women from every background fighting against all manner of oppression, and inspirational rhetorical prose meant to uplift, empower, and motivate. It would be a great book to buy one day, I thought to myself after a friend sagely warned me to stay true to my passion and not succumb to "should," but would it pull me along a journey that captivated and intrigued me, would it get at what was most relevant in my life and the lives of others I talked to, forcing us to face and embrace, confront and understand? Would it help me to learn more about myself, and thus help me to learn more about the nature of female empowerment? Doubtful.

And so what you have in your hands now is the book that I struggled for two years to even allow myself to bring into being. The one that came out of the late-night wonderings and intense conversations about difference, desire, and the things we fear most within our emerging selves. I hope the journeys in this collection encourage you to reach into the spaces of yourself where you are most afraid to go, to create feminist space in which you can be real. I hope these writers encourage you to pull your truths, your questions, and your so-called demons out, out into the open, where you can get a better look and lead us all into the future.

—rebecca walker

to be real

Uniqueness and freedom have as their consequence that one can never regard other people merely as means, but must always treat them as ends in themselves. As beings they have the fundamental authority to define their existence and its meaning themselves, including their own values and their own morality. In this way it becomes not morality but ethics—understood as the meta-discussion of morals and how they function together in a common system, which is the universal basis for any discussion of values. We must therefore accept that we can find no universal morality.

—Cybernetics and Human Knowing

You have to give up the life you've planned to find the life that's waiting for you.

—Joseph Campbell

To Be Real

danzy senna

growing up mixed in the racial battlefield of boston, i yearned for something just out of my reach—an "authentic" identity to make me real. Everyone but me, it seemed at the time, fit into a neat cultural box, had a label to call their own. Being the daughter of both feminist and integrationist movements, a white socialist mother and a black intellectual father, it seemed that everyone and everything had come together for my conception, only to break apart in time for my birth. I was left with only questions. To Be or Not to Be: black, Negro, African-American, feminist, femme, mulatto, quadroon, lesbian, straight, bisexual, lipstick, butch bottom, femme top, vegetarian, carnivore? These potential identities led me into the maze of American identity politics, and hopefully out the other side.

When I was eleven years old, an awkward child with knobby knees and a perpetually flat chest, I was preoccupied with questions of womanhood and what kind of woman I would become. Even then, I was aware of two kinds of power I could access as a female. There was the kind of power women got from being sexually desired, and the kind women got from being sexually invisible—that is, the power in attracting men and the power in being free of men. I also noticed that women fought one another for the first kind and came together for the second. Even as a child, I knew people craved power. I just wasn't sure which kind I wanted.

I liked the power of looking pretty, but wasn't certain men were worth attracting. I didn't like the effect they had on the women around me. Like most of my friends, I lived in a fe-male-headed household. My mother raised us with the help of other women, a series of sidekick moms who moved in and out of our lives. In the evenings, we all converged in the kitchen, an orange-painted room on the second floor of our house. In the kitchen, laughter, food, and talk formed a safe space of women and children. On those occasions when men did enter the picture—for dinner parties or coffee—the fun of wild, un-abashed laughter and fluid gossip seemed to float out the win-dow. In walked huge, serious, booming creatures who quickly became the focus of attention. The energy of the room shifted from the finely choreographed dance of womentalk, where ev-eryone participated in but no one dominated the conversation, to a room made up of margins and centers. The relative kind-ness of men didn't change the dynamic of their presence. From my perspective, it appeared that they immediately be-

came the center of the kitchen, while the women were transformed into fluttering, doting frames around them. The
women who had a moment before seemed strong, impenetrable heroines, became, in the presence of men, soft and powerless girls.

My confusion about which kind of power I wanted to have
—which kind of woman I wanted to be—is reflected in a diary
entry from that year. In round, flowery script I wrote vows.
"Always wear lipstick. Never get married." The prospect of
being able to turn heads, to be asked out on dates—to be
desired—was an aspect of my impending adolescence which
looked thrilling. Lipstick became the symbol of this power in
my mind. At the same time, I noticed that once Lipstick
Women had attracted men, often they became old and beaten,
pathetic, desperate creatures, while the men remained virile
and energized. At ten, I hoped there was a space in between
the two extremes—a place where I could have both kinds of
power—a place where I could wear lipstick and still be free.

My mother and her friends seemed to have settled for only
one of these forms of power—the power of feminism—and
their brazen rejection of the "lipstick world" insulted and embarrassed my burgeoning adolescent consciousness. I remember one dusky evening in particular, when a group of women
from the local food cooperative came banging on our door.
They wanted my mother's support in a march protesting violence against women. She liked these tough, working-class
women and what they stood for, so while other mothers called
their kids into dinner, ours dragged us into the streets. My
sister, brother, and I were mortified as we ran alongside the
march, giggling and pointing at the marching women chanting
"Women Unite—Take Back the Night!" The throngs were letting it all hang out: their breasts hung low, their leg hair grew

wild, their thighs were wide in their faded blue jeans. Some of them donned Earth shoes and T-shirts with slogans like "A Woman Needs a Man Like a Fish Needs a Bicycle." They weren't in the least bit ashamed. But I was. I remember thinking, "I will never let myself look like that."

Shortly after the march, I began to tease my mother. "Why can't you be a *real* mother?" I asked. It became a running joke between us. She'd say, "Look, a real mother!" pointing at prim women in matching clothes and frosted lipstick at the shopping mall. We'd laugh together, but there was a serious side to it all. I wanted my sixties mother to grow up, to stop protesting and acting out—to be "normal." I loved her, but at the same time craved conformity. In my mind, real mothers wore crisp floral dresses and diamond engagement rings; my mother wore blue jeans and a Russian wedding ring given to her from a high-school boyfriend. (She had lost the ring my father gave to her.) Real mothers got married in white frills before a church; my mother wed my father in a silver lamé mini-dress which she later donated to us kids for Barbie doll clothes. Real mothers painted their nails and colored their hair; my mother used henna. And while real mothers polished the house with lemon-scented Pledge, our house had dog hair stuck to everything.

My mother scolded me, saying I wanted her to be more "bourgeois." Bourgeois or not, to me, *real* equaled what I saw on television and in the movies, whether it was the sensible blond Carol Brady or the Stephen Spielberg suburban land-scape—a world so utterly normal that the surreal could occur within it. At night, visions of white picket fences and mothers in housedresses danced in my head. I dreamed of station wagons, golden retrievers, and brief-case-toting fathers who came home at five o'clock to the smell of meat loaf wafting from the kitchen. But *real* was something I could never achieve with my white socialist mother, my black intellectual father who visited on Sundays, and our spotted mongrel from the dog pound, because most of all, real was a white girl—and that was something I could never, ever be.

I was fourteen when I first sat perched on a kitchen stool and allowed a friend to put an iron to my head—a curling iron, that is. She wasn't pressing my hair straight. Just the opposite. She was trying to give my straight, chestnut-brown hair some curl, and I wasn't taking no for an answer. So far, I had been mistaken for almost everything—Italian, Greek, Jewish, Pakistani —but never for black. My features and hair brought me forever short of Negritude. In a 1980s twist on the classic tragic mulatta, I was determined to pass as black. And if that wasn't possible, at least with my hair-sprayed "crunchy curls" I could pass as Puerto Rican. I remember lying in bed at night and smelling Spanish cooking from the apartment downstairs; I would close my eyes and fantasize that I was actually Puerto Rican, that everything else had been just a bad dream, that my name was Yolanda Rivera, and that I lived in the barrio.

I had dropped my quest for a "real mother" and yearned for something within my reach: a real ethnicity, something other than the half-caste purgatory to which I had been condemned. Now I yearned for Blackness, which, like femininity, was defined by the visible signifiers of the times. In my father's era, these had been a daishiki, an Afro, a fisted pik. No longer. This was still Boston in the 1980s and to be authentically black meant something quite different. Now you had to wear processed hair and Puma sneakers. I remember gazing at my best friend's straightened black hair, at the sheen of the chemicals and the way it never moved, and thinking it was the most beautiful hair I had ever seen. I believed the answer to that ubiquitous question "How can I be down?" lay in cultural artifacts: a Louis Vuitton purse, a Kangol, a stolen Ralph Lauren parka.

On my first day of high school, I went decked out in two-toned jeans, Adidas sneakers, and a red bomber with a fur-lined collar. My hair was frozen in hard curls all over my head and I wore frosty pink lipstick. I snapped my bubblegum and trailed after my sister. She is a year older than me and like most firstborn children, had inherited what I saw as the riches: kinky hair and visible blackness. We sauntered into the cafeteria where everyone hung out before class began. Doug E. Fresh beats boomed from someone's radio. Old friends greeted my sister with hugs; she introduced me and, to my relief, everyone smiled and commented on how much we looked alike. A dark-skinned boy with a shaved-bald head asked my sister where she had been hiding me, and I blushed and glanced away from his steady brown-eyed stare. There, across the cafeteria, my gaze fell on a girl, and we stared at each other with that intensity that could only mean love or hate.

She looked a little like me, but right away I knew she was more authentic than I would ever be. With an olive complexion, loose dark curls, and sad brown eyes, she sat in a cluster of pretty brown-skinned girls. She was smoking and squinting at me from across the hazy cafeteria.

I whispered to my sister: "Who's that girl?"

"That's Sophia."

Sophia whispered something just then to the girls at her table and they giggled. My cheeks began to burn.

I nudged my sister. "Why's she staring at me?"

"Cause David, her boyfriend, has been eyeing you ever since you came in here."

The bald-headed boy—David—winked at me when our eyes met and I heard my sister's voice beside me warn: "Just keep your distance and it'll be okay."

It wasn't. As the year progressed, the tension between me and Sophia escalated. It was as if we took one look at each other and said, "There ain't room in this school for both of us." From her point of view, I threatened her position not only with David, who had a fetish for light-almost-white girls, but also her position in the school. She, like me, had gotten used to her role as "the only one." Her "whiteness" had brought her status within the black world, and she didn't want that threatened by anyone, and certainly not by me with my crunchy-curls.

In a strange way I idolized Sophia, though I would have never admitted it at the time. To me, she was a role model, something to aspire to. She represented what I had spent my whole life searching for: she was the genuine article. While I lived with my white mother in a rambling brown-shingled house, Sophia lived with her black mother in an inner-city townhouse. While my curls were painstakingly acquired, Sophia's were natural. While I was soft, Sophia was hard-core. And of course, while I was the tragedy trying to walk-the-walk and talk-the-talk, Sophia didn't need to try.

David became our battleground. I told my friends and family that I was in love with him and that I despised Sophia. The truth is that Sophia was the real object of my desire. I wanted to be her. But it was just dawning on me that certain things could not be manufactured. By curling my hair, wearing heavy gold hoop earrings, and a bomber jacket, I could not re-create her experience. My imitation of her life could only go skin deep. So my desire for her was transformed into an obsessive envy. If I couldn't be her, I would beat her.

One day I discovered obscenities about me splattered on the girls' room wall—just the regular catty slander, nothing too creative, saying I was a bitch and a ho. But there was a particular violence to the way it had been written, in thick red marker around the bathroom mirrors. In tears, I went to find my big sister. Always my protector, she dragged me to the girls' room after lunch period to set things straight with Sophia once and for all. We found her in there with her girls, skipping class and preening in front of a mirror.

Sister: "Did you write this about my sister?"

Sophia: "She been trying to get with my man all year. That bitch had it comin' to her."

Sister: "I asked you a question. Did you write this about my sister?"

Sophia: "Yeah, I did. And what are you gonna do about it?"

Soon, in the bright spring sunshine, my sister and Sophia came to blows while I stood on the sidelines with the rest of the black population of our school. I had been warned by Sophia's rather hefty cousin that if I jumped in the fight, she would whip my ass. I didn't jump in. And after all was said and done, my sister ended up with a broken nose, Sophia with two black eyes and a scratched up face. The war was over and I got out without a scar. My sister had protected me, and I knew I was a coward, a fake. And as I sat holding my sister's hand in the hospital waiting room, I knew it wasn't blackness I had failed in. It was sisterhood.

By the time I got to college, in 1988, the mythology of the 1960s had made a comeback. The era loomed in my imagination as a sort of renaissance of free love, black power, and feminist empowerment. I had developed a *political consciousness* that recognized the evils of the Revlon Three-Minute-Relaxer and the bourgeois slave mentality of the modern housewife. I no longer thirsted for ghettocentric credentials or a mother who baked cookies on weekday afternoons. I had become a full-fledged, button-wearing, fist-waving activist. The climax of this phase came toward the end of my freshman year, when I was arrested and charged with trespassing. Along with fifty other students, I had barricaded myself into the university president's office building for eight hours with a list of demands for full-time ethnic studies faculty. It was an exhilarating and ultimately successful act, and one I don't regret.

But as I was being dragged out of the building in handcuffs, I had a flash of déjà vu, the uncanny feeling that I had experienced something like this before. Then, as I stepped on to the back of the police bus and stared at the rows of sweaty, grimy-faced "radicals," I realized that in fact the whole protest had seemed simply a cheap imitation of the 1960s protests I had seen and heard so much about, not only in war stories from my parents, but also on television and in the movies. It was a crude imitation of my parents' life experience. While our protest was about actual issues, we had recycled the language and tactics of another era, leaving the whole event with a NutraSweet aftertaste—close, but not quite the real thing.

My collegiate quest to prove myself as a radical, in the image of my parent's generation, was in fact an extension of the same old dilemma I faced as a child when I promised myself that I would always wear lipstick but never get married. Once again, I found myself falling within the borderlines of identities, forever consigned to the Never-Never Land of the Mulatto Nation. How could I be black but look so white? How could I be a feminist but continue to wear lipstick and shave my legs? How could I feel attracted to men as well as to women?

To escape from these dreaded multiplicity blues, I had once again constructed a "real" image of myself. As a "radical Afrikan" I took over school buildings and, ironically, developed a fierce disgust for miscegenation. Given my origins, it might seem odd that interracial couples got under my skin. But my parents had split up somewhere between the end of the sixties and the beginning of the seventies. The dream of interracial loving was over, and I, the progeny of *Guess Who's Coming to Dinner*, found myself repulsed and disdainful of interracial couples—and in particular, of black men dating white women. My friends and I would hiss vicious assumptions at the sight of a black man with a white woman:

"She wants to fuck her way into the black experience. He wants to fuck his way out."

Whenever I was dissing Jungle Feverettes with my fellow black nationalist buddies, I was always careful not to mention my own trail of white boyfriends. Lucky for me, I had burned all the evidence—the "Squeeze" albums, the love letters S.W.A.K.ed from Oregon, the prom pictures of me and that guy from Israel. . . .

Born into a world where racial and gender boundaries were nebulous, my friends and I sought to construct authenticity where there was none. Into this vacuum, we recovered the language of our Golden Age, the 1960s, appropriating its vocabulary for our world, when in fact it didn't quite apply. Back in the 1960s, enemies and friends seemed more clearly defined, whether they actually were or not. To be black or female generally placed one outside of the power structure. To call oneself a feminist meant something inherently transgressive. No longer. As a generation, in our music and in our politics, we continue to talk of black and female empowerment, with the assumption that certain cultural signifiers, certain catch phrases, have meaning and resonance—though the fact is that they no longer do.

The outmoded belief in the sanctity of blackness and the goodness of women was unmistakable in the Clarence Thomas/Anita Hill hearings. Thomas came to be viewed by some (both black and white, liberal and conservative) as a black martyr, another "brother" lynched by the system, because of his physical "blackness" and his oft-told tale of rising up from poverty—in other words, his "authentic Negro experience." These cultural signifiers camouflaged the fact of his actual beliefs and policies, which have always been diametrically opposed to traditional "black resistance politics." Anita Hill, on the other side of the coin, became touted as a "feminist martyr" when in fact she had been consistently allied with the right wing, traditionally anti-feminist movement. The fact that she was a woman critiquing Thomas for sexual harassment catapulted her to feminist icon status. Furthermore, the fact that she is black made it okay for white feminists to lambaste Thomas without any of the liberal discomfort they might otherwise have felt in charging a black man with a sex crime. Both groups—those who supported Thomas because of his blackness and those who supported Hill because of her femaleness—were basing their support on a biological given rather than an ideological and actual affinity.

I recently saw an advertisement for a hair dye that depicted a smiling thirty-something woman with shining auburn hair. Under her face were the words, "We put up with our husbands. We put up with our mother-in-laws. We shouldn't have to put up with gray hair." This advertisement is representative of an emerging feminism—often referred to as "Power Feminism"—which resembles little more than a new language for free-market individualism. This feminism, if nothing else, reveals the true limitation of identity politics when they don't involve a critique of power imbalance. In mainstream venues from *Newsweek* to *Vogue* to MTV, this "new face of feminism" is being celebrated as an improvement on the rigidity of the 1970s militancy. *Cosmopolitan* calls it "capitalist feminism"; *Esquire* magazine prefers to call it "Do Me Feminism." Glamorous young women are congratulated as having outdone their mothers, on having won women's liberation without breaking a nail.

And unavoidably I feel a certain identification with this "new feminism." It is like a welcome sign to my generation of young women, allowing us to at once differentiate ourselves from our feminist mothers and at the same time achieve mainstream power in our careers and love lives. It allows us the self-righteousness of being political activists without the economic sacrifice or social marginalization that has so often come along with that role. It is a feminism no longer on the defensive, with a fun, playful aesthetic that acknowledges the erotic and narcissistic pleasure women receive from beautifying themselves, a pleasure not to be denied.

This new "power feminism" certainly seems a sexy alternative to the 1970s party-pooping rigidity, where revolution came defined by strict dress codes. It may, in fact, be the resolution of the conflict I felt as a child—the space where I could wear lipstick and be free. But I have to wonder: what exactly has changed to allow feminism to become so fashionable? And the answers I find disturb me more than they comfort me. Certainly sexism hasn't disappeared. I need only to turn on MTV to see images of women as objects. Violence against women is on the rise in the streets and in the home, and big-budget films like *Single White Female, Basic Instinct,* and any number of the *Fatal Attraction* rip-offs reveal a culture of misogyny, racism, and homophobia that is as deep as ever. The beauty industry grows as a multimillion-dollar industry every day, as the race/class divide in America gets wider. So why has feminism suddenly become okay in the eyes of the mainstream?

The obvious answer lies in the fact that the power feminists are not necessarily the same women who were locked out of the power structure in the first place. The power feminism phenomenon represents not a "new school" in feminism, but rather a very old school imbedded in whiteness, privilege, "beauty," and consumerism of which the mainstream media has always been in favor.

In Manhattan, I see playgrounds filled with black and Latino women caring for white children. The white women who employ these nannies are busy working on their careers— "thinking like winners" as Naomi Wolf prescribes. At the newsmagazine for which I recently worked, there is almost an equal number of white women and white men in power. In their tailored suits, crimson lips, and stiletto heels, these women smash through the glass ceiling to become top editors on the esteemed twelfth floor of the magazine. They publish article upon article celebrating capitalist-feminism and like true superwomen, have children at home being cared for by West Indian nannies. For the women they employ, power feminism offers few solutions to the problems they face in feeding their children, paying the rent, getting home safely in a dangerous city. As British feminist Susan Watkins writes in *Red Pepper* magazine, "In fact, the 'trickledown' effects of power feminism are having little impact on the worsening living and working conditions of the majority of women in the U.S." Feminism isn't necessarily on the side of the dispossessed—"real" feminism can also be a cloak for conservatism, consumerism, and even sexism. Without recognition of power in all its different forms, and of the unexpected places power can come from, we are only fooling ourselves.

> pass (pas. pas) v. passed, passing, passes. -1. to move on
> or ahead; proceed. 2. to be accepted as being some-
> thing one is not. 3. to cease to exist; to die.
> —*The American Heritage Dictionary*

It is perhaps because of, not in spite of, the intense confusions of my childhood and adolescence that I have come to embrace feminism in my twenties. Today I no longer yearn for a "real" mother; I can see now that I had one all along. I also no longer believe in a single "authentic Negro experience." I have come to understand that my multiplicity is inherent in my blackness, not opposed to it, and that none of my "identities" are distinct from one another. To be a feminist is to be engaged actively in dismantling all oppressive relationships. To be black is to contain all colors. I can no longer allow these parts of myself to be compartmentalized, for when I do, I pass, and when I pass, I "cease to exist."

A black gay British friend of mine, David, took me to the Gay Pride March in London not too long ago. As we marched with the hordes of uniformed gay white men—cropped hair, tight jeans, white T-shirts—we realized that from a distance this march could have been a white male supremacist march—a fact which made us acutely uncomfortable. But we were even more uncomfortable when the march finally entered Brixton, London's black neighborhood. There, a Jamaican bystander focused his vitriolic homophobia on David, calling him a "fucking sodomite" and various other names as he threatened him with violence. As we walked, many other black Brixtonian bystanders focused on David in their hatred, paying little attention to the white gay marchers around us. David's sameness as another black person made him more offensive to them, not less, and the white men who made up the majority of the march were protected in some strange way by their "alien-ness" to the community at large.

Who were our allies and who were our political enemies at this moment? Were we more identified with the working-class black community who threw insults and threatened violence, or with the middle-class gay white male community that gawked at the blacks with fear and loathing? Was David "more black" or "more gay" at that moment? Of course he was both and much more. But what really mattered was that we walked safely back to his flat in Brixton, through the confusion and violence of the world around us, together.

Back at his flat, David and I spoke of our feelings of alienation from both communities. David suggested that in our post-modern condition we should no longer speak in terms of "men and women," "blacks and whites," "gay and straight," but rather in terms of "powerful" and "powerless," positions which are themselves in a constant state of flux and can become obscured if we are not vigilant. Any of us, despite our biological traits, can hold and abuse power at any one moment. As my mother says, "Whoever can, will."

In this way, it is not my "half-breed" lipstick-carrying feminist muddle that is too complicated, but identity politics which are too simplistic, stuck in the realm of the body, not the realm of belief and action. I have become suspicious of kente cloth and womyn symbols, the sale and mass consumption of cultural artifacts. My yearning to be real has led me in circles, to red herrings called identity, those visible signifiers of liberation that can be bought and sold as easily as any other object. Breaking free of identity politics has not resulted in political apathy, but rather it has given me an awareness of the complexity and ambiguity of the world we have inherited—and the very real power relations we must transform.

Femmenism

jeannine delombard

waves—which, by definition, curve alternately in op- posite directions—embody contradiction. For me femmenism is where the third wave of Western feminism and the third wave of American lesbianism intersect. Femmenism is the rip-tide that drags nature and nurture, essentialism and construc-tivism, and all other binary oppositions out to sea. Femmenism is nothing if not contradictory. Femmenism is looking like a straight woman and living like a dyke. Femmenism is being attracted to someone of the same sex who is very much your opposite. Femmenism is calling yourself a girly-girl and insist-ing that others call you a woman. Femmenism is playing up your femininity even when you know it can and will be used against you. Femmenism is using the master's tools to dismantle the master's house. Femmenism is political but not correct.

memoirs of an out-of-sync girlhood

I can still remember the day I learned what the word *lesbian* meant. I was in the third grade and had just kissed my best friend Erica on the lips. Suddenly everyone in my homeroom was screaming "Eeeeyew! Lezzies!" and making gagging noises. I didn't know what "lezzy" meant, but I could tell it wasn't good. When I discovered later that "lezzy" was short for "lesbian" and what *that* meant, I was more confused than ever. Despite the ugly way I learned it, I thought "lesbian" was the most beautiful word I had ever heard. Not even the image it conjured up, just the sound the vowels and the consonants made together. And when I did consider its meaning, I thought the word even more beautiful. For me, as a child, beautiful meant feminine, and what could be more feminine than two women making love?

The irony, of course, is that I was thinking all this in 1975, when the second wave of feminism was cresting, and many women (especially lesbians) were challenging traditional notions of femininity. Although she was no feminist activist, my mother considered herself a liberated woman and, looking back, I realize I must have driven her slightly crazy with my girliness. Not only did I embrace all things feminine, but I hated everything that I perceived as tainted with masculinity. I would only wear pants under duress and absolutely refused to wear jeans under any circumstances, although my mother and almost every other woman I knew wore them every day. Needless to say, I hated boys, and I hated it even more when some friend of my parents would chuckle knowingly and say that *that* would change soon enough.

I clearly recall the battles my mother and I would have over "appropriate" clothing and toys. I wanted to wear pouffy pastel party dresses and Mary Janes every day of the week; she bought me corduroys and hiking boots. I routinely begged for —and was just as routinely denied—what I saw as the staples of girlhood: Barbies, a nurse kit, and Tinker Bell play makeup. Instead, I received entire clans of politically correct dolls (the Sunshine Family was white and the Happy Family was black, but their hair and facial features were the same). Even my literary heroes were wrong. I aspired to be just like clever, stylish Nancy Drew, whom my mother dismissed as prissy and dependent; she thought Laura Ingalls, the boisterous tomboy from the "Little House on the Prairie" TV series, a much better role model.

I grew up in a home where gender roles were anything but strict, and breaking out of them was strictly encouraged. Fresh out of the hospital, my mother, attempting to diaper a very small, squirmy baby with a very large, pointy diaper pin, passed out cold. My father, the oldest of seven children, finished the job neatly. I know this story not because it is a rare example of active parenting on my father's part, but because it illustrates how labor was divided in our household—on the basis of ability as much as gender. It was my father who stayed home with me (he was a student at the time) while my mother went off to work as a teacher in the local elementary school. (Later, when my father also began to work out of the home, a photograph of Divine—in her trademark teal blue eyeshadow and body-hugging tulle dress—always hung above his desk.)

By a strange twist of sociocultural fate, my mother and I were in a similar situation: both of us could have gotten much of what we wanted as children if we only had been born boys. In the fifties, my mother's affinity for masculine clothing and activities was considered unnatural; in the seventies, my desire for ultra-feminine toys and accessories was perceived much the same way. Listening to "William Wants a Doll" on my Free to Be You and Me record, I understood that for a boy to plead for a baby doll was daring and original, while for a girl to do so would be old-fashioned and unimaginative. I have no doubt that, had I been born a boy, my parents would have tried to interest me in tea sets and Betty Crocker ovens in an effort to steer me away from G.I. Joes and Hot Wheels. Dominated by a new kind of double standard, my childhood taught me that avoiding gender roles can be every bit as frustrating, limiting, and ridiculous as adhering to them.

drowning in the second wave

I came out in 1985, when I was a freshman at Vassar and political correctness was sweeping American campuses. Three years earlier at a Barnard women's studies conference, sex activists like Joan Nestle, Pat Califia, and Amber Hollibaugh had battled it out with hard-line feminists opposed to pornography, S/M, and butch-femme. These pivotal "lesbian sex wars" marked an end to old-style lesbian feminism with all its rigidity and uniformity, ushering in an era of sexual experimentation, diversity, and inclusiveness. Located just two hours up the Hudson from Barnard, Vassar's lesbian community remained blissfully unaware of these changes, thus avoiding the difficult challenges the conflict would have posed to our identities, our politics, and, last but most assuredly not least, our sex.

At Vassar and, I suspect, other college campuses of the time, the political often superseded the personal. For many of us, coming out didn't mean sleeping with a woman or even having a crush on one; it meant walking that longest mile every Thursday evening to the Gold Parlor, where LFL (the Lesbian Feminist League) met.

LFL is where I first heard about butch-femme—as an antiquated relic from the dark ages of lesbian herstory. While LFL's facilitator admitted that some poor misguided souls still engaged in such "role playing," the message was that butch-femme would soon be a thing of the past, and not a minute too soon. When the topic came up again a couple years later, one woman, a histrionic British exchange student, told (complete with tears and supportive back-rubbing) of her traumatic experience as a femme—a cautionary tale for those of us tempted to enter into such an oppressive relationship.

Not that our own politically correct unions were particularly liberating. Like most other LFLers, I was in "a long-term, committed monogamous relationship" with a woman whom I resembled in thought, action, and dress. We shared our clothing (oversized men's shirts, bulky knee-length Greek fisherman's sweaters, and baggy Indonesian pants) and our politics (protesting the KKK in Philly, celebrating gay pride in New York, and marching for choice in D.C.). We even went to therapy together. Monogamy was no problem for me; having been date-raped at the age of fourteen by a man at least twice my age and cowed into sexual intercourse by numerous other males since, I approached *all* sex with more than a little trepidation. Our intimate, passionless relationship seemed to confirm the "Dear Abby" stereotype that women prefer snuggling to sex.

I had come to college with all my junior femme accessories in tow: trunks of kitschy 1950s prom dresses; countless fishnet stockings; black velvet pumps with four-inch heels; and, for everyday wear, skin-tight mini-skirts in a variety of colors. But after a year at Vassar, I was being chased out of women's rest rooms because with my buzzed hair, ripped jeans, leather jacket, clunky black shoes, and six-foot frame I looked like a man. By the time I graduated, I had not only entirely new political convictions (and a wardrobe to match), but a severe eating disorder and impenetrable (so to speak) sexual anxieties.

Looking back on all this now, I can't help but think that, for many of us, certain aspects of lesbian feminism were *enabling* (to use a term popular in the twelve-stepping eighties) rather than *empowering* (to use another). While even an ardent femmenist like myself is hesitant to add to the already considerable amount of time, energy, and paper that has been spent debating lesbians' sartorial preferences, I think it's worth pointing out that the standard dyke or lesbian feminist uniform—baggy, rumpled clothes, Birkenstocks, no makeup, unstyled hair—may have contributed to the negative body images many of us had (and may still have).

Studiously indifferent to our appearances, swaddled in loose, drab clothing, we were not androgynous, just asexual. For me, and, I suspect, for numerous others, the dyke aesthetic was economically as well as politically expedient: with a few minor adjustments, the same outfit could camouflage my body as it passed from anorexic scrawniness to bulimic bloat and back again.

Outwardly proud of our bravery and daring as lovers of women, we concealed our awkward bodies and unspoken anxieties under yards of fabric. Choosing not to wear makeup or "do" our hair not only articulated our rejection of patriarchal notions of femininity, but saved us from having to face ourselves in the mirror every day.

renaissance woman

Two years after leaving college, in my second year of graduate school, I carried on a long-distance affair with a bartender I had met when I finally got up the nerve to go alone to Hepburn's, Philadelphia's only women's bar. Our relationship was a homecoming for me in many ways. This woman introduced me to a gay demimonde of drag queens, moving parties, leather bars, and after-hours clubs. In this new, glamorous, and sexually charged environment, I felt suddenly free—free to shed the formerly de rigueur, frumpy dyke uniform and don the slinky Spandex mini-dresses I'd been longing to wear. To my delight, this woman and her gay male friends not only refrained from doing an in-depth political analysis of my internalized heterosexism, but actually rewarded me by treating me like the prom queen I'd always dreamed of being. Finally, I felt like I had found the real me. I had come out years before as a lesbian, but I didn't really come to terms with my sexuality until I came out as a femme.

Apparently, I'm not alone. As Karen Everett and historian Lillian Faderman have pointed out, the lesbian community is in the throes of a butch-femme renaissance. And as it turns out, I am a typical renaissance woman: a middle-class academic. But it's more than my class status and bookishness that set me apart from my pre-Stonewall predecessors, who were predominantly working-class bar dykes. On the one hand, I have benefited—often in ways I am not even aware of—from more than two decades of feminism and gay rights activism.

On the other hand, however, I feel a little like a freak in my own community, renaissance or not. During American lesbianism's first wave, young or newly out lesbians could count on being initiated into the mysteries of butch-femme court-ship, dress, manners, and sex by a more experienced mentor. Today, although I know a lot of women I would describe as butch, and countless "lipstick lesbians," I know of only one self-identified butch-femme couple. (And the last time I saw them, the butch hit on me and the femme gave me laundry tips.) As a rule, my lesbian friends' response to butch-femme ranges from polite dismissal to scornful ridicule. To them, butch-femme is a label, it's role playing, and they want no part of it.

Not that I can blame them. Anyone who's had a pleasant walk with her lover spoiled by some jerk yelling, "Which one of you is the man?" knows the frustration of having one's lesbian-ism taken for a cheap imitation of heterosexuality. Likewise, anyone who's been called "sir," or worse yet, "little boy," sim-ply because she has short hair, a flat chest, or unpierced ears knows how alienating *that* can be. But butch-femme is not about aping traditional notions of masculinity and femininity any more than it is about mimicking heterosexuality.

Nor has it ever been. From the late 1930s to the early 1960s, bar dykes implicitly understood butch and femme as two distinct lesbian-specific genders. Then, as now, you'll occa-sionally hear butch women jokingly call their evenings together "boys' night out." But unlike gay male culture, where drag queens and gay men often refer to each other as "she," both butches and femmes use the female pronoun when speaking of themselves and other lesbians.

I remember a conversation I had a couple of years ago with a friend who had just come back from a lesbian cruise. She said that you had to identify as either butch or femme to participate in the on-deck games. She refused to play at all and was angry because, as she put it, "I didn't pay $7,000 to have someone tell me I have to choose between butch and fuckin' femme." Although I am no more anxious than the next dyke to return to the days when butch and femme were the only options open to lesbians, I do wish that they could be accepted as two legitimate choices among many.

A year ago I expressed this wish in a review of Joan Nestle's groundbreaking anthology, *The Persistent Desire: A Femme-Butch Reader*. About a month later a woman wrote a letter to the editor of the alternative newspaper in which the review appeared, calling my article "dangerous" and accusing me of "proudly broadcasting restrictive, insulting, and oversimplified terms for behavior (Butch & Femme) without including some of the subtle intricacies, the complexities that truly make up a [lesbian] relationship." Ironically, the point I was trying to make in that essay is that butch-femme is nothing if not intricate, subtle, and highly complex, despite the fact that it is often oversimplified as a monolithic set of prescribed, restrictive behaviors by straight people and lesbians alike.

If lesbians see butch-femme as a capitulation to heterosexual norms, most of the straight world believes that butch-femme lurks at the core of *every* lesbian relationship, while the rest see it as a kinky, exotic sex game, better left in the bedroom closet along with the strap-on dildo, the handcuffs, and the edible underwear. Like pornography, everyone has an opinion about butch-femme, but no one seems very clear about what exactly it is.

My lover and I are no exception to the rule. Although we laughingly refer to *The Persistent Desire* as "the manual," we both have the sense that we are making up what it means to be butch and femme as we go along.

For me, being a femme means that I take pride in wearing just the right shade of lipstick, drawing the perfect black line above my eyelashes, keeping my legs smooth, and smelling good. Being a femmenist means knowing I am just as attractive when I don't wear makeup, shave, or put on perfume.

Being a femme also means that I want to be with a woman who appreciates it when I do these things—not silently, but openly and enthusiastically. A woman who sends me flowers; helps me out of cars; and knows how to take care of all the details, like choosing the right wine, tipping the bartender, and calling a cab. Being a femmenist means both making sure that I know how to do all these things myself *and* getting an erotic charge out of having them done for me.

Being a femme does *not* mean that I would rather be with a man, nor does it mean that I am attracted to masculine women. Unlike most of my friends, I prefer curvy, voluptuous women to buff, hard-bodied ones. But that doesn't mean I want to kiss a lipsticked mouth or caress a stockinged knee. Although I enjoy playing up my own femininity, I like to be with a woman who keeps hers under wraps, a gift for me alone to open and enjoy.

If butch women aren't masculine or even (in lesbian-feminist parlance) male-identified, what are they? To me a butch woman is one who exudes confidence, authority, independence, and a certain sexual cockiness. These may be considered masculine qualities, but I only find them attractive in women.

I remember one night my bartender girlfriend made a call from a pay phone at 3 A.M. Six feet tall, she was wearing heavy work shoes, black jeans, and a bomber jacket, her long blond hair hidden in her wool cap. As she was dialing, she tensed as a tough-looking young man approached, only to relax when he greeted her with, "Evening, officer." The man, making an assumption about her authority, not her gender, was responding to her butchness, not her "masculinity."

The same thing happens when my lover and I go out to dinner: no matter how we are dressed, invariably the server will take my order first, have my girlfriend taste the wine, and present her with the bill (even when I have requested it, credit card in hand).

According to the old dyke saying, there are more butches on the streets than between the sheets, which is just fine with me. What I love most about the woman I have been living with for the past two years is that underneath her crisp, starched shirts, behind her precise, controlled gestures is someone who is not only considerate, gentle, and patient, but beautifully, undeniably female. Far from simplifying our relationship, butch-femme layers it with a tantalizing intricacy and a highly erotic contradictoriness. If my girlfriend and I choose to split up our household chores fairly evenly, the division of labor in our bedroom is more complex. Suffice to say that when the sight of my lover's nude body makes me as hormonal as a thirteen-year-old boy, I feel perfectly free to act like one.

Life as a femme on the streets is seldom as pleasant or as safe as it is between the sheets. On the one hand, being a femme increases exponentially my much-publicized invisibility as a lesbian. Almost every day, and usually several times a day, all sorts of heterosexual men strike up conversations with me, comment on my appearance, or shout lewd remarks at me. Since to them I don't look like a dyke or even a liberated woman, they automatically assume that I look the way I do to provoke male attention and approval. For me, being a femme in public means constantly weighing my personal comfort against my personal safety. On the other hand, my lesbian invisibility is suddenly, dangerously, stripped away when I am with my lover. We found this out the hard way one night on vacation in France, when we were returning to our Left Bank hotel from a bar in the Marais, Paris, gay district. Conscious of the late hour, we resisted the temptation to stroll arm-in-arm or even touch hands. As we were walking in front of Notre Dame, a man passing in the opposite direction jammed his hand between my legs and roughly grabbed my crotch. Before I could get any words out, he was walking—not running—away, clearly unafraid of what my lover or myself might do to him.

I am convinced that the man attacked me because my girlfriend and I were so obviously lovers, not just because we were "unaccompanied" women. With that one gesture he challenged my lover's right to my body as much as he violated my right to myself. And it worked. For a few days, whenever my girlfriend touched me, all I could feel was that hand.

As a femme, I know that this kind of attack can and will happen again; as a femmenist, I am both willing to do everything I can to ensure that it doesn't and capable of understanding what's at stake when it does anyway.

riding the third wave

For years people gay and otherwise have tried to determine whether sexuality is a product of biology or environment. Like many gay men and lesbians, I realize this is a moot point. Perhaps I would not have become a lesbian had I been born in a different era, culture, or even family, but I certainly would not be who I am without some very—shall we say—basic instincts.

Likewise, my femmenism. Although my early girly tendencies felt very instinctive to me, perhaps I would not have become a femme if my parents and the feminist movement had not pushed me so hard in the opposite direction. Perhaps being a femme is my way of rebelling against my parents; maybe it's just part of the current antifeminist backlash.

But I don't think so. I owe a lot to my first-wave foremothers: the turn of the century cultural feminists who based their politics on their femininity as well as the bar dykes of the forties and fifties who developed butch-femme into an art form. But I owe even more to my second-wave sisters: the feminists of the 1960s and '70s who separated gender from sex and sex from sexuality, and their lesbian counterparts who recognized in their homosexuality a source of pride, not shame.

This, it seems to me, is what femmenism is all about. Unlike my first- and second-wave predecessors, no one force-fed me femininity. Quite the contrary: I had to fight for it tooth and nail. I'm not claiming to have grown up in a vacuum: certainly, feminism or no feminism, there was still a lot of social pressure for me to get with the age-old restrictive feminine program. And I don't doubt that some of my femme identity comes from that pressure. But also unlike my lesbian/feminist predecessors, my female socialization was countered by feminism, a critical apparatus that enabled me, indeed forced me, to question every step I made along the long and winding road of gender-role identification. Having grown up in such an environment, I realize that my femmenism has not only been carefully nurtured, it is also perfectly natural.

This essay is dedicated in loving memory to Emily Polachek.

Brideland

naomi wolf

brideland exists primarily in the bridal magazines, which conjure up a fantastic, anachronistic world that really exists nowhere beyond itself. It is a nineteenth-century world, in which major late-twentieth-century events, like the sexual revolution and the rise of the financially self-supporting woman, seem to have transpired only glancingly, to be swept away by a dimity flounce like so much unsightly grit. It is a theme park of upward mobility; in Brideland, in the events surrounding The Event, everyone is temporarily upper middle class: everyone routinely throws catered events and hires musicians and sends engraved invitations and keeps carriages or vintage cars awaiting. At the ceremony itself, things become downright feudal: the bride is treated like a very queen with her court of "maids." She has, perhaps, a child to lift her train, a child to bear her ring, and a sparkling tiara upon her hair. Cinderella is revealed in her true aristocratic radiance at last, and, in the magazines, she is perpetually arriving at the ball.

Brideland has very little to do with the relationship or even the marriage; it is, like any theme park, eternally transient: you enter, you are transformed completely, and then, presumably, you depart. It is a world of lush feminine fantasy, eerily devoid of men, who appear, if at all, as shadow figures retrieving luggage or kneeling before the bride in a state of speechless awe. Brideland has an awful lot to say about what women want that they are not getting, and it taught me a thing or two about myself.

My own initiation was abrupt. Shortly after we made our announcement, I picked up one of those magazines, mostly to find out what the rules were that I was bound to be breaking. As I turned page after page, I started to change. Long-buried yearnings surfaced, a reminder, which little else gives me, that until I was six, I inhabited a world unchanged by the 1970s' women's movement. Somehow, I had picked up atavistic feelings about The Bride that I would never have recognized in my conscious, feminist, and more skeptical mind.

By page 16 my capacity for irony was totally paralyzed. I tried hard to activate it but, as in a dream, I was powerless; it wouldn't budge. By page 32 I was hypnotized; by the time I reached the end, the honeymoon section—for the magazines are structured chronologically, as if they want to be sure you know what comes first—I had acquired new needs; blind, overwhelming, undeniable needs. The fantasies I had put away in 1966 with Bridal Barbie resurfaced with a vengeance. I needed . . . garters! And engraved stationery—engraved, not printed! And fetching little lace mitts; and a bouquet that trailed sprays of stephanotis! And heavens, maybe a veil or mantilla of some kind—down my back, of course, not over my face—would not be as unthinkable as I had thought.

You must understand: this is coming from a woman who had viewed all traditional wedding appurtenances as if they represented death by cuteness. While I am the product of an egalitarian marriage, and fervently believe in the possible goodness of life partnership, I have had such a strong resistance to all things matrimonial that when I pass Tiffany's I break out in a cold sweat. I could imagine eloping; or a civil ceremony; or even an alternative ceremony so creatively subversive that it would be virtually unrecognizable for what it is. But not—never—a wedding.

Part of my aversion comes from my ambivalence, not about the man—about whom I have no doubts—but about the institution. How can I justify sealing such a private, precious relationship with a legal bond that lets a man rape his wife in fourteen states? How can I endorse an institution that, in the not-too-distant past, essentially conveyed the woman over to her husband as property, denying her even the right to her own property? How can I support a system that allows me to flaunt my heterosexual relationship brazenly, but forbids deeply committed gay and lesbian friends of mine to declare their bonds in the same way? How can I ask my love to be sanctioned by a legal order that leaves divorcing women to struggle in a desperately unevenly matched battle in sexist courts for money and custody of children? And, less profoundly, but no less urgently, if I were to do it, what on earth would I wear?

Brideland lulls the reader into a haze of romantic acquisitiveness that leaves most such political considerations firmly outside the threshold. The magazines' articles about the origins of different rituals leave no doubt as to the naked patriarchalism of the ceremony's origins. Bridesmaids were originally dressed similarly to the bride so as to confuse marauders who would wish to abduct the woman. Groomsmen were warriors whose role was to help the bridegroom fight off the would-be kidnapers. The cedar chest and mother-of-the-bride embroidered handkerchiefs—even the beading and faux-pearling and glitter down the bodices of many dresses—are all vestigial reminders that brides and their trousseaus were essentially chattel to be bartered, bearing a specific value. Even the word *honeymoon* derives from the Old English custom of sending the couple off for a month to drink honeyed ale, as a way to relax sexual inhibitions and, presumably, ease the anxieties of virginal teenage brides who most likely had had little contact with their mates, and whose attraction to them was generally considered an irrelevance. But in the glossy pages, these fairly unnerving details fade into quaintness.

The centerpiece of Brideland is, of course, the dress, and it is this that has elicited my deepest buried fantasies. For a reason that for a long time was mysterious, I felt that I had to, but absolutely had to, create a wedding dress that had an eighteenth-century bodice, three-quarter-length sleeves, and an ankle-length skirt with voluminous panniers. I have since homed in on the trace-memory, and realize that the transcendentally important look of my dress on the critical day was predetermined by a drawing of a milkmaid in the A. A. Milne (creator of Pooh) children's book, *Now We Are Six*.

But many brides, certainly judging from the evidence of Brideland, have strong feelings about The Dress, and find themselves, as I did, having a far more mystique-laden reaction to all the trappings of the territory than their secular, self-sufficient daily living had prepared for them. Why is this? What does Brideland offer a modern woman that she does not get elsewhere?

The answer lies, I think, in the shape of the classical wedding gown. When a woman has a formal wedding, she is essentially dressing up like Queen Victoria. The bell-shaped crinoline, the corsetlike bodice (trust me, if you doubt this; I've tried one on), the sweetheart neckline and elaborately coiffed hair, the flouncing and bustling to the rear, the hundred tiny cloth-covered buttons—this is all High Victoriana. Men wear spats, morning coats, top hats. In other words, a formal wedding is the last ritual event in the contemporary world, except for certain ethnic holidays, in which the participants dress up in period costume.

Why would a bride tend toward the Victorian or Edwardian rather than, say, the Early Etruscan? The reason has to do with the modern era's denigration of female sexuality. We live in an age in which female sexuality is held incredibly cheaply; it is on tap; you can gain access to it at the flick of a switch. While few people want the bad old days of enforced virginity to return, I think there is a terrible spiritual and emotional longing among them for social behavior or ritual that respects, even worships, female sexuality and reproductive potential. We are no longer Goddesses or Queens of our own sexuality.

Paradoxically, swaddled in the white satin of the formal bridal gown, we take on for a moment that lost sexual regalness. For the Victorian era, with its superficial repressiveness, was the last time that great store was placed on the preservation and prohibition of female sexuality. To the extent that it was strongly taboo, its power was strongly socially manifested.

In Brideland, unlike with our boyfriends at the beach, we are hard to unbutton, to get at, to even feel through the whaleboning. We are made into treasure again, and jewels adorn our breasts. In white, we retrieve our virginity, which means metaphorically, the original specialness of sexual access to us. We carry bouquets of roses and other lush flowers, which have always symbolized female sexual parts and their fruitfulness. The veil is the metaphor for the hymen, which veils the innermost feminine self. In photo after photo, as in the cliché of engagement, men—those masters of the universe—are on bended knee, offering polished gems. This is a very old archetype that the modern world has banished in the rush of the sexual revolution and the least-common-denominator leveling of *Debbie Does Dallas* on cable: in Brideland, men worship the goddess of female sexuality once again.

Who wouldn't want to drift in those currents for a while? The dream of the formal wedding, and the culture that surrounds it, demonstrates on some level how barren the world is for women when female sexuality is stripped of its aura. One would not want to go back to the feminine mystique; but perhaps the knowledge that we have lost the sense of the value of female sexuality, and that we are suffering from that as if from a vitamin deficiency, will lead us to find new rituals, new experiences, new ceremonies in which we can announce to the world that we are sexually priceless—and not just for one expensive day.

Kicking Ass

veena cabreros-sud

i have this thing with violence. i look for fights on the train. I dare Joe Pervert on the street to touch me so I can kick his balls. I go to firing ranges for fun. I confront a guy who's talking shit about me and my girlfriend and tempt him to punch me by telling him he can't get his dick up. I should have a gun tattooed on my forehead. I've got this problem with violence, you could say.

To be young, brown, female, and free is about violent contradictions. The lifelong Gandhian turned guerrilla. Not a new discussion, nor even an engaging question, for many. And no wonder. After so many rapes, murders, bodies dumped in alleys, screams ignored by the neighbors, boobs on display at the corner-store deli, you get a little tired. You start looking for a quick fix beyond chronically underfunded women's services for battery, child care, health care which become, understandably, Burn Out Central. When I called a battered women's shelter as a teenager, the intake woman told me it was in my mind and I should just go to a doctor to get myself checked out. She sounded either a) exhausted and overwhelmed by the number of calls she was getting; b) overworked, underpaid, and bored shitless by her job; c) sick and tired of hearing crying women who had been banged up by boyfriends, husbands, lovers, etc. Probably all of the above. Me, too. I've gradually given up, you might say, on others taking care of me. Those proper, slower, legal means to justice. They have, in many ways, cost me dearly in terms of energy, years, and hope.

Sometimes I wonder if the violence in our lives can truly be addressed by more money, more time, more shelters, more services. I wonder how deeply what Toni Morrison calls "rememory"—the very real existence of past oppression, though its actual form may no longer be there—goes. The ability for violence to live for hundreds and maybe thousands of years through its survivors, as in Morrison's *Beloved*, where a former slave cautions her child about a plantation that is no longer physically in existence but may very well enslave her children. It's kind of like alcoholism: something that gets passed down from mother to daughter, father to son, not easily erased from our collective consciousness by affirmative action or celebrations of multiculturalism. A Third World heirloom.

When I turned ten, my father took me to a firing range and taught me how to shoot a gun. Neither he nor my mother have liberal views on violence; they simply couldn't afford to. As a child in the Philippines, she was tortured by Japanese soldiers during World War II; in India, he grew up under the British empire, which jailed his prepubescent brother. They have no illusions about what power will do to those in its grip. I grew up with an intense dislike of Brits and countless dreams of torture. The former a generalization, of course; the latter, a very real inheritance, as tangible as a trust fund, of my mother's endless dreams of running from Japanese soldiers, their bayonets gleaming in the moonlight, being chased to the top of a mountain, surrounded on all sides by a faceless Imperial Army, and then—at the last minute—being able to fly. That part, of course, is only a dream. They gave me, in essence, a childhood *sans* soft-focus innocence, minus the inculcated belief that adults will not poke, prick, and fuck you over, the instinct always to fight back on every front, from teasing pre-K homeboys to racist teachers who ignored me in class.

Fight, fight, fight, don't ever not fight, was our motto. Being a colonial, a slave, a survivor—or the progeny of one—is not easily forgotten. It becomes reinforced, relearned by living in a highly militarized and segregated culture where even small children like my son ingest the necessities of survival, self-defense on the playground. If you're over four, baby, you pay full fare. He's learned it well, a lesson I've taught with pride and some sadness: the reality that his flesh is vulnerable to cruel words and bullets, that the world will not cherish him as I do. We wonder why our children are so angry. They've got their own rememories, trapped in a rice paddy being tossed above bayonets or in an imperial jail where a boy is dying of hepatitis while the Limey guard butters his scone. Generation X can't touch this.

Most white feminists look at me disdainfully when I recount some of my choice violent moments. They are appalled, morally repelled by this unbecoming behavior. One even giggled, holding her breast bone ever so lightly and saying she is a nonviolent type, blah blah blah. The messages are, on the surface, 1) I'm educated and you're not, 2) I'm upper class and you're not, and 3) I'm a feminist and you're not (since her brand of feminism is equated with nonviolent moon-to-uterus symbiosis). My "men" can do the fighting but I, gentle maiden, shan't; the new feminism remaking a generation in the image of the suburban, wealthy, sophisticated, genetically genteel. No one protected me when a loved one cracked my head on a public street one night; not even the college-educated, Upper West Side white women strolling by and pretending not to see. I don't like getting hit either, but what are you gonna do when someone grabs your tits? Meekly whisper you won't stoop to your attacker's level? And what level exactly is that? If that's the way "women" react, how do we classify the elderly Filipinas on a subway train who, when Joe Dickwad grabbed my ass, congratulated me for whacking him as hard as I could, screaming obscenities, and chasing him—to his utter shock and dismay—through the station? They were the few who seemed to acknowledge, respect, and allow for "aggressive" forms of resistance instead of strapping on moral straightjackets for the nineties which we "women" must squeeze into. If that's a woman, I'm not one. I am an animal who eats, sleeps, fucks, and fights voraciously—I assume a "good" woman does it gently and in missionary position only. To deny our instinct for self-protection is to slam the door on all desires, to create a lustless, cookie-baking, June Cleaver in drag. A combo Stepford Wife/Virgin Mary. The polite, "good" woman who goes eek at the mousies. In reality, we seem more like exhausted, overworked, protective, hungry women and mothers who cling to our children longer than they would like and would willingly, even eagerly, protect them and ourselves with a sledgehammer.

But the broader implication is this: that one's own collaboration with mass-approved violence—i.e., institutional racism, First World nationalism, and apathetic complacency—doesn't count. Climb the corporate ladder, buy American, tune out on Prozac—these silences equal death. But there's a popular illusion that "violence" is limited only to the physical, the actual contact of skin on skin. What about the daily devastation of poverty, the lack of child care, the shortage of clean air, the sight of children going without—and one's own active or passive participation in these devastating institutions? If Jane Six Pack hits you, she's a lower-class bitch. If Jane Six Pack sits in her air-conditioned stockbroker suite investing in Latin America, it's affirmative action.

In many of the well-protected enclaves where feminism is discussed, a woman's response to violence with violence is not viewed as one of the many expressions of resistance nor as a natural, human response to daily humiliation, but as a sociopolitical faux pas. The crazy woman. I felt for the man who shot those commuters on the Long Island Railroad. How taboo. If you listened past the *New York Times* opinions on the subject, many others did also. Terrorized as I am by my understanding and horrified as I am by the act of seemingly random violence, I'd like to go beyond dismissing him as the Crazy Man. Because then I would be the Crazy Woman and we would be living in a society of Crazy Millions. Perhaps the challenge is to question why America has created so many crazies. And to ask how much longer can we live together in a country made up of segregated worlds.

The solution is hardly get a gun, Sally. Because the answer would be armed yupettes en masse blowing away mostly brothers of color in midtown. It is more a question or a series of inquiries into how we can incorporate our daily resistances, the hitting back; the spitting in a boss's coffee; the ugly contortions of our loud, angry, cuss-ridden mouths, to create an opening, a space where "we" are allowed our multiple forms of resistance which go beyond tame-able, controllable, mass consumable, and ultimately nonthreatening feminism. How this seemingly modest defiance becomes stepping-stones to redefining who the enemy is, what is resistance, why we fight back in the first place. The guerrilla girl who makes do with everything and turns away *nada*. Everyone is an ally in her world: the farmer who contributes rice, the teenager who pisses in the soldiers' drinking water, the infuriated, crazy woman who's lost her family, because all are translatable acts of rage to the next essential step. Where the ivory tower debutantes are disenfranchised of their inherited power to define and "we," the alternately poor, colored, Third World, loud, violent, nasty girls, reclaim the power of holding the compass.

A researcher I spoke with a few years back told me about a women's organization in Bengal, India, which—when confronted with frequent rapes in the women's-only section of trains—armed themselves with baseball bats and beat the shit out of any men who tried to enter the women's section. First World feminism has yet to take that basic step, to incorporate the resistances of women of color and not only the atrocities. Ultimately, our minor rebellions make the count less unequal. They are the blueprints for the very physical and very tangible reappropriation of our skin, outside, inside, everywhere, and in every way that it is ours and ours alone. If you can own your bad attitude, why can't you own the world? At the end of the day, power concedes to nothing except to power. It's a useful thing to know.

An Odd Break with the Human Heart

elizabeth mitchell

muddy, wild-eyed, some of them hairless, all of them shoeless, my dolls must be somewhere waiting for me. They're probably in my parents' attic, slumped against each other, my distinct levels of affection for each of them written on their bodies. Missing limbs indicate a favorite; smooth hair marks one received too late for me to care.

If I had as much free time now as I had during childhood, when I could devote half the afternoon to reading and riding my bike, and the other half to staring at the ceiling and imagining it flooded, I'm sure I would collapse under the weight of my guilt. It's not that I did my dolls wrong, but that I secretly resented them. They made me a mother too soon.

As a child, dolls were my children. Empathy came easily then, and adults fostered it with their encouragement of maternal gestures. Is the baby tired? Is it sick? Does it want to go outside? The classic picture books that were read to me undercut my annoyance with my orphanage of stuffed playthings and exaggerated my guilt: a toy bear on a store shelf is heartsick until a little girl finally sees beyond his frailties and brings him home. A despondent velveteen rabbit is abandoned by a child who did the unspeakable: he grew up. I would take these tales to heart and then spend the afternoon silently batting a vacant-eyed doll in a shoebox swing.

My brothers, in contrast, could be entertained by their toys, educated at whatever minor level by their racetracks and craft kits and mechanical gadgets. The world was new to me too, the strength of my arms and legs untested, but I was given the responsibility of caring for another object that contained only what I invested in it. How would I now work out the politics of who would sleep in my bed? How would I talk to my toy? I would have wished for a magnifying glass; instead I was coached to play with a mirror. What could I possibly learn? That my primary responsibility was to others, that I should shower love on something that gives me nothing in return?

My three-year-old niece often worries over a fluffy white rabbit. She tends to a number of other dolls and animals, too, but when she invited me out for a walk on the day she received her first tricycle, it was the rabbit that came along, packed into the front basket so that it could get some air. Every time we approached a buckle in the sidewalk, my niece would dismount the tricycle and wheel it over, explaining to me that she didn't want the rabbit to get too violently jarred. She had made the doll a voodoo icon of herself. Clearly, she was too scared to negotiate these obstacles her first time out, but the feeling was better projected on to some other entity—as if, already, it would be unseemly for her to elicit concern about her own worries. She had made her empathy total. Watching her efforts, I, like a traitor, felt overwhelmed by how sweet she was in her compassion, but I felt troubled too, by how prepared she was for the life of a girl. Through dolls, the heart muscles of females are strengthened, ensuring that they will be ruled by compassion and, through that compassion, by others, for the rest of their lives.

Like it or not, we women are community-oriented. We are easy marks, for example, for high-powered peer pressure. Madison Avenue bombards us with messages about acceptable appearance, and we respond with astronomical spending on skin and hair. And if you look at the most antisocial behavior—violent crime—you'll find that we play a correspondingly minimal role: women account for only 6 percent of the national total. It would be impossible to say whether our instinct to serve and preserve communities is essential (i.e., biological) or simply socialized, but it is undeniably powerful.

I find it telling that even many of the most militant feminists are unable to act selfishly. Eileen MacDonald's book on female guerrillas, *Shoot the Women First,* derives its title from a warning supposedly issued in the last few decades to anti-terrorist squad recruits in Germany. Intelligence-gathering networks found that once women had crossed over into the guerrilla life, they became more dangerous than their male counterparts. They would not hesitate to begin an exchange of fire; they persisted more passionately in the struggle; and they were more willing to take chances. Most of these women based their beliefs on feminism. And they were drawn to the rebel's pose. Astrid Proll, an early member of the anticapitalist Red Army Faction, which first bloomed in Germany in the seventies and continued its advocacy of violence into the early nineties, told MacDonald: "You must understand that then the most fantastic thing in the world was not to be a rock star, but a revolutionary."

MacDonald found that these women were impelled to transgress their traditional roles as peacekeepers because they felt doubly oppressed—both politically (because of ethnicity, ideology, or religious belief) and socially (because they were women). What allowed them to move from internalizing their protest to projecting it to the public realm, one could argue, was their sense that there was no true community to protect in the first place. Nothing of worth could be destroyed in the violence because the very foundations of society were so dangerously fissured. Their violence was loaded with ideological meaning, the culmination of a political diatribe. But even among these women, who had risked everything and broken every taboo, they persisted in seeing themselves as servants of a principle. Their cause was frequently referred to as a surrogate, a child, even a "son." The women were acting on his behalf.

The women of my mother's generation seemed given to this same sort of communal effort, winning victories for the feminist movement, for their sisters, for their daughters. They had the comfort of knowing that what they fought for was needed by all members of their gender; sexual freedom, equal opportunity in the workplace, access to all the institutions of power. They also had more clear-cut antagonists to act against: people, usually men, whose goal it seemed was to siphon off their strength, experience, and knowledge. The world has by no means become perfect for women, but the troubles, at least for middle- and upper-class women in the United States, have grown less glaring. What values do we all seek as a gender, we have to wonder, and how do we fight for them? Who is now the enemy?

Lately, I have felt the need for a new type of female rebel because I recognize that the limitations that tether me may be both harder to identify and to sever than the ones that my mother and her generation fought against. Now that we've broken the barriers that once kept us out of law schools and board rooms, we have unearthed another, more hidden source of many of our limitations: the human heart. Suddenly, as the curtain parts, we see a deeper and more beguiling force at work in constructing a self for ourselves. These are the commitments to our loved ones and friends, and their dreams for us of a self that fits into their lives neatly and cozily, like a puzzle piece. These are the wishes of a parent or the sway of feminism on our career choices.

To overcome these forces, and to look at our lives autonomously, we need to shrug off what we women have been trained to care about above all else: other people, their thoughts, feelings, and concerns. We need to put the training we received when we cared for dolls into perspective. Or we will be compelled to experience only shadow lives.

This is not to say that everyone I know is held back by ties to their community. Many women I know have identified their own ambitions and—more importantly—their own desires, and have dared to be self-interested. But many others have not. None of us would question our abilities to do a job as well as a man, but too often we don't risk leaving our ministering roles to pursue our own vision. While we are able to focus on what we know would make us feel satisfied, we remain addicted to institutions—to schools, workplaces, and other symbols of accomplishment. The rules of our lives have been changed by the women's movement, but for many women, these rules have brought with them a new set of limits, not a new sense of freedom.

Obviously, many factors influence the degree to which one's life is dictated by others. Financial need can limit certain freedoms, as can a family that is close and protective. The people I know who have traveled the farthest, taken the biggest risks, and spoken with the most freedom have often felt ostracized from society or their families. This is not to say that a terrible mother or father will make you ultimately happy; but family troubles may lead you to feel liberated.

I personally have never been away for very long from my hometown in Connecticut—probably ten months at most. Nor have I returned there for more than a few weeks at a time in the last decade. I go back for short visits, my eye selecting the fragments of landscape that seem most evocative of my youth: the thin clapboard houses, the clean yards, the sandy roads, the gray bark of trees, a sky that seems stained a perpetual, petulant dun color. It probably is not. The state has a reputation for quaint and verdant scenery; I'm sure I am just imagining the bleakness.

The weight I feel settling fully in my heart as the car races toward home is neither sentimentality, nostalgia, nor hostility. This is where the entire clan on my mother's side was born, raised, and currently lives. Down the street from my parents' house is my elementary school; ten blocks away is the publishing company where I held my first job, breaking the gender barrier as their first office girl. At the bottom of the hill is the Catholic church where my parents were married, I was confirmed, and where, as a teenager, my anger reverberated with the organ pipes. The similarity of each day in these towns seems to blend toward eternity. When I wander around here, life doesn't look empty; it seems uncomfortably full of meaning, and a pervasive solemnity tends to wash away my hope for a self-realized future.

I was not born into sisterhood: I closed a line of sons. And so my search for a feminist self is most naturally not a communal enterprise but one against, and for, my mother and her generation. My mother keeps me on a long leash. To some extent, she seems to use me as a proxy to fight her demons of self-doubt and insecurity, and to battle the sexism and limitations that she has seen but would hate to name as discrimination. I move away from home, traveling farther, earning more, putting off motherhood. She's very proud. Then I hear the soft swish of the chain through the dust. I am not exactly towed back in, but held at the run of my tether. I hear that she's been asking my brothers, "Has she talked yet of children?"

That anxiousness for me to give birth, I know, is a cipher for another desire. Now that I am in my late twenties, everyone wants to extol to me the glory of babies. My uncle reminds me frequently that he has a carriage waiting for my use. My four-year-old nephew asks me why I don't have a child yet, since after all they're fun and you can play with their toys. Even my chatty cab driver tells me I should breed soon.

In our society, babies have come to represent everything but unmaturated human beings. They function as the nexus for debate and discussion in a world changed by feminism. Few people expect women's love relationships to resemble those of our grandmothers or our mothers, but most still wonder how anyone could reject children. For my mother and many in her generation, babies are our safety net. If everything goes wrong in this wild new world of female emancipation, at least I can say that I bore children. For some, a baby provides the guarantee of domesticity; a child will anchor me at home, where my loved ones or family can find me. For my nephew, it is the doll that I need to qualify as a real girl.

For me and most of my female peers, having children lies down the road, like a can we keep kicking and catching up to. But I don't want all the hope of life to reside in the beginning of a new human being. I want that anticipation to reside in an unborn part of myself, whether it be intellectual, spiritual, or emotional. I want to push myself toward this self-realization, but I am hounded by anxieties, among which three are particularly powerful: one, that the notion of self-realization is an illusion, ultimately indistinguishable from self-aggrandizement. Two, that because my self-interest is hazy to me, my movement toward what I think I want will actually lead me on a path to what I dread; that my dreams of complete freedom, like my childhood fantasies of being a back-up dancer for the Beatles, will expose themselves as wrongheaded with the years. And three, that the sobriety of the community where I was born, or rather, of which I was born, will call me back. With only a touch of grim humor, my elders repeatedly espoused certain scraps of advice: "Always remember, no job is fun. Working a 'dumb job' is better than pursuing a less secure, desired job. Life isn't going to be exciting every minute." None of these are outrageously dark in and of themselves. But together, they compose a drumbeat of resignation. Nathaniel Hawthorne would be proud that the old New England spirit lives on.

Feminism enters this world like a life raft. Its message, in stark contrast, seems to be wholly optimistic. If you remain strong, self-reliant, angry at the right times, supportive, and, when given the opportunity, ambitious to break new ground for the gender, then everything will work out well. You will feel at peace with yourself. But whether intended or not, feminism usually celebrates power; it holds up politically motivated women to idolize: the founder of a feminist journal or the leader of a local uprising. Simultaneously, it encourages a suppression of the ego in homage to the greater good of sisterhood. And those images are infectious, especially to those of us who have not given up on feminism yet, who want it not just to change institutions but the quality of all women's lives. To be a great woman, I should prioritize the common good, whether that involves a communal task or merely rising higher in my profession, functioning as a symbol of my gender in the social hierarchy.

I should place my life on the altar of our continued struggle, but in my heart I only want to be an explorer of the world, free to move where I want. I am less concerned with making enough money to buy beauty than in finding beauty in the Badlands or the frozen Baltic Sea.

Back when I was in third grade, our teacher would run a column in the class-produced newsletter, listing each child's dreams for the future. Veterinarians were in abundance, as were mothers and race-car drivers. At that age, such visions of an imaginary future are considered adorable. Parents like to look at the lists and chuckle at how bold, how perfect, or perhaps how prescient their children's choices are. By high school, no one seems to care much about what teenagers aspire to; they'd rather judge "Most Popular" or predict "Most Likely to Succeed." At that point, society has asserted its interest, clearly letting us know what is expected of us. By young adulthood, we've usually come up with new visions of a fulfilling life—and learned to keep those fantasies to ourselves.

By the time we're adults, feminism has given us confidence, but oddly only within the context of competition with men—and primarily within social constructs that already exist. When, for example, I am offered the opportunity of power in the workplace, no matter how minor, I feel urged to take it, like an addict, to demonstrate the talents of my gender, to stand as a marker for the shifting demographics in the white-collar workplace, to take the path my mother's generation hewed for me: to a desk, a regular paycheck, a Rolodex.

I am well aware that I could perform in a job as well as a man, but can I achieve autonomous, personal excellence? Without clear markers for this kind of success, many women in my generation, including myself, feel ill at ease. If one can refer to a graduate degree, a title of employment, a project involving many other people, then one's efforts are taken seriously. We are differentiated from our mother's generation or the generation before that. We feel secure with the definitions of success that have always existed in this country.

When I consider these definitions, these traditions, these constraints, I feel the urge to call upon women to rebel, but I struggle to define what the benefit of rebellion would be. The old rewards seem too empty. I suspect the true goal would be the perpetual pursuit of joy. In seeking joy, the agonies would not disappear—perhaps, in fact, happiness would rarely materialize—but the human gesture would be toward delight, and that pursuit, I believe, must begin with the individual. Groups or movements can bring equality. Only individuals can achieve ecstasy.

• • •

Part of the challenge of living out one's own vision is that it demands an odd break with the hyperactivity of the human heart. We women have the profound ability to see ourselves everywhere—in every person, in virtually every role, in the way that my niece could see her own fears reflected in a stuffed rabbit.

Compassion, love, and empathy are all important values, and extremely attractive. But in women, they can become debilitating, even dangerous. Why do women stay in threatening relationships, for example? I don't want to simplify this. There are obviously a zillion reasons, among them financial dependency, the fear of being alone, and the terror of retribution. But also, I believe, is that flicker of compassion that forfeits all self-preservation. And why does that empathy spark? Because the other person had austere parents, a hard day at work; because he or she breathes, because he or she merely exists. In love, as an adult, I challenge myself not to give away my heart like a pacifier. I try to stop the hair trigger of my empathy, to keep myself from offering my affection purely as the salve that will restore peace to a troubled soul. It's necessary to offer compassion, but love should not be confused with pity.

We need to identify where our own passions lie and isolate them from what we think other people want for us. What do *we* want to do with our lives? Whom do *we* choose to love? These questions are not easy to sort out, nor can anyone predict what is right for another person. In fact, to do so would be antithetical to this call to action. But we should give each other respect and leeway, recognizing that the true pursuit of a fully realized self, when it is in process, is often less automatically attractive or valued than the empty exercise of power.

Of course the process will never cease, I recognize that my life will not be easily partitioned into the before and after of an epiphany inspired by a life led by true desire. Perhaps my veil of anxiety will never lift. I will await myself the way I linger for a friend on a mountain lookout, allowing them the moment when they will recognize the mysterious cue that allows them to leave. Am I done yet? Am I ready to go back and sort through the aspirations and ambitions that my loved ones bequeathed me, as they did the dolls, and figure out which ones are worth my respect, my time, my effort?

To some extent, I suppose I have already begun this process. Despite the fact that there are many influences from my community I have put off, part of what I am taking on in at least temporarily rejecting the demands of my family, my friends, my gender, is an option my mother—who loves to travel but rarely does, who adores journalism but gave it up for marriage and children—has always wanted me to have: the exquisite agony of being an individual and the awful luxury of feeling unsettled.

Missionary Position

gina dent

unlike many people, i don't remember a time when i "became" a feminist. I can recollect moments when individual feminist issues took their place in my consciousness as significant questions, problems, debates, or decisions. I can recall when I first read Angela Davis's *Women, Race, and Class*, and when, recovering from surgery, I discovered Alice Walker's *In Search of Our Mother's Gardens*. In college, I began to take courses on Black women, and I learned to narrate my life through those stories. But it never "happened" to me the way it seems to have "happened" to those women who came to feminism in the generation before me. In some ways, my experience feels closer to the one my grandmother might have described. Like her, I grabbed at every means I could to make the life that I was living hold more possibility. And I used whatever strategies I could uncover to strengthen my sense of being in the world. In other words, I was doing feminism before I was talking feminism—and long before intellectualizing feminism became part of the basis for my career.

That's what makes me stop now to consider just what it was that I was doing before I was calling it feminism—and why it is that many women, especially young women, are doing what looks to me like feminism and not calling it that. This is not a new issue, after all, this problem of doing but not claiming feminism. In the written history of U.S. feminism, there is at least one parallel case that might help to explain what I mean: the case of Black American feminism.

In response to ongoing complaints and queries by the white feminist community about the participation of Black women, Black women have made a number of arguments, most of which conclude that while it may not look the same as white feminism (the Feminism that gets to wear a capital "F"), and while it may not always call itself feminism, Black feminism does indeed represent a parallel movement toward women's emancipation. Black feminism, or "womanism," includes me and my grandmother, since it has never based itself on a self-conscious description of particular movements or strategies. It intersects with and embraces ways of existing in the world that claim nothing to do with women's emancipation, and it charts these stories as evidence of "womanish" wisdom and struggle. This is important, because while it is sometimes true that we are living it before we are speaking it, the reverse can also be true—we can understand something theoretically long before we actually live it. There are things that I have read about Black feminism (things still noticeably absent from written Feminism) that I am only now beginning to make use of, which is why it is critical that we write the contemporary histories of all feminisms in such a way that they include the many kinds of people who are doing them, and not only those who are speaking the name of Feminism in the language and manner we have come to accept. These narratives of feminism will help to sustain the next generation of women and men who might find themselves in them, who might be encouraged and supported by them. As I was. And who might be instructed and enabled by them. As I am.

The rest of my story is about the combined tendency in the world of public information toward what I am loosely calling "confession," about its uses and abuses, and about how it contributes to the problem of doing feminism without saying it and saying feminism without doing it. It seems to me that in order to answer the question of why young women are not claiming feminism, we have to consider it from the other side—what is it that feminists are doing that gets labeled Feminism? I think much of what they (we) are doing is making confessions.

These confessions are not always intended to work toward the shared goal within feminism of making more information available to those who have been denied access to it and the right to produce it. A confession is not, after all, about the exchange of information. A confession is about form, not content. It is about the act of confessing, about the experience of that moment of revelation, and about those before whom the revelation is made. This practice of making confessions concerns itself little with the factuality of the story, or with the desired outcome of its telling, but rather with the performance of telling itself. At the moment of confession, one can imagine the self extending outward and into a community that assumes it has something in common with you and that you in turn identify with.

But each community sets limits as to what can be confessed. Some things are too outlandish, some not serious enough. Some things will brand you as a nonbeliever, others will require remedies that exceed the power of the circle. Confessions always have their scripts, and nothing in them nor in their mode of presentation can violate the circle of commonsense. They must fall on the ears of the other so naturally that any transgression will titillate but not shock, surprise but not disappoint. You must know what to do even though you must never talk about what to do. And you must know what price your confession will exact.

In the small world I inhabit, these rules of confession have disrupted the validity of many feminist gestures. Loosely interpreting the most common feminist edict as a mandate for public performance, there has been an overarching reduction of the feminist ethic to a limited confessional practice based on the phrase "The personal is political." That slogan, now twisted to serve not the collective cause of feminism but the individual causes of many who appear best to represent, serves to validate statements that used to get disciplined out of theoretical and scholarly circles. But where there is no process through which legitimate self-exploration is translated into collective benefit, the feminism drops out of Feminism and the personal fails to become political. The current practice of confession instead works to establish the bounds of what I think of as "missionary feminism," a feminism that puts forward its program so stridently, guards its borders so closely, and legislates its behavior so fervently that many are afraid to declare its name.

Let me illustrate what I mean. Not long ago, I went to Minnesota to attend a conference on feminism and the law. An amazing array of women from the United States and Canada had come together—women who were Black, white, Asian, Latina, Native American, Arab-Canadian, and so forth. Poised to begin our morning panel after an encouraging dinner the night before, the first group of speakers went around the table and introduced ourselves to the audience, giving some context for why we had been invited and why we had chosen to come. Then came the first round of comments. Not long into this exchange, I asked a general question in response to remarks made by one of the panelists. My question was based on the academic inquiry into the production of women's agency. How, I wondered aloud, can we describe another woman's life as a crisis in need of remedy without doing violence to that woman by naming her condition for her? In what moments are we, as feminists, authorized to speak for other women about what we, as theorists and activists, interpret as their oppression?

I asked this question after I heard one of the speakers tell a story of a woman whom she had heard being beaten by her husband, though who later, when the speaker asked this woman about what had been done to her, made up another story to cover for her husband. And I asked this question based on the comments of a woman who identified herself as formerly "prostituted" and who now devoted her energy to helping to change the lives of others currently in the position in which she formerly found herself. But I asked the question more generally, because contained within it were many stages of the process of assimilating intellectual feminism, the culmination of which, I now felt, something I had learned before I had experienced.

What happened shortly after I raised these points both surprised and frustrated me. Now I realize I was unprepared for what followed because at the time I had not yet begun to think of feminism in terms of its dynamic of confession. I had not yet understood that personal revelation and the characterization of one's own life was also meant to authorize other remarks that might be made. Much later, I was made aware that I had violated a sacred rite—what the organizers later referred to as the "coming to voice" of another woman.

The irony of their words was impressed upon me further by the fact that all the women gathered in Minneapolis had responded to the promise that our words would be documented in the published transcript of these roundtables. When the publication of the transcript was replaced by a summary article authored by the conference organizers, their emphasis on "coming to voice" became the kind of ritualized complaint —supported by its rhetoric, its form, and by the audience that would permit it—that many of us had worked against while we were there.

It is not that I had never known of this concept. After all, my early African-Americanist and feminist education was based largely on the loose application of this principle in establishing the legitimacy of the material I was studying at the time. And I had always respected the sacredness of other people's stories in group situations designed to encourage healing and private exploration, in rape crisis centers, in women's groups, in friendships. I could not recall, however, the experience of this ritual in so public an atmosphere, and certainly not at an academic conference at the time destined for publication. I understood the expression "coming to voice" as referring to a process that had already culminated. It was impossible to imagine the performance of the moment of "coming to voice" as unconnected to the whole series of moments that preceded it, to "private" revelation toward self-conscious action that might possibly culminate in public speech or activity, but might just as easily result in some otherwise unremarked-upon "private" transformation. That is, I understood the idea of the personal becoming political differently, as happening at a later stage in the feminist process.

I had no idea that in responding to my Minnesota friend's confession in this way, questioning activities she was involved in on behalf of other women based on theoretical principles she had drawn from interpreting her own experience, and placing those principles up for intellectual discussion, I had broken what many considered a feminist code, not as it was explained to me but as I have come to understand it. What I had done was place her story—of having attempted to enter a strip club the night before the conference with a group of women protesters from her own organization—up for contest. What I had done was treat her individual, personal, even intimate story as the basis for a public discussion in which the boundaries were unclear, in order to arrive at a theoretical model for feminism in general. But I did this because I made the assumption that her position on the panel and her leadership of an organization assured that she had moved already through a number of stages of "coming to voice." For me, this public forum was an opportunity to discuss our responsibility as feminists who had turned to our work—of various kinds—as a space to work out these issues on another level. In the hierarchy of feminist praxis, we had moved to another stage.

But I had misunderstood. This was not a feminist reworking from the ground of that intellectual intervention, "the personal is political." This was a confession. And before I knew what I had done, and in the midst of the discussion that followed my question, the woman who had made the confession left the room in tears, refusing ever to return.

From the moment I asked my questions, there were two

conferences, it seemed: one that lumbered along, attempting to address various issues of feminist praxis; and another that sought to reconstruct the story of my colleague's leaving. Over the remainder of our time together, which had then only just begun, I and others were reminded of this extended moment in phrases such as, "We should think about what we have done to her." "We," of course, was euphemistic, and I and the other women of color who spoke on my behalf began quickly to see where responsibility was going to be laid. The difficult question of agency I had raised was then answered for me simply, though in a manner I could not have anticipated. Just as the woman I questioned had been "prostituted," "we" had done this to her. Which is how I came to realize just who this Feminism was for.

"So you see this as racial?" was the response that I received when I risked pointing this out in a more private circle (as if the emotional codes of early Feminism which held that certain emotional responses, i.e., crying, laughter, anger, were more natural and legitimate than others had not already been thoroughly examined as racially, culturally, and economically biased). In this space, a decidedly Feminist space, I had broken the code. The woman who left was affirmed because she used it, and it worked to her advantage.

In the number of defenses of myself that I felt compelled to give over the remainder of the weekend, I made use of some of the feminist knowledge that I had only understood intellectually before. I was able not only to address prostitution, a Feminist issue, but my treatment as a contradiction, a Black feminist issue, both strong enough to have forced a woman out of a room, but weak because I was a young Black woman. They spoke to me as a young Black student, hiding within their condescension the racialized difference of our theoretical feminist interpretations. Here, generational and professional status served to confuse what would otherwise be a discussion of differences among equals. In the end, it did not matter what I was able to argue, because until now, the only public story of feminism was the one that insisted I had broken the code.

And I had broken it in more than one way. Her confession was about the issue of prostitution, an issue deeply entrenched within the nexus of issues most controversial in the feminist community. Her declaration, "I was a prostituted woman," was about what had been done to her as a victim. Her feminism had taught her to define the harm and to determine who was responsible for it. And it had given her a missionary zeal to purge this evil from the lives of all women on their behalf.

So I ask here quite seriously: how and when did feminism become a religion? When did we begin to proselytize, on the basis of this moral obligation we have, to save? And I ask the same question now that I asked that morning in Minneapolis, in a still more public forum: how do we address the question of women's agency, of attributions of false consciousness and delusional thinking in racial and feminist and class-based terms? In other words, How do we teach and encourage feminism without assuming that those who do not proclaim it—or who proclaim in a way other than we might expect—do not use it, without assuming that those who are not its missionaries are living in "sin"?

By declaring that "the personal is political," feminist theorists held that to start from your own point of view was to help explain something larger than yourself; to legitimate that which was not yet part of the public dialogue; to make the language of politics less remote; to widen the sphere of viable life choices.

It was an intervention that declared that there were significant things that happened in interpersonal relationships that had profound political ramifications because they affected large numbers of similarly situated people at the same time. "The personal is political" gave women a way to establish themselves as a class of beings in the world. And understanding ourselves as a class moved us from just doing it through talking about doing it into theorizing about our doing it. This meant that more women (and even men) could get hold of this information and try to incorporate it into their lives. It was the pedagogy of the oppressed.

In the current period of what some consider crisis (perhaps better labeled stasis), personal revelation is often dressed up as the grounds for greater public action and theorizing, leaving us with the problem of the public consumption of feminist ego and the private experience of apathy, even paralysis. This lack of interest in and identification with feminism, at least in its most public incarnation, is at least partly caused by Feminism's inability to claim its victories in moving past them, and the increasing tendency for feminists and others to accept a description of feminism that appears to circumscribe ideas too impractical, remote, radical, or theoretical for everyday use.

The fact that everyday feminism doesn't always look like the Feminism that appears in books anymore is partly a function of the generational shift that has led to the description of the feminist movement in waves. This generational language hides other differences within it—national trajectories, sexual orientation, professional status, etc. In effect, then, the problem is not so much in the gap between generations of feminists, but in the efforts of feminists having now matured into many levels of activity in many places and, consequently, the hierarchy in the way those activities are claimed. Establishment feminism, then, is not simply white and bourgeois, as Black feminists have argued in the past. The "third wave's" attempts to grapple with that hierarchy require more than the old ways of analyzing race and class. The current diversification of descriptive American identities, and the (at last) more commonly accepted notion of the impossibility of ascribing to any of those identities a single perspective, necessitates another kind of language for feminism. Which makes it doubly hard to point out racist effects—the substantive work that racism does —since these effects are also partly generational and theoretical (at the level of the language), and they will have to be pointed out in a climate where many believe we are beyond them.

It may be difficult for many to accept a new description of oppression that cross-cuts constituencies within feminism, one that doesn't automatically align power relations with race, nationality, sexuality, or ability, but sometimes with an invisible demand for a particular mode of feminist practice. As one such mode, then, confession becomes not only a dynamic within feminism but a means of policing its borders.

If speaking in the name of feminism means that what is spoken must follow the rules of confession, then the demand for all feminists to do so is also a process of conversion. And conversion in this sense is not what many will argue it must be: the willing acceptance of a new way of life based on an understanding and belief in feminist principles. Instead, it becomes the unself-conscious acceptance of the way that feminism is done. Feminism as such is no longer a free-form nexus of ideas and strategies but a *way* of living in the world that can hide its origins in racism, classism, heterosexism, etc. It is no surprise, then, that there is on the part of many women an equally unself-conscious distancing from the circle of feminist confessors and from the name under which these rituals are declared.

I say that this acceptance and this turning away are unself-conscious because I think much of the basis upon which these circles have parted is rarely discussed or analyzed, or even decided in a particular moment. It doesn't "happen" in some moment of awareness. It happens more in the way that I recall my own acceptance of feminism, without particular notice. It is, of course, a part of how our identity is formed, but in this generation it is interpolated through means far less direct.

When I have spoken to other women who do not consider themselves feminists, about the issues and decisions in our lives that I consider to be intimately connected to feminist practice, we can often agree about what to do in a particular moment even when we cannot agree about what to call it. The question, then, is the one that seems to appear everywhere in this post–civil rights generation: where is the movement? The downside of feminism's dispersion from the generation that theorized it into the generation that absorbed it in practice is that feminism's history has become much harder to write. It is not the women's movement but AIDS activism, rape crisis centers, discussions of unequal health care, and even more importantly, other things much harder to categorize, the smaller things we do on a daily basis that form the patterns of our lives. And while some of us would band together these smaller and larger acts and label them as expressions of the truth of our gendered lives, and therefore evidence of the continued impact of feminism, others would see this attribution as blind avowal to a faith that requires its inflationary public tithing.

But there are many closet feminists, private worshipers who cherish the routine application of feminist principles in their lives though they would never confess in the circle. Still more serious a fault to some, they have no missionary zeal. Even if they could recognize their faith and name it to themselves, they would never jeopardize their life's careful balance by the open admission of idolatry. They would certainly never devote their time to proselytizing in its name. This is not to blame them. Not this time. They share their secrets with each other, their friends, partners, and children. They, perhaps as much as any others, maintain the fragile thread of faith that is made visible only in rare personal and political moments.

That thread is the only evidence we have that there could be a movement, that, were we able to unleash that energy by attending to some of our exclusionary and disciplinary tendencies, we might find that we were stronger than we thought. We might find that we would have the grandmothers and the daughters along with the mothers. We might find that we would have the sons, too. Not all of them. But enough of these women and men to feel less insecure about our fate and thus less constrained to the tireless defense of our name.

Those who "do" feminism without proclaiming it are women I often run in to in the course of my day. They can analyze, as well as any I have heard, the dynamics of race and sex in their offices, talk about the way men in their classes dominate the discussion, and conspire to maintain their public space. Perhaps most significantly, they do not see themselves as weak enough to merit protection. And they relish all the privileges that civil rights and feminism have brought them. But when they do this, even when they do this together, they do not discuss its relevance to feminism. They do not have to, and they do not want to. But I hold on to this fragile thread of their faith because it is the one thing that connects them and me, the one thing that makes it possible for me to believe that there will be another history written, or many small ones, though one that may not be catalogued in the way we might expect. To hold on to that thread, we must work to make feminism a faith worthy of proclaiming, and less of a religion that takes its edicts from the hierarchy.

I propose, then, that we begin to think critically about how to take the religion out of feminism, how to break down the illusion that we comprise a community that has agreed upon its rules of existence. From my Minnesota story, we may extrapolate at least two problems for feminism: first, how to deal with the emotional need for feminism that is currently expressing itself as religious fervor; and second, how to rethink our positions around sex and woman's pleasure without assuming we can describe and determine a single missionary feminist point of view—the missionary position. I take from this a lesson for feminism: if we continue to operate in it as if it is a religion, we lose our ability to translate its pleasures and joys to future generations, and we risk its dissolution in the name of religious freedom.

Feminism has allowed us to begin to understand how the designation of some things as public and others as private has shielded power used against women and prevented us from exerting our own power elsewhere. But the authority to dispense information has disappeared with the ever-growing abuse of the power of the disciples in the ritual of confession. We must admit that the posture of confession is not necessarily personal revelation; it is the staging of an event designed to have a certain effect. It addresses a deep need, but disguised underneath it are often attacks against those who stand outside of the circle.

My Minnesota missionary attempted to gain the authority to take control of our collective stories simply because she was speaking from personal pain. When these gestures are legitimated by an audience of converts, they create the appearance of putting oneself on the line. They may well come from the good intention of promoting another way of being in the world, but confession is less about changing conditions than converting souls. There is no purity in that.

Giving It Up: Orgasm, Fear, and Femaleness

donna minkowitz

His throat grunted painful noises, an awful pleading whine that went ignored as he felt his buttocks spread roughly apart. A searing pain raced through his body as the hardness of one of his attackers tore roughly into his rectum. "Shake back, bitch!" a voice urged. "Give him a wiggle!" His rapist expressed delight as his body flinched and quivered from the burning cigarettes being applied to his side by other inmates gleefully watching.

the relation of real violence to fantasy—and to the violent quality of orgasms—makes many of us deeply uneasy. If I tell you this quotation comes from a supposedly nonfiction account of prison rape—Wilbert Rideau's *The Sexual Jungle*—

will that make you more ashamed of having been turned on by it?

It's not surprising to me that rape has always been a potent metaphor for coming. Despite my outrage at the verdict, the 1992 gang rape trial of college football players in Glen Ridge, New Jersey, was a bonanza for my fantasy life, with both a baseball bat and a mocked-at, retarded victim. My inner movie screen has also thrilled to fourth-grade memories of Linda Blair's ordeal-by-broomstick in *Born Innocent*, the Menendez brothers and their slippery parents, and Snoop Doggy Dogg's lyric about "fuck[ing] the fleas off the bitch." There are also more enduring representations of that hideous strength. Late at night, I turn the lights down low, uncap some Astroglide, and pull out Andrea Dworkin, trawling for passages like this:

> What I told her when she made me talk to her is how once you went to jail they started sticking things up you. They kept putting their fingers and big parts of their whole hand up you, up your vagina and up your rectum; they searched you inside and stayed inside you and kept touching you inside and they searched inside your mouth with their fingers and inside our ears and nose and they made you squat in front of the guards to see if anything fell out of you and stand under a cold shower and make different poses and stances to see if anything fell out of you and then they had someone who they said was a nurse put her hands up you again and search your vagina again and search your rectum again and . . . then the big one who had been watching and laughing took the speculum which I didn't know what it was because I'd never seen one or had

anyone do these awful things to me and it was a big, cold, metal thing and he put it in me and he kept twisting and turning it and he kept tearing me to pieces. [*Mercy,* pp. 71–72, Four Walls Eight Windows, 1991]

Is it horrible to say that reading about real-world rape and torture sometimes turns me on? Some accounts make me sick, some make me angry, and still other accounts make me sick, angry, and aroused at the same time. On some occasions, arousal is the only emotion I feel. Is that inhuman of me?

"Inhuman"—the fear of becoming like a beast. Out of control, swinish, a brute . . . the animal I provoke when I allow myself inside the gates. It's not just unsafe to open these gates —it's shameful. Men, church, state, and art have told us for centuries that we're disgusting when we get out of control— bestial, dirty as only the body can be dirty. How can women give it up enough to let someone see us writhe, claw, moan, and beg, the bitches in heat we've fought forever not to become?

I'm fifteen years old and faking orgasms with my first girl-friend. Every time she touches me in some way that might actually arouse me enough to lead to a real one, I make her stop. The sensations feel so threatening that I would rather be frustrated than experience them for even a second. Once the danger has passed, I'll thrash around in ungratified perfor-mance.

The first time my girlfriend goes down on me, it feels almost like pain. But it is not pain. It is—too much. Being in need and out of control like this feels all wrong. It's as though an insect stung me there, or maybe I broke something. This can't be a natural feeling. I can't imagine voluntarily repeating this.

Sixteen years later, I have learned how to come. I've been practicing, conscientiously, for six years. It's gotten easier to endure, but even now I understand why nineteenth-century doctors warned that masturbators would go mad or revert to a more primitive life-form, and why the religious right still believes this. When Dr. James Dobson of Focus on the Family warns that sexual liberation will provoke an epidemic of rape, "cross-species fetuses," and even serial murder, he could be speaking straight out of my fears.

When I touch myself, I am waving a red flag at a bull. Forcing, soothing, and seducing myself through this nightmare might be the most macho thing I've ever done. But it's the kind of macho that appears to require a woman's full-bodied bravery—sometimes called "masochism." The difference between bravery and masochism has always puzzled me, but perhaps that's because women have never been taught to jettison our feelings at the moment of impact. How do you open yourself to a threat? One lover told me, "When you come, you put your hands in fists." I'm not surprised that my need for defense is so great at a time when forces I can't control are turning me into an animal being I don't recognize.

Learning how to masturbate felt a little like those torture simulations the Army does for its fighter pilots in training. "You will survive this," I would comfort/warn myself. "I can't survive this," I'd protest and taunt back. But I couldn't tell which voice was seducing, or which was torturing the other.

If I felt this forever, I would go insane, said a nonmacho being somewhere inside me. Extreme arousal has always made me think of William Burroughs's disquieting riffs on "the algebra of need," a phrase he coined to describe the exigencies of heroin addiction:

> In the words of total need: "Wouldn't you?" Yes you would. You would lie, cheat, inform on your friends, steal, do anything to satisfy total need. Because you would be in a state of total sickness, total possession, and not in a position to act in any other way. . . . A rabid dog cannot choose but bite. [*Naked Lunch*, Introduction]

Perhaps the algebra of need meant even more to me in terms of that need that shadows sex, the equally discomfiting demand for emotional connection.

Looking at the thesaurus entry for Necessity, I find I could easily masturbate to it: "Necessity, compulsion, duress . . . choicelessness, no choice, no alternative, Hobson's choice . . . involuntary, instinctive, automatic, unwilled . . . urgent need, 'necessity's sharp pinch,' matter of life and death . . . inevitable, unavoidable, inescapable."

But why would arousal feel like torture to begin with? When I first began exploring my own obstreperous numbness, I thought I might have been sexually abused as a child. Now I conjecture it may have more to do with a less dramatic occurrence: getting hit. Whenever I remember a fist coming down on me, I sense myself losing control of my own body, feeling things happen to its surfaces and vitals that I have no ability to order and no capacity to stop. To have another person make you experience pain against your will is to experience enormous helplessness: even if we can't control anything else in the world, we can usually control our own bodies, and losing that control to another person can make you feel like you have lost everything, lost utterly, ceased, in a way, to be a human being.

Losing control while experiencing pleasure can feel just as dangerous. Helplessness is helplessness, and the vulnerability of arousal feels all too similar to the shaky sensations of violence and the air of defeat they bring.

Yet part of me wants to resist the inclination to trace my terror to this one cause—a putative Original Abuse that would explain everything that frightens me about the abyss. Does the fear of violence and enthrallment impel only those who have been physically battered? In fact, all women grow up under the shadow of the rapist looming just beyond our ken—or his alter ego, the lover who will break us to his will. These two personages may be very different in real life (being in love is a lot different from being raped), but in the psychological realm they could be kissing cousins. In our culture, the anguish of closeness is huge whether the entity closing in threatens with coercion or compatibility.

Many of us shiver when we hear the wolf of intimacy at our door, but women more than men have good cause to cover their ears to its sexual roar. One reason it sounds more threatening to us is women's more intimate acquaintance with all kinds of violation of our physical boundaries. I remember my ex-lover Julia abruptly withdrawing her wet vulva from my stroking hand. She was having a flashback of sexual abuse from age four. And I call to mind another lover, Ellen, inexplicably becoming angrier than I'd ever seen anybody be in bed. She'd been transported, she explained later, and was confusing me with the man who'd raped her. Whether or not the abuser's hand has actually pressed against our labia—or slammed into our face—our identity as women is constituted by the threat of violence. From childhood we are made to understand that other people will try to control our bodies, and that many will succeed. Unlike boys, we are never taught to fight back when our physical self-sovereignty is threatened.

That is why our identity is an identity of incoherence, and why it's so hard to give it up to the other's mouth or her hand or just the universe watching as you lose control by yourself. Losing control of our sexual feelings can be so devastating that we fear we'll lose something even more central to us: our moral integrity.

Out-of-control desire, Catharine MacKinnon asserted in a 1993 *Ms.* article, was responsible for some of the most horrific atrocities of this century: the mass rapes in Bosnia. She attributed the systematic physical and sexual abuse of Muslim and Croatian women by Serbian military men to an overweening sadistic desire triggered solely by pornography:

> When pornography is . . . normal, a whole population of men is primed to dehumanize women and to enjoy inflicting assault sexually. The *New York Times* reported finding "piles of pornographic magazines" in the bedroom of Borislav Herak, the captured Serbian soldier who calmly admitted to scores of rapes and murders. . . . Pornography is the perfect preparation —motivator and instruction manual in one—for the sexual atrocities ordered in this genocide. [*Ms.*, July/ August 1993, p. 28]

MacKinnon quotes one informant who remembers "a thick sex book that made the rounds" in a Serbian military prison. "It showed," she said, "men with animals and women with animals, how you get AIDS." Images like these, MacKinnon says, are what drive the Serbian soldiers to rape. Because these men have let go their humanness enough to fantasize about having sex with animals, about *women* having sex with animals, and about "how you get AIDS," they have turned into uncontrollable rape-beasts whose ethics are the ethics of the jungle. [p. 29]

As MacKinnon sees it, loss of control permeates the Serbs' encounter with sexual desire. The "thick sex book" was "so read that it was completely falling apart" [p. 29]. For MacKinnon, the Serbs' desire has unleashed a monster within them that resulted in some of the most heinous abuses of this century. But there is a difference between feeling and action that MacKinnon fails to see: namely, the difference between getting turned on by images of domination, and getting turned on by such images and then raping people. And the difference between me and those Serbian prison guards is that although I may have similar sexual responses, I am not going to rape or brutalize anyone. Through letting myself experience orgasm and S/M, I've learned that I can trust myself to feel whatever desires I have. Faced with temptation, I do *not* become that fictive beast whose conduct has no limits.

But MacKinnon implies that if people ever get the sexual satisfaction we really want, we will not be able to stop ourselves from taking it by force. We will need to be locked up to protect the innocents who haven't tasted blood. I know this terror intimately, because it's one of the oldest parts of myself. It is what kept me from knowing my emotions, enjoying my girlfriends, or trusting my body for my first ten sexual years. It is not a rational fear, but it is a very powerful one. It is the feeling that may lead so many of us to fantasize having sex in chains.

Whatever humanness is, it is not about smothering the bundle of emotions society has called "the beast" that dwells inside us. Seen by the half-light of repression, this unnamed thing may well look like a monster, crammed so far down inside our internal prison that it has taken on all the characteristics of the tortured, the filthy, the damned.

It looks less and less like a monster when I hold it in my arms.

The author would like to thank Ann Powers for her many insights and suggestions.

Pushing Away the Plate

min jin lee

bus stop.

It is usually bright and slightly cool in the mornings when I
wait for my bus at the Seventy-second Street and Lexington
Avenue bus stop. I try to get on the M101 Limited bus when I
go to work. This bus going downtown makes local stops from
Seventy-second to Sixtieth Street, but it makes express stops
from Sixtieth Street to Fiftieth and from Fiftieth Street to
Grand Central Station without halting every two blocks. Despite its Park Avenue address, my office has another entrance
on Lexington Avenue between Forty-fifth Street and Forty-

sixth Street so when I get on the Limited bus, I get off at Fiftieth Street and walk a few blocks toward the shiny glass building which houses my office. But on the one or two days when I miss the Limited bus, I get on the local one, and my normal ten-minute ride extends easily to twenty minutes.

Although I get a bit annoyed at myself, because I'll start my day a little late, secretly, the longer ride is a small treat, because I know that I will see interesting people on my bus— old and young, rich and poor—and I shall have time to craft stories in my head about them. I'll concentrate on the rich pattern of a woman's chenille suit or gaze at the lightly textured balding spot of a man's head and imagine her or his life outside of the bus that we share. Sometimes, I get lucky and find a comfortable window seat for myself, and then I'm not annoyed at all. I daydream for a luxurious twenty minutes before reaching my destination, my shared office with its heavy, dark wooden desk piled high with documents to draft, review, and revise.

When I am seated in my window seat, I begin to think about the passengers and I discover that I forget my own size. The people around me seem to grow in their girth and breadth and my body diminishes slowly. I feel tiny and girlish, rather prim but curious about my surroundings. The worn seat of the bus swallows me up and I've become invisible. I am formless and all eyes. Around me are all these seated and standing adults who are on their way to work. Some women are breathtakingly beautiful. Their hair doesn't move as they shift the sliding weight of their printed alligator leather handbags on their narrow shoulders. The lanky, beautiful women wear expensive sunglasses and smell of musky perfume. They look as if they work in the fashion or publishing industry. Then, there are women who look fatigued; their shapes are heavy and full and they often wear clothes that look uncomfortable and tight. The tired women look like housekeepers or home-care nurses. These women carry worn plastic shopping bags emblazoned with THANK YOU FOR SHOPPING HERE on them. Mingled everywhere, I notice women who wear suits. The suits are often navy or gray. Sometimes, the suits look very new on the wearer. The women who wear the suits are between the ages of twenty-five and forty-five. They carry cordovan leather briefcases with squared-off handles, which slide in and out of an envelopelike opening. The briefcases have long shoulder straps. I am amazed at the number of professional women who carry them. On the outer pockets of the briefcases, glossy fashion and life-style magazines peep out behind the unread newspapers.

As the bus advances toward my stop, I remember that I am five feet nine inches tall and weigh almost one hundred and forty pounds. My large physical frame emerges from the seat of the bus, and as I straighten the skirt of my dark suit, I remind myself that I am a corporate lawyer and not a tidy immigrant girl in a shapeless outfit. I maneuver my body toward the front of the bus and disembark.

The stroll from the bus stop to my building takes two minutes and this time is enough for me to wake up, take the tortoiseshell headband off my nearly dry hair, and straighten my posture. I am a lawyer, I am a lawyer, I am a lawyer. I recite this like a mantra for two interlocked purposes: to state affirmatively that I am a female white collar professional and to nullify the negative statement belying my mantra, that I am just a young woman who has no idea what she is doing in this shiny glass building in midtown Manhattan. I start my second diurnal chant, I belong here, I belong here, I belong here.

As I get off the elevator which opens up to the wood-paneled lobby of the law firm and greet the receptionist, who sits behind an impressive oval desk made of burl wood, I feel tense knots of uncertainty with respect to my new role as an attorney. As I walk in, other young women approach the reception desk. They are laughing and their formerly loud conversations of their subway, bridge, and tunnel rides cease, and they bend a little to sign in on the attendance sheets on a clipboard. I don't sign in because the receptionist marks a check in a box for me; lawyers do not keep track of their own presence or absence, only secretaries, paralegals, and other members of support staff do. On certain mornings, the insecurity looms over and around me and I feel like a spool bound tightly under coils of dark cotton thread. On other mornings, the uncertainty enters my head intermittently in brief spurts. On a quiet month, weeks can pass without the lingering feelings of doubt, and I wonder when I shall feel less like a guest at a *bal masque*.

land of lakes.

A partner with whom I often work walked into my office a few weeks ago. He asked me how I was feeling. I lied. I replied to him that I felt fine. The corporate group had been working furiously to finish many fiscal year-end transactions for one of our big clients. As a result of the large volume of transactions, none of us were sleeping very much. The associates, legal assistants, and word processors worked straight through several weekends, and all of us complained unceasingly about our jobs. I did not feel fine. The partner then smiled and said, well, then you are going to go to Minneapolis and close this deal. He proceeded to tell me the name of the transaction and then dropped a few documents on my desk, already littered with various stages of transactional documents. He said, as he walked out the door, go speak to the senior associate in charge of the deal and find out what you are supposed to do. A secretary made airline reservations for me to fly out to Minneapolis the next morning. I had never been to Minnesota before.

I was told by a senior associate that I would meet a representative of the corporate client, Jim, at the hotel. Jim's secretary and my secretary, via facsimile, arranged for us to meet at the lobby of the Minneapolis Radisson Hotel South at 7:30 the next morning. Jim was on time. He shook my hand and introduced himself. I had expected him to be older, somewhat heavier. I remembered reading in some memorandum that Jim worked in our client's Texas office, so I mentioned as we marched toward the parking lot that I had heard on the television news report that the Texas Rangers had beaten the visiting team. Jim said mildly, oh. Then, I asked him if he was a baseball fan, and he said no. Then, I said, oh.

Once we got into his maroon-colored rental car, he mentioned how difficult it was to travel so much. There was no time to see his wife and kids, he said. This was my second business trip, ever, but I extrapolated my experience and let on that I knew how he felt. He told me a little bit about his family and said that his daughter's swim meet went well the day before but it had been held outdoors and the temperature the day before was over 110 degrees in Plano, Texas. I told him that I had never been to Texas before. He then said in a clear and slow voice, well, don't come now, it's too hot. As he drove, we spoke about the beautiful weather we were experiencing in Minneapolis, the Land of Lakes. When we stopped at an intersection, I asked him how far we were from the closing site, and he said it would take about ten more minutes to get there. At that point, I took out the neatly written notes I had prepared that morning in my hotel room while I ate my breakfast of hot

oatmeal and coffee. I started listing the business and legal issues that he should be aware of at this closing.

The reasons why I had decided to become a corporate
lawyer as distinguished from a litigator are actually quite simple: one, I like to start and finish things within a reasonable
amount of time, and two, I don't like to fight. Closings symbol-
ize perfectly the first reason. Nearly all of the issues of this
Minneapolis transaction were already negotiated and all of the
documents had been drafted, now, the parties to this deal
would join around a table and sign the many pieces of paper
framed by crisp manilla legal-sized folders and give or take
certified checks denominating large sums of cash. In a boxy
rented Chevrolet, Jim and I sped toward the office of the lawyer of the seller; I was the lawyer of the buyer, and Jim was,
effectively, the buyer; we were on our way to the closing site to
meet the seller and his lawyer. There, we would end our pos-
turing, bantering, arguing, drafting, commenting, and revising:
we would bring about closure.

The sun shone brilliantly over the asphalt-covered parking
lot. I thought about wearing my mirrored sunglasses but decided against it. Jim remarked on the clearness of the day. We
arrived early and we stood in front of the building which
looked dark and empty. On the side of the building where the
entrance was located, there was a small metal plaque screwed
into the wall stating the name of the seller's lawyer and on the
end of his name, were the letters, J.D., signifying that he was a
juris doctor, a graduate of law school. The façade of his office
was not very impressive. When we walked into the roomy and
cluttered office, a cheery middle-aged woman greeted us: you
must be the people from New York. Jim didn't correct her by
telling her that he was in fact from Texas. I extended my hand

to shake hers. She looked like someone who could have been a relative of my fourth-grade schoolteacher, Mrs. Maher. Her name was Peggy and she asked us if we would like coffee. I nodded yes while I looked around the room. Jim said no. Peggy led us to the closing room.

The seller of the business had already arrived. A portly man with lots of wrinkles under his eyes. He looked older than my father and I felt very young again. Jim and I looked like teenagers in comparison. I crossed my arms and straightened my shoulders. Feeling a little nervous, I tried to recall what Cynthia and Carol, two senior associates at the firm, had said to me before I had left New York for Minneapolis: "You have to take control of a closing, don't let anyone rush you or push you around. It's your show, take charge." The seller asked us how our flight was. We spoke for a while about the Mall of America, the largest indoor shopping center in North America, located only a few miles from the closing site. Peggy chimed in at this moment to say that Jim and I should go there after the closing. We said that we might if we had any time before our respective flights, mine to Manhattan and his to Dallas. I noticed again how excited everyone in Minneapolis got when they talked about the Mall. I had scanned a brochure about it at the hotel lobby as I was checking in, so I asked a few questions about Snoopy Park, the indoor amusement attraction. Apparently, or so it was told to me, many people from places as far away as Germany or Japan fly into Minneapolis airport just to go shopping and fly right back to Munich or Osaka after a day of retail purchases.

I walked out of the closing room leaving Jim and the seller to talk about the heat in Texas, because I had to find a phone to call my office in New York. I was asking Peggy for permission to use one of the phones when the seller's lawyer introduced himself loudly by paraphrasing his secretary: you must be the lady from New York. Yes, I am, I said.

We couldn't actually start the closing since we were waiting for the Federal Express delivery person to bring the buyer's check, which was being flown in from another state. Everyone seemed to be in good spirits, and I began to think that my first closing of a transaction would actualize the expectations that I had of becoming a corporate lawyer. Unlike a lawsuit where there is a guaranteed loser, in this kind of transaction, I ruminated, we would all walk away winners: the buyer gets the business and the seller gets his check. Interrupting my thoughts with an odd question, the seller's lawyer asked me if I spoke other languages besides English. I replied Spanish, a menu knowledge of French and Italian, and a reasonable comprehension of Korean. Before I had a chance to ask him the same question, he exclaimed, I go to Korea all the time. Amused, I asked him why. He replied, for the shopping. At this point, my client and his client were listening to us intently. The check had not yet arrived and I was getting a little bored so I listened to him tell me about Korea.

I love Itaewon, he began his description, with his eyes weirdly sparkling. I tuned him out and tried to recall what I knew about Itaewon. It is the section of Seoul where most of the merchants sell knock-off designer handbags, fake Rolex watches, T-shirts with Chanel No. 5 printed on them, and brand-name sneakers to tourists and to American G.I.s who are stationed near the demilitarized zone. I also knew that at night, Itaewon transforms from the bazaar of imitation goods into streets full of electric lights and neon signs advertising go-go girls and discotheques. I had been to Itaewon a few times when I was last in Korea. Clearly, it was reinforced to me by my elders that a girl does not go to Itaewon by herself. During the day, when I went to buy souvenirs, I was accompanied by my mother's best friend, and on the rare occasions that I went to Itaewon at night to go to certain approved of discotheques, I would be permitted to go only with large groups of people, many of them relatives. My uncles and aunts who lived in Korea narrated detailed and chilling stories about Korean-American girls getting kidnaped and being sold into prostitution. Over and over again, I was told that good girls do not go to Itaewon. When the seller's lawyer finished telling us what he remembered of Itaewon, I walked out of the room to check if the delivery man had arrived. From that point on, I noticed that the seller's lawyer began to touch me.

All of us waited for the check for nearly an hour. I asked the seller's lawyer to revise a set of resolutions he had drafted to include another concept. He agreed and handwrote my comment in and asked Peggy to type it up. Wordlessly, he draped his arm around my waist and said that while we waited he would give me a tour of his office and show me all the things he bought in Itaewon. He directed my body toward his office and I made sure that the office door was wide open. He pointed to a huge brass elephant that must have weighed almost two hundred pounds which seemed to guard his desk. I bought that in Itaewon, he boasted. Dismayed and slightly bewildered by his choice of decorative arts, I asked him if he was a Republican. He said he was an Independent.

He relinquished my waist only to place his hand on my forearm to pull me toward another direction, look, I bought this clock from Korea. It was an old-fashioned schoolhouse clock with a small copper door at the base of its face and across the clock face the following word was etched into the plate glass, Federal. It seemed likely that the clock was made and purchased in Korea, but it looked so American. He then touched my back and directed me toward the closing room because Peggy told us that the check had arrived. I walked briskly away from the palm of his hand, which I felt was imprinted on the small of my back. When I saw the violet and orange striped express-mail package on Peggy's desk, I told Jim that the closing check had arrived.

Signing the legal papers and handing the seller the certified bank check took less than twenty minutes. I gathered all the folders and called New York to report to the partner and the senior associate that the deal had closed. The partner told me that I should get on an earlier flight and head back to the office to pick up some more documents and then fly out to Los Angeles that night from New York to close another deal. The senior associate asked me how it went, and with my client standing next to me, I spoke into the receiver to say that the closing proceeded smoothly. I picked up my closing briefcase, which felt much lighter since I was leaving the seller and his lawyer two copies of everything I had brought with me, and told Jim that I would not be able to go with him to the Mall of America due to the change in my plans. Jim kindly drove me to the airport.

pushing away the plate.

As a young girl growing up in New York City, I dreamed of becoming many things. Between the ages of eight and twenty, I wanted to be: a cabinetmaker, an architect, a teacher, a judge, a dancer, a carpenter, a television writer, a stained-glass maker, an industrialist, a chef, and an actor. Yet in my varied and exhaustive catalogue of careers, I never wanted to be a wife or a mother. In my adolescence, donning puffy white dresses with lace veils or nursing doll babies never held much interest for me. To my surprise, however, and sometimes, dismay, I have done things and become things I had not expected, and lately, I hesitate to rely on the conviction I felt when I was eight or twenty.

As my mother had often said, girls who never anticipated marriage always got married before the others who had longed to wed. As the middle girl of three daughters I fulfilled my mother's sage observation. In the words of my Korean kin, I was the first one to leave my father's house to go to my husband's house. Christopher and I were married in the fall of last year and as quickly as our wedding ceremony passed in mere hours, our one-year wedding anniversary is fast approaching.

In thinking back to my week-long wedding festivities, the most unsettling recollection I have from all of the events is the closing remark of my father-in-law's toast offered at the rehearsal dinner.

My father-in-law, an elegant man who had been a member of the Foreign Service, raised his glass of white wine to toast the engaged couple. Especially for the rehearsal dinner, I had my hair styled in a chignon and had my makeup applied professionally that afternoon at the coiffure at Bergdorf Goodman's, and as I sat in my seat in the bird and flower print wallpapered room at the Sky Club, which is perched on top of the former Pan Am building, I felt certain that all the guests' eyes were focused on my expensively decorated head. Nervously, I tucked a wisp of stray hair back into place and waited for my father-in-law to finish. Displaying the grace of a man who has spoken publicly many times, he thanked everyone for coming and stated how joyful he was about the upcoming wedding. He ended his toast by wishing Christopher and me many years of happiness and finally, many, many grandchildren. The guests cheered at this point and suddenly, I felt all the pairs of the families' eyes directing their gaze from my head to my stomach. I smiled uncomfortably.

As a New York business lawyer, I have come to know many professional women who work in my field. Despite our common career and business interests, when I talk to these women, I have noticed that we rarely speak about structuring private placement offerings, the varying tranche interest rates created from manipulating asset pools, or the financing of off-shore deals. With the exception of griping about certain projects, annoying colleagues, or the hours that we labor, the rising star of all conversation topics is motherhood. A week does not pass by where some female lawyer I know either from work, graduate school, or professional association mentions the motherhood question and its actual or perceived effects on her career and marriage.

In my single, brief year as a professional in New York City, I have learned the following from the female attorneys I have encountered: most women attorneys want children and the same women believe that having children will harm, delay, halt, obliterate, or overshadow their legal career. This dialectic of maternal desire and anticipated professional destruction invades the conversations I have with my friends, colleagues, and acquaintances who are female lawyers, and I find that the tension between such a powerful longing and an all-too-possible obstruction is transforming my budding thoughts about motherhood.

This is the drill: when you go to one of the top-ten law schools and you are the top third of such a law school, it is understood in the profession that certain courses are charted for you. In the fall of your second year in law school, you interview at a law firm for a summer associate position in a place like New York City for the summer months following your second year. If the firm likes you, the partners ask you to return when you graduate after completing your third and final year; this is called "the offer." If you accept the offer, you take the bar examination after you graduate and start your career at the law firm in which you were a summer associate, but now you are deemed an associate. After eight or nine years or so of being an associate at the firm, you may be considered for partnership, and if all works out well, you become a junior partner. Keep in mind that there are many variations to this outline, but this is the stuff you are weaned on in law school if you are interested in the private sector—the goal, you are informed, is partnership. At the very minimum, however, to make partner, you must be on the track for partnership.

Fortunately or unfortunately, not everyone makes partner. In fact, fewer and fewer people are asked to be partner each year, and as I continue working, I notice everywhere that fewer and fewer women are in fact partners, and since more and more female associates get off the partnership track, the future seems assured that there will always be fewer women partners. Whether it is a true theory or not, it is commonly believed that women associates leave the track to have children, either to stay home with them until the children are five or so, or to get jobs which are physically less demanding. So as a first-year associate, I look around me and I look above me and I notice we have come a long way but we have a long way to go.

I hear male associates whisper that women are in some ways lucky, since they don't have to stay on the track, especially the married ones, and to my shock, I can't say that I always disagree with them. In material terms, as a married woman with a husband who can support me, I would have shelter, food, and comforts even if I quit my job today. Nevertheless, I have always been hungry for more than my material needs.

Lately, I have been contemplating the sheer irony of my foresisters demanding the right to get on the track and then for me to realize how brutal it is to stay on it when you want other things, too, like, children, for one. And I hear my girlfriends asking themselves as I ask myself, why stick it out? Why should I have to bill so many hours, why should I give up relationships, why should I always be politically neutral, why should I wear these incredibly boring clothes, why should I give up having children or perhaps, worse, watch another woman raise them? Are my female colleagues and I the intended heirs of the legacies of Susan B. Anthony, Emma Goldman, Angela Davis, Charlotte Perkins Gilman, Harriet Tubman, and Betty Friedan? Have we eaten our fill of our portion of equal opportunities and are we pushing away our plates?

Somewhere down deep, deep beneath the fear of failure and the pain of humiliation, I ask myself seriously if I still believe that I can do anything. I heard a clear voice cheering me on to keep at my goals as it pushed me forward when I was in elementary school, junior high school, and high school. I heard such a voice get dimmer, fuzzier when I got to college and law school. Lately, I hear a voice that doesn't sound familiar to me in my head—no, it says, no, girl, you can't do it all, no one can do it all. So, Harriet, Susan, Charlotte, Angela, Betty, and Emma, did you hear such a nasty voice? Would you have even attempted to bill 2,500 hours a year, stay married, and raise children? Ladies, did I miss your point?

I never thought I wanted to be a wife. It just wasn't on my list of things to do. And now that I am a wife, I feel privileged to feel such a profound level of intimacy and friendship. Because I was wrong about the institution of marriage, now I think, although I never thought I wanted to be a mother, my adolescent certainty against such a prospect has flagged. I'm not so sure anymore. Yet the downside of choosing mother-hood has been spelled out to me. My female colleagues, alumnae, and girlfriends seem convinced and are warning me that, if I want children, I have to make a choice, I must give up my space on the track to drive a station wagon in suburbia.

It is spring in Central Park and I am staring at the marvel-ously painted horses of the merry-go-round, and as I wait in line to take my turn, I watch the brass ring revolve around the striped axis. I think to myself, I don't know if I want to be a partner and I don't know if I want to be a mother and I don't know if I can be both at the same time, but I know that right now I feel cornered. I sway in time to the tinny music and I wait patiently for my ride to start.

pain au chocolat.

I was late for church this morning. I had forgotten that the morning service was moved up to 10:30, so I walked in half an hour late. When I walked out of the service at noon, I felt disoriented, as I usually do when I'm not on schedule. Unlike the mildewy weather of yesterday afternoon, today was breezy and light. So instead of taking a taxi directly to work like I had done yesterday, I decided to walk down Fifth Avenue and pick up a few tubes of my favorite lipstick at Henri Bendel before heading to the office.

Whenever I enter this New York department store, I feel like I've stepped into a beautiful gift box. The floor-to-ceiling Lalique windows gleam behind the gilded cherubim standing on glass and pewter shelves holding four-ply amber-colored cashmere sweaters. Neat rows of obscure French perfumes with exotic names suggestive of vegetation indigenous to Morocco and Tunisia frame the curving staircase.

Day after day of reading black and white corporate documents, it is refreshing to see colors and textures and smell floral and citrus scents from sensually shaped crystal flacons. I am out of my office and it feels good to be giddy and not so serious about the world of business transactions. At this moment, I am concerned solely with the shade of my lipstick.

After I purchased two tubes of my favorite lipstick, Auburn by MAC, I ascended the stairs clutching my miniature brown and white striped shopping bag and my brown briefcase. Treat of all treats, I decided to have a cup of coffee at the café located on the second floor of the store. I was going to savor being a lady of leisure for at least thirty more minutes this Sunday afternoon before I trudged toward my office to finish drafting more documents for the four acquisition deals I had to close before the end of the month.

The host seated me near the frosted glass windows. From my table I had a view of a full street block of the Fifth Avenue Book Fair which was being held outside. Decadently, I ordered a coffee and a pain au chocolat.

Ever since I left college, I get a little sad when I see stores or vendors which sell books. I stared out of the window and saw all these people milling about the stalls covered with cheerful canopies that were filled with stacks and stacks of fresh new books. I felt a tinge of envy of all those people on the street below who had the luxury of spending the day at the book fair. Stealing these thirty minutes or so to eat my brunch at this posh café filled me with guilt since I had so many items to cross off on my list of to-do's back at the office.

Sitting at a table covered with demask linen and sipping a

cup of bitter hot coffee cut by the sweetness of a flaky crois-
sant, I contemplated my guilt mingled with envy. My envy is
easy to explain. When I was in college, I wanted to be a fiction
writer more than anything else. I took writing courses, wrote
essays, and published my stories in little campus magazines.
When I announced my decision to write, my parents made it
very clear that they would not support such an unsound and
baseless decision either economically or emotionally.

My father had said to me: "You're too young, you haven't
lived your life yet. What could you possibly have to say? No
one would care to read your books. All you've ever done was go
to school, you can always write when you get older. You should
go to law school. Learn a trade." And I believed him.

Frankly, I was envious not only of the people outside my
window who had the leisure to peruse the tables laden with
books, but also of the authors of such books. When I was
twenty years old, becoming twenty-five seemed very far away,
and by then, I had imagined that I would have written at least
two acclaimed novels with moving plots and serious characters.
I had not yet done so, and in lieu of such a grandiose feat, I
had learned a specialized trade so that I would no longer eat
my father's bread. I had learned to put bread on my own table,
bread which happened to be at the moment a layer of chocolate enrobed in layers of buttery pastry. As I poured more hot
coffee from the well-polished pewter pot into my porcelain cup
resting on its gold-rimmed saucer, I shifted my gaze from the
view from the window to the restaurant menu.

I had guessed that the waiter was a native French speaker
from his accent when he had stopped to take my order. Hence,
when he had asked me what I would like, I tried to pronounce
"pain au chocolat" as artfully as possible, recollecting the
acerbic comments made by a college friend who was French

whenever he heard people attempting to pronounce such common menu terms. *Pain,* how could a word meaning sustenance to one man, mean hurt to another man, I wondered.

My mingled guilt is not so easy to explain. On average, as a junior associate, I work almost six days a week and each day I am at my office well over twelve hours. Surprisingly, at the end of each day, I cannot finish everything which needs to get done. My peers have the same curse it seems, so like them, I return, begrudgingly, to work on the weekends and attempt to catch up. Since I have started my job as a young lawyer, I rarely stop working and I never stop thinking about my work. No matter how hard I try, I can't finish it all.

When I was growing up in Korea, I heard the story of *Kongji and Potji* which is about the virtuous girl, Kongji, whose father remarries a horrible woman who has an evil daughter, Potji, who abuses this girl and through certain miracles, Kongji ends up marrying a nobleman who rescues her from such hardship. Kongji is the good and beautiful heroine and each time her stepmother hands her one onerous task after another, a team of toads or a bevy of birds descends upon her home and aids her in completing the nearly impossible tasks.

There are moments when I feel like Kongji. Certain senior associates and partners begin to resemble Kongji's stepmother, and drafting half a dozen documents or plowing through boxes of due diligence review in one night begin to parallel having to fill large clay vessels with hidden cracks with water or hulling a hundred bags of rice by hand. At my office, there are no fairy toads to sit in the bottom of the vessels to prevent the seepage so I can fill the jars with water, and there are no friendly birds to hull the mountains of rice with their tiny beaks. The evenings advance quickly, and I am alone drafting my agreements and reviewing the piles of documents. When my eyes give, I finish what I can and head home.

New York City is magical at the very early hours of the morning. The damp, tar-paved streets glisten with the reflections of the lighted storefronts. In the quiet taxi ride returning home, I remind myself gently that I am historically privileged to have this job. After all, I tell myself, my forbears could not have imagined that their girl-child descendant would be an attorney. At the same time, I try not to hear the calm voice of my father, who expected such an outcome.

Getting Off on Feminism

jason schultz

When it comes to smashing a paradigm, pleasure is not the most important thing. It is the only thing.

—Gary Wolf, *Wired* Magazine

minutes after my best friend told me he was getting married, I casually offered to throw a bachelor party in his honor. Even though such parties are notorious for their degradation of women, I didn't think this party would be much of a problem. Both the bride and groom considered themselves feminists, and I figured that most of the men attending would agree that sexism had no place in the celebration of this union. In fact, I thought the bachelor party would be a great opportunity to get a group of men together for a social event that didn't degenerate into the typical anti-women, homophobic male-bonding thing. Still, ending one of the most sexist traditions in history—even for one night—was a lot tougher than I envisioned.

I have to admit that I'm not a *complete* iconoclast: I wanted to make the party a success by including at least some of the usual elements, such as good food and drink, great music, and cool things to do. At the same time, I was determined not to fall prey to traditional sexist party gimmicks such as prostitutes, strippers jumping out of cakes, or straight porn. But after nixing all the traditional lore, even *I* thought it sounded boring. What were we going to do except sit around and think about women?

"What about a belly dancer?" one of the ushers suggested when I confided my concerns to him. "That's not as bad as a stripper." I sighed. This was supposed to be an occasion for the groom and his male friends to get together, celebrate the upcoming marriage, and affirm their friendship and connection with each other as men. "What the fuck does hiring a female sex worker have to do with any of that?" I shouted into the phone. I quickly regained my calm, but his suggestion still stung. We had to find some other way.

I wanted my party to be as "sexy" as the rest of them, but I had no idea how to do that in the absence of female sex workers. There was no powerful alternative image in our culture from which I could draw. I thought about renting some gay porn, or making it a cross-dressing party, but many of the guests were conservative, and I didn't want to scare anyone off. Besides, what would it say about a bunch of straight men if all we could do to be sexy was act queer for a night?

Over coffee on a Sunday morning, I asked some of the

other guys what they thought was so "sexy" about having a stripper at a bachelor party.

"Well," David said, "it's just a gag. It's something kinda funny and sexy at the same time."

"Yeah," A.J. agreed. "It's not all that serious, but it's something special to do that makes the party cool."

"But *why* is it sexy and funny?" I asked. "Why can't we, as a bunch of guys, be sexy and funny ourselves?"

" 'Cause it's easier to be a guy with other guys when there's a chick around. It gives you all something in common to relate to."

"Hmm. I think I know what you mean," I said. "When I see a stripper, I get turned on, but not in the same way I would if I was with a lover. It's more like going to a show or watching a flick together. It's enjoyable, stimulating, but it's not overwhelming or intimate in the same way that sex is. Having the stripper provides a common emotional context for us to feel turned on. But we don't have to do anything about it like we would if we were with a girlfriend, right?"

"Well, my girlfriend would kill me if she saw me checking out this stripper," Greg replied. "But because it's kind of a male-bonding thing, it's not as threatening to our relationship. It's not because it's the stripper over her, it's because it's just us guys hanging out. It doesn't go past that."

Others agreed. "Yeah. You get turned on, but not in a serious way. It makes you feel sexy and sexual, and you can enjoy feeling that way with your friends. Otherwise, a lot of times, just hanging out with the guys is pretty boring. Especially at a bachelor party. I mean, that's the whole point, isn't it —to celebrate the fact that we're bachelors, and he"—referring to Robert, the groom—"isn't!"

Through these conversations, I realized that having a female sex worker at the party would give the men permission to connect with one another without becoming vulnerable. When men discuss sex in terms of actions—who they "did," and how and where they did it—they can gain recognition and validation of their sexuality from other men without having to expose their *feelings* about sex.

"What other kinds of things make you feel sexy like the stripper does?" I asked several of the guys.

"Watching porn sometimes, or a sexy movie."

A.J. said, "Just getting a look from a girl at a club. I mean, she doesn't even have to talk to you, but you still feel sexy and you can still hang out with your friends."

Greg added, "Sometimes just knowing that my girlfriend thinks I'm sexy, and then talking about her with friends, makes me feel like I'm the man. Or I'll hear some other guy talk about his girlfriend in a way that reminds me of mine, and I'll still get that same feeling. But that doesn't happen very often, and usually only when talking with one other guy.

This gave me an idea. "I've noticed that same thing, both here and at school with my other close guy friends. Why doesn't it happen with a bunch of guys, say at a party?"

"I don't know. It's hard to share a lot of personal stuff with guys," said Adam, "especially about someone you're seeing, if you don't feel comfortable. Well, not comfortable, because I know most of the guys who'll be at the party, but it's more like I don't want them to hassle me, or I might say something that freaks them out."

"Or you're just used to guys talking shit about girls," someone else added. "Like at a party or hanging out together. They rag on them, or pick out who's the cutest or who wants to do who. That's not the same thing as really talking about what makes you feel sexy."

"Hmm," I said. "So it's kind of like if I were to say that I liked to be tied down to the bed, no one would take me seriously. You guys would probably crack up laughing, make a joke or two, but I'd never expect you to actually join in and talk about being tied up in a serious way. It certainly wouldn't feel 'sexy,' would it? At least not as much as the stripper."

"Exactly. You talking about being tied down here is fine, 'cause we're into the subject of sex on a serious kick and all. But at a party, people are bullshitting each other and gabbing, and horsing around. The last thing most of us want is to trip over someone's personal taste or start thinking someone's a little queer."

"You mean queer as in homosexual?" I asked.

"Well, not really, 'cause I think everyone here is straight. But more of queer in the sense of perverted or different. I mean, you grow up in high school thinking that all guys are basically the same. You all want the same thing from girls in the same way. And when someone like you says you like to be tied down, it's kinda weird—almost like a challenge. It makes me have to respond in a way that either shows me agreeing that I also like to be tied down or not. And if someone's a typical guy and he says that, it makes you think he's different—not the same guy you knew in high school. And if he's not the same guy, then it challenges you to relate to him on a different level."

"Yeah, I guess in some ways it's like relating to someone who's gay," Greg said. "He can be cool and all, and you can get along totally great. But there's this barrier that's hard to cross over. It kinda keeps you apart. And that's not what you want to feel toward your friends, especially at a party like this one, where you're all coming together to chill."

As the bachelor party approached, I found myself wondering whether my friends and I could "come together to chill"— and affirm our status as sexual straight men—without buying into homophobic or sexist expressions. At the same time, I was doing a lot of soul-searching on how we could challenge the dominant culture's vision of male heterosexuality, not only by deciding against having a stripper at our party, but also by examining and redefining our own relationships with women.

sex and the sensitive man

According to the prevailing cultural view, "desirable" hetero men are inherently dominant, aggressive, and, in many subtle and overt ways, abusive to women. To be sexy and powerful, straight men are expected to control and contrive a sexuality that reinforces their authority. Opposing these notions of power subjects a straight guy to being branded "sensitive," submissive, or passive—banished to the nether regions of excitement and pleasure, the unmasculine, asexual, "vanilla" purgatory of antieroticism. Just as hetero women are often forced to choose between the images of the virgin and the whore, modern straight men are caught in a cultural tug-of-war between the Marlboro Man and the Wimp.

So where does that leave straight men who want to re-examine what a man is and change it? Can a good man be sexy? Can a sexy man be good? What is good sex, egalitarian sex? More fundamentally, can feminist women and men coexist comfortably, even happily, within the same theoretical framework—or the same bedroom?

Relationships with men remain one of the most controversial topics among feminists today. Having sex, negotiating emotional dependency, and/or raising children force many hetero couples to balance their desire to be together with the oppressive dynamics of sexism. In few other movements are the oppressor group and the oppressed group so intimately linked.

But what about men who support feminism? Shouldn't it be okay for straight feminist women to have sex with them? Straight men aren't always oppressive in their sexuality, are they?

You may laugh at these questions, but they hold serious implications for straight feminist sex. I've seen many relationships between opposite-sex activists self-destruct because critical assumptions about power dynamics and desires were made in the mind, but not in the bed. I've even been told that straight male feminists can't get laid without A) feeling guilty; B) reinforcing patriarchy; or C) maintaining complete passivity during sexual activity. Each of these three options represents common assumptions about the sexuality of straight men who support feminism. Choice A, "feeling guilty," reflects the belief that straight male desire inherently contradicts the goals of feminism and fails to contribute to the empowerment of women. It holds that any man who enjoys sex with a woman must be benefiting from sexist male privilege, not fighting against it. In other words, het sex becomes a zero-sum game where if men gain, feminism loses.

Choice B represents the assumption that hetero male sex is inherently patriarchal. Beyond merely being of no help, as in Choice A, straight male sexuality is seen as part of the problem. Within this theory, one often hears statements such as "all heterosexual sex is rape." Even though these statements are usually taken out of context, the ideas behind them are problematic. In essence, they say that you can never have a male/

female interaction that isn't caught up in oppressive dynamics. Men and women can never be together, especially in such a vulnerable exchange as sexuality, without being subject to the misdistribution of power in society.

The third choice, "maintaining complete passivity," attempts a logical answer to the above predicament. In order to come even close to achieving equality in heterosexuality (and still get laid), men must "give up" all their power through inactivity. A truly feminist man should take no aggressive or dominant position. He should, in fact, not act at all; he should merely lie back and allow the woman to subvert male supremacy through her complete control of the situation. In other words, for a man and a woman to share sexuality on a "level playing field," the man must remove all symptoms of his power through passivity, even though the causes of that inequality (including his penis!) still exist.

I know of one feminist man whose girlfriend *insisted* that she always be on top when they had intercourse. Her reasoning was simple: a man in a dominant sexual position represents sexist oppression incarnate. Therefore, the only possible way to achieve female empowerment was to subvert this power through her dominance. She even went so far as to stop intercourse before he reached orgasm, as a protest against male sexual entitlement.

The above story represents the *assumption* that sexism functions within male sexuality in a uniform, unvarying way, and that straight women must adapt and strategize within their personal relationships accordingly.

Does it have to be this way? Must male heterosexuality always pose a threat to feminism? What about the sensitive guy? Wasn't that the male cry (whimper) of the nineties? Sorry, but all the media hype about sensitivity never added up to significant changes in behavior. Straight male sexuality still remains one of the most underchallenged areas of masculinity in America. Some men *did* propose a different kind of sexuality for straight men in the 1970s, one that emphasizes feelings and sensitivity and emotional connection. But these efforts failed to affect our ideas in any kind of revolutionary way. Now, instead of a "sexy" sensitive guy, men's magazines are calling for the emergence of the "Post-Sensitive Man," while scientific studies tell us that women prefer Clint Eastwood over Michael Bolton.

Why did sensitivity fail? Were straight women, even feminists, lying to men about what they wanted? The answer is "yes" and "no." I don't think sensitivity was the culprit. I think the problem was men's passivity, or more specifically, men's lack of assertiveness and power.

In much of our understanding, power is equated with oppression: images of white supremacists dominating people of color, men dominating women, and the rich dominating the poor underline the histories of many cultures and societies. But power need not always oppress others. One can, I believe, be powerful in a nonoppressive way.

In order to find this sort of alternative, we need to examine men's experience with power and sexuality further. Fortunately, queer men and women have given us a leg up on the process by reenergizing the debate about what is good sex and what is fair sex. Gay male culture has a long history of exploring nontraditional aspects of male sexuality, such as cross-dressing, bondage and dominance, and role playing. These dynamics force gay men to break out of a singular experience of male sexual desire and to examine the diversity within male sexuality in the absence of gender oppression. Though gay men's culture still struggles with issues such as the fetishizing of men of color and body fascism, it does invite greater exploration of diversity than straight male culture. Gay culture has broader and more inclusive attitudes about what is sexy and a conception of desire that accommodates many types of sex for many types of gay men. For straight men in our culture, there is such a rigid definition of "sexy" that it leaves us few options besides being oppressive, overbearing, or violent.

Part of the success that gay male culture enjoys in breaking out of monolithic notions of male sexuality lies in the acceptance it receives from its partners and peers. Camp, butch, leather, drag-queer culture is constantly affirming the powerful presence of alternative sexualities. Straight male culture, on the other hand, experiences a lack—a void of acceptance—whenever it tries to assert some image other than the sexist hetero male. Both publicly and in many cases privately, alternative straight male sexualities fail to compete for attention and acceptance among hetero men and women.

hot, heavy, and heterosexual

Without role models and cultural messages to affirm them, new forms of desire fail to stick around in our heads and our hearts. Therefore, straight men and women need to get hot and heavy for an alternative male heterosexuality. Often, women who desire nontraditional types of straight men fail to assert their desires publicly. If and when they find these men, they do so through friendships, long-term relationships, or by accident. They rarely seek them out in bars, one-night stands, or house parties. Sexual desire that results from a friendship or long-term relationship can be wonderful, but it fails to hold the popular "sexy" status that active dating, flirtation, or seduction does. If we truly hope to change straight male sexuality, we must move beyond private one-on-one affirmations and change public and cultural ones.

Unfortunately, it's easier said than done. Whenever I've tried to assert a nonoppressive sexuality with women, I've sunk into a cultural quagmire. I get caught riding that fine line between being a Sensitive New Age Guy and an asshole. Many straight women (both feminist and not) still find an aggressive, dominant man sexy. Many straight women still desire a man to take charge when it comes to romance or intimacy, especially when initiating intercourse. Yet many of the same straight feminist women constantly highlight the abuse and discrimination that many of these men inflict. They often complain about a man who is misogynist while affirming his desirability. This dichotomy of desire is confusing and frustrating.

Admittedly, much of my frustration relates to my own experience. I've always found fierce, independent women attractive—women who say they want a man to support them emotionally, listen to them, and not fight them every step of the way. Yet in reality, these women often lost respect for me and for other men who tried to change our sexuality to meet these needs.

I'd try to play the game, moving in as the aggressive man and then showing a more sensitive side after I'd caught the person's attention. But more often than not, the result was frustrating. I didn't catch a clue until one night when I had an enlightening conversation with one of these women who called herself a feminist. I asked her why guys who tried to accommodate the political desires of straight feminists always seemed to lose out in the end. She said she thought it was because a lot of young straight women who confront gender issues through feminism are constantly trying to redefine themselves in relation to culture and other people in their lives. Therefore, if they pursue relationships with men, many consciously seek out a *traditional* man—not only because it is the kind of man they have been taught to desire, but because he is familiar to them. He is strong, stable, predictable, and powerful. As the woman's identity shifts and changes, she can use the man she is dating as a reference point and source of strength and stability.

If she chooses to become involved with a feminist man who feels the same need to examine assumptions about gender (including his own masculinity) on a political and personal level, both partners are in a state of flux and instability. Both are searching for an understanding of their relationship, but each questions how that relationship is defined, even down to assumptions about men, women, sex, and commitment. Within this shifting matrix, straight feminist men who explore alternative ways of being sexual are often perceived as passive, weak, and in many cases, undesirable. In the end, it seems much easier to choose the traditional male.

out of the breeding box

We need to assert a new feminist sexuality for men, one that competes with the traditional paradigm but offers a more inviting notion of how hetero men can be sexual while tearing apart the oppressive and problematic ways in which so many of us have experienced sexuality in the past. We need to find new, strong values and ideas of male heterosexuality instead of passive identities that try to distance us from sexist men. We need to stop trying to avoid powerful straight sexuality and work to redefine what our power means and does. We need to find strength and desire outside of macho, antiwomen ways of being masculine.

Take the notion of "breeding." Many cultures still assume that the male desire to breed and procreate is the primary purpose of sexuality. This idea, based on outdated notions of Darwinism and evolutionary prophecy, forces us to think of heterosexual men as having a single sexual purpose—ejaculating inside a fertile woman. Be hard, be strong, and cum into any woman's vagina you can find. It's all about sowing seed and proving heterosexuality through the conquest of women. Through this mechanism, reproductive sex is seen as "natural" and most desirable; all other forms of sexual interaction are seen as warm-ups or "foreplay." Breeding prioritizes heterosexuality, and within straight sex, limits its goal to the act of vaginal intercourse.

Yet in a pro–birth control, increasingly queer-friendly world, breeding has become a minuscule aspect of sexuality. Few heterosexual men and women have sex strictly to breed, and gay men and women almost never do. Within this new context, notions of what is "sexy" and what straight men desire have much more to do with how we fuck or how we feel than with what we produce.

Even among young people who have no intention of creating children, breeder assumptions continue to define male heterosexuality. For instance, many of my friends, especially queer ones, will harass me after I've been dating a woman for a while and give me flack for being a "breeder." They assume that the reason I'm with her—the goal of my relationship—is to make sure I cum inside her. Even if I don't want a child, even if I hate intercourse, the assumption about my male heterosexuality is that I will at least act like I'm trying to procreate when I'm having sex. Any possibility of a hetero nonbreeder sexuality doesn't exist. I'm forced into the breeding box, no questions permitted.

I've tried to confront these assumptions actively, but it's difficult. Usually I respond with something crass, such as, "Funny, I don't feel like breeding, just fucking." Or by talking about how *I* prefer to be penetrated sometimes. This may seem extreme, but that's how challenging it feels to try to present a different idea of straight male sexuality—one that isn't predicated on notions of being vanilla or being a breeder.

My critique of breeding is not an attempt to discredit fatherhood. Parenting is as much a part of the revolution as any other personal act. My point is that if we want hetero men to change, we have to give them viable choices. There has to be a difference between acting straight and acting like a breeder. And breeding is just *one* of the many assumptions that our culture applies to male heterosexuality.

It's up to straight men to change these assumptions. Gay men and lesbians have engaged in a cultural dialogue around sexuality over the last twenty-five years; straight women are becoming more and more vocal. But straight men have been almost completely silent. This silence, I think, stems in large part from fear: our cultures tell us that being a "real" man means not being feminine, not being gay, and not being weak. They warn us that anyone who dares to stand up to these ideas becomes a sitting target to have his manhood shot down in flames.

breaking the silence

Not becoming a sitting target to have *my* manhood shot down was high on my mind when the evening of my best friend's bachelor party finally arrived. But I was determined not to be silent about how I felt about the party and about new visions for straight men within our society.

We decided to throw the party two nights before the wedding. We all gathered at my house, each of us bringing a present to add to the night's activities. After all the men had arrived, we began cooking dinner, breaking open beer and champagne, and catching up on where we had left off since we last saw each other.

During the evening, we continued to talk off and on about why we didn't have a stripper or prostitute for the party. After several rounds of margaritas and a few hands of poker, tension started to build around the direction I was pushing the conversation.

"So what don't you like about strippers?" David asked me.

This was an interesting question. I was surprised not only by the guts of David to ask it, but also by my own mixed feelings in coming up with an answer. "It's not that I don't like being excited, or turned on, per se," I responded. "In fact, to be honest, watching a female stripper is an exciting and erotic experience for me. But at the same time, it's a very uncomfortable one. I get a sense when I watch her that I'm participating in a misuse of pleasure, if that makes sense."

I looked around at my friends. I couldn't tell whether the confused looks on their faces were due to the alcohol, the poker game, or my answer, so I continued. "Ideally, I would love to sit back and enjoy watching someone express herself sexually through dance, seduction, flirtation—all the positive elements I associate with stripping," I said. "But at the same time, because so many strippers are poor and forced to perform in order to survive economically, I feel like the turn-on I get is false. I feel like I get off easy, sitting back as the man, paying for the show. No one ever expects me to get up on stage.

"And in that way, it's selling myself short sexually. It's not only saying very little about the sexual worth of the woman on stage, but the sexual worth of me as the viewer as well. By *only* being a viewer—just getting off as a member of the audience— the striptease becomes a very limiting thing, an imbalanced dynamic. If the purpose is for me to feel sexy and excited, but not to act on those feelings, I'd rather find a more honest and direct way to do it. So personally, while I would enjoy watching a stripper on one level, the real issues of economics, the treatment of women, and the limitation of my own sexual personae push me to reject the whole stripper thing in favor of something else."

"But what else do you do to feel sexy?" A.J. asked.

"That's a tough question," I said. "Feeling sexy often depends on the way other people act toward you. For me, right now, you guys are a huge way for me to feel sexy. [Some of the men cringe.] I'm not saying that we have to challenge our sexual identities, although that's one way. But we can cut through a lot of this locker-room macho crap and start talking with each other about how we feel sexually, what we think, what we like, etc. Watching the stripper makes us feel sexy because we get turned on through the dynamic between her performance and our voyeurism. We can find that same erotic connection with each other by re-creating that context between us. In such a case, we're still heterosexual—we're no more having sex with each other than we are with the stripper. But we're not relying on the imbalanced dynamic of sex work to feel pleasure as straight men."

I took a deep breath. All right, I thought. Here we go. "What makes me feel sexy? I'll tell you. I feel sexy when I say how much I love licking chocolate off a partner's back. Not just that I like to do it, or talking about how often I do it, but that it feels amazing to taste her sweat and her skin mixed in with the sweetness of the chocolate. I feel sexy when I think about running my fingers through her hair in the shower, or watching her put a condom on me with her tongue. I feel sexy remembering how my muscles stretch and strain after being tied down to the bed, or the difference between leather, lace, and silk rubbing up and down my body. That's some of what makes me feel sexy."

The guys were silent for a few seconds, but soon afterwards, the ice seemed to break. While most of the guys weren't completely satisfied with or prepared for my answer, they seemed to feel that it was a step in the right direction. They agreed that, as heterosexual men, we should be able to share with each other what we find exciting and shouldn't *need* a female stripper to feel sexy. In some ways it may have been the desire to define their own sexuality that changed their minds; in others it may have been a traditionally masculine desire to reject any dependency on women. In any case, other men began to speak of their own experiences with pleasure and desire, and we continued to talk throughout the night, exploring the joys of hot sex, one-night stands, and even our preferences for certain brands of condoms. We discussed the ups and down of monogamy versus "open" dating and the pains of long-distance relationships.

Some men continued to talk openly about their desire for straight pornography or women who fit the traditional stereotype of femininity. But others contradicted this, expressing their wish to move beyond that image of women in their lives. The wedding, which started out as the circumstance for our gathering, soon fell into the background of our thoughts as we focused away from institutional ideas of breeder sexuality and began to find common ground through our real-life experiences and feelings as straight men. In the end, we all toasted the groom, sharing stories, jokes, and parts of our lives that many of us had never told. Most importantly, we were able to express ourselves sexually without hiding who we were from each other.

Thinking back on the party, I realized that the hard part was figuring out what we all wanted and how to construct a different way of finding that experience. The other men there wanted it just as much as I did. The problem was that we had no ideas of what a different kind of bachelor party might look like. Merely eliminating the old ways of relating (i.e., the female sex workers) left a gap, an empty space which in many ways *felt* worse than the sexist connection that existed there before; we felt passive and powerless. Yet we found a new way of interacting—one that embraced new ideas and shared the risk of experiencing them.

Was the party sexy? Did we challenge the dominance of oppressive male sexuality? Not completely, but it was a start. I doubt anyone found my party as "sexy" as traditional ones might be, but the dialogue has to start somewhere. It's going to take a while to generate the language and collective tension to balance the cultural image of heterosexual male sexuality with true sexual diversity. Still, one of my friends from high school —who's generally on the conservative end of most issues—told me as he was leaving that of all the bachelor parties he had been to, this was by far the best one. "I had a great time," he said. "Even without the stripper."

public pleasure and the pursuit of political change

> We need to affirm one another, support one another, help, enable, equip, and empower one another to deal with the present crisis, but it can't be uncritical, be-

cause if it's uncritical, then we are again refusing to acknowledge other people's humanity. If we are serious about acknowledging other people's humanity, then we are committed to trusting and believing that they are forever in process. Growth, development, maturation happens in stages. People grow, develop, and mature along the lines in which they are taught. Disenabling critique and contemptuous feedback hinders.

—Cornel West

The bachelor party was but a small example of the dialogue straight men need to—and can—create. Some of the most amazing conversations I have had have been with other straight and bisexual men about the *pleasure* of sex with women. These conversations have been far from passive, boring, or placid. They have ranged from the many uses of cock rings to issues of consent within S/M and B&D acts to methods of achieving multiple male orgasms. The difference between these conversations and typical sexist male dialogue is that our discourse strives to bypass the mythological nature of straight male bravado and pornographic fantasy and to emphasize straight men asserting themselves as strong voices for equality *and* pleasure in cultural discourses on sexuality.

These public dialogues have been immensely helpful in dispelling overemphasized issues like impotence and premature ejaculation; such conversations have also allowed us to move past the degrading and pornographic lingo used in high school locker rooms to describe sex with women and have pushed us to focus our energy on honest questions, feelings, and *desires*. These are the kinds of voices straight men must claim publicly.

When it comes to sex, feminist straight men must become participants in the discourse about our own sexuality. We have to fight the oppressive images of men as biological breeders and leering animals. We must find ways in which to understand our diverse backgrounds, articulate desires that are not oppressive, and acknowledge the power we hold. We must take center stage when it comes to articulating our views in a powerful voice. I'm not trying to prescribe any particular form of sexuality or specify what straight men should want. But until we begin to generate our own demands and desires in an honest and equitable way for feminist straight women to hear, I don't think we can expect to be both good *and* sexy any time soon.

Sexism and the Art of Feminist Hip-Hop Maintenance

eisa davis

i belong to the church of hip hop. just as people my parents' age remember precisely where they were when JFK was shot, my fellow believers and I can recall every detail about the first time we heard "Rapper's Delight." Hip-hop beats are always thumping somewhere in my chest every time I feel at home with myself, under lyrics that stir politics, music, and theatrical performance into a hearty gumbo that tastes different each time I try it. Hip hop gave me a language that made my black womanhood coherent to myself and the world; hip hop revived me when my soul was blanched from neglect. So I knew something was up when I found myself at the record store, a vein in my temple near to bursting, trying to decide whether to buy Snoop Doggy Dogg's *Doggystyle* or Queen Latifah's *Black Reign* with my last $15.

This didn't make any sense. Latifah had virtually saved my life in college: her music and public image were intimately, almost inextricably, connected to my awakening personal and political identity. How could I walk out on her at this critical moment, this election of the marketplace, by casting a cash vote for sexism, violence, Snoop and Dre? What could have precipitated this Cardinal Sin?

Back in my sophomore year in college, Latifah was the woman I had been waiting for, the woman who could be me. Black, female, nineteen-year-old royalty. With her hair and sexuality tucked underneath crowns, knee-high boots, and military garb trimmed with kente, she tore up every single track on *All Hail the Queen,* her debut album, her deep voice commanding complete respect. She not only inspired idolatry in young women like me and in our parents, but she got props from the hard rocks: the B-boys with Ph.D.s in vinyl archaeology, and the exclusively male jury of rappers, producers, and magazine editors in whose ears the hip-hop canon is constructed.

The first time I saw Latifah in person, I left my feminism and classical political theory class early so that I could hear her speak over the electric fence between a (white) feminism that many Harvard students and faculty wanted to hear her advocate, and a (black) womanism that the nebulous B-boy council and many black students needed her to defend so that she could retain her ghetto pass. White women wanted her to prioritize sexism and "transcend" racism; black men wanted her to address racism and spirit away her knowledge and experience of sexism. She navigated the thicket of competing loyalties and emerged completely intact, being everything to everybody, occasionally clipping or silently blotting out her answers altogether so as not to put anyone out.

I bumrushed the stage after her talk, to meet her, hoping that some of her energy, strength, boldness, and creativity would osmose into me. On that day, Latifah seemed so perfect to me because she evoked a recognizable ideal: the quintessentially strong, virtuous woman my grandmother always exhorted me to become. The woman everyone loves—from a distance. Never loose, never trivial, never bitchy or butchy. The talented, disciplined, powerful woman who is too generous and down-to-earth to constitute a threat. The woman who keeps her panties up and practices the art of no, who polices any moral injustice or infraction of etiquette and never misses an opportunity to speak up for herself or any oppressed groups in words that are clear, just, and listened to.

Latifah was like a young Rosa Parks getting open on the mike, a symbol with whom everyone could identify. Her Afrocentric imaging, full-bodied voice, and collaboration with some of hip hop's pioneers (such as KRS-One, De La Soul, and Daddy-O of Stetsasonic) set her apart from female rappers like Lyte and Shante who'd come before her. She meant safety and strength to me, a way for me to come out as a black woman. Not that I was planning on rhyming any time soon. But she was my age, and that made her the first mainstream black female role model with whom I could identify in a practical way. Latifah was a step toward an entirely new epistemology for me. My political awareness and self-esteem began to put on some weight as I started to connect more meaningfully with my mother and my aunt, took a trip to West Africa with my family, moved into an artsier, blacker dormitory, took classes in African-American history and culture, sat twelve hours for microbraids, and fell in love with a black man.

When I got Latifah's next album, *Nature of a Sista'*, I laid on my couch and cried because she was talking about men! I couldn't believe that she was singing about love, loneliness, and relationships and occasionally even sounding like Madonna to top it all off. R&B was moving toward her; she (and hip hop) were moving toward R&B. All the iconography was changing, tending toward a heightened corporeality in an expanding discourse on sex. And just like Lyte and her lipstick, Janet and her belly button, Latifah was only a woman after all. She had gone "soft," the ultimate insult in the hip-hop phallo-universe, experiencing the same wounds and joys I was petrified of revealing to myself, let alone to the world. I felt betrayed. How could she do this to me? A little makeup now and again was fine, but did she have to display the holes in her heart, and the reality that she needed a man from the bully pulpit of hip hop?

And yet I had identified so powerfully with Latifah that after I listened to the album a few more times, the shock eased and I started to absorb, unconsciously at first, a wider concept of my own femininity through Latifah's own expanding notions of self. By accepting Latifah's growth, by allowing her to be someone I didn't want her or myself to be while still admiring her, I made a subtle but distinct break with my inherited tradition of who I, Black Woman, was supposed to be.

Then came Latifah's movie roles, her business acumen, and *Living Single*. As her identities began to compound instantaneously in the Hollywood dream bank, I lost that initial sense of connectedness. She still managed to balance the needs of her hard-core and lay feminist contingencies while making an empire of herself, keeping Nielsen ratings high and the mall rats in stitches every Thursday night. But who was she? I no longer recognized myself in her work or in her persona.

Which brings me back to my dilemma: *Doggystyle* or

Black Reign? Was I in the mood for bluesy misogyny over the fattest, most addictive beats known to humankind, or did I want to hear "positive" messages I already knew nestled into Latifah's latest product? The devil or Daniel Webster? Toxic chocolate sundae or nine-grain granola?

I ended up buying *Doggystyle;* seven hours later, I was singing "g'z up hoes down." But I did acquire a free copy of *Doggystyle* later that week and traded it in for *Black Reign* so that I could have both, which is what I wanted in the first place. In my post-Latifah phase, I don't fit into a puritanical, dualistic feminism that recognizes only indignant innocence (buying *Black Reign*) or unenlightened guilt (buying into *Doggystyle*). I don't have to choose.

My dilemma, then, was not one of rational consumerism, or how to voice my own opinion best, given the products and their attendant philosophies. While that remains an important issue, the actual dilemma I was experiencing was how to explain that I don't feel oppressed by Snoop or defined by his conception of women—without denying that in Snoop's world, he is defining me and all women, even if he separates the queens from the hoes in his life off wax. How can I love me some Dre beats with sexist Snoop lyrics while responding to him in language that criticizes the misogynist reality he's been born into and continues to build for himself?

When I was introduced to Latifah in 1990, Afrocentric racial consciousness and progressive gender politics joined hands in hip hop, and the version of female empowerment I had borrowed from my elders wouldn't even allow me to say or hear bitch. Even in jest. Even as a verb. But now, like many women I know, I have acquired an immunity to sexist lyrics. While some may call this immunity a weariness, or a numb defeat, could it be the first inexplicable taste of inner power? I can't stuff my ears with cotton and refuse to hear those who have different politics than I do. I don't want to censor or dismiss my culture, my language, my sense of community regardless of the form in which it comes. Hip hop, after all, is the chosen whipping boy for a misogyny that is fundamental to Western culture. Why should I deny myself hip hop but get a good grounding in Aristotle? I'd rather listen and listen well, and have a conversation with the artist-philosophers who are repeating the sexist ways they have been taught, and then have chosen, to see the world.

As part of my work as a journalist, I've had some illuminating discussions with Ice Cube, Scarface, Apache, Snoop, the members of Brand Nubian and many other rappers regarding their use of sexist lyrics. These conversations have underscored the need to be sensitive to the rapper's or listener's specific context when deciphering lyrical meaning. The terms "bitch" or "ho" (or "nigga") can be used playfully, lovingly, even fictively at times. "Bitch" can even be used as an anodyne for lost love (for instance, on "Bitches Ain't Shit").

The second point I've heard from male rappers is that there really are bitches and hoes. And they need to be told about themselves. Even rappers who are socially conscious qualify these lyrics by saying things like, "This song isn't for an African queen like you or like my lady or like my mama," but this, as Jeru the Damaja says, "is for the "bichez." In other words, if you're not a bitch or a ho, why do you have a problem? (Just insert the word "nigga" flying out of a white mouth and watch the script flip.) Why do you come when you weren't being called in the first place? I only disrespect those who disrespect themselves. I'm a correct black man, a god, only a nigga on weekends. I learned my history. Now why can't these bitches get themselves together?

This response has little validity for me, because while I am immune to a sexist reality on record, I'm not yet free, to steal from The Coup. When used jokingly between equals, these terms are fine, and when I'm getting my groove to "Bitches Ain't Shit (But Hoes and Tricks)" in a club, I'm cool. But don't let a black man call me "bitch" other than in jest. The word can become a sledgehammer, sometimes even a bullet that grazes my heart. It's as if, for one unbearably painful moment, I believe him more than I believe myself.

I also don't buy the claim that there are "real" bitches and hoes. I think it is a trap that punishes women for playing their expected roles in figuring the rapper's persona. Onstage, hip-hop artists invite women's desire and pursuit, bragging about their conquests far in advance of the reality. But when the women go back to the hotel after the show and get what they came for, the artists reject the women who have legitimated their player persona, channeling their own morning-after disgust into a litany of bitches and hoes.

There are no excuses for lyrical sexism. I can't fantasize that it's dead, embalmed, and on exhibit at the Smithsonian, or convince myself that it's an historical, cultural condition that black women have to accept in order to understand and stand by "our" men. Yet I still feel virtually untouched by this verbal and visual violence toward women, and I believe this feeling springs from an increased sense of freedom rather than from apathetic resignation.

As sexist as these lyrics and attitudes can be, my immunity is fortified by a growing number of male rappers who consciously and humorously espouse a chauvinism they know to be antiquated because they are beginning to understand that their position is as fragile and as powerful as a woman's. Male hip-hop artists recognize that they are the hunted; they flesh out all of white America's fears by carrying out, lyrically, unthinkable acts of sociopathic destruction. The fantastical crime setting of gangsta and horrorcore rap, starring protagonists who drip with testosterone, features a masculinity that defines itself by an ability to annihilate any challenger, female or male. When this protagonist commits sexual and violent crimes, he satisfies a specifically black male yet generic desire for total power. This protagonist also embodies the newly formulated national enemy: in the absence of the Red Threat, the specter of the criminalized black male steps into its place. Thus the criminalized enemy is contained and made fictive, consumed, pitied, or condemned by the haves, and disowned or celebrated by the have-nots. Misogyny here becomes a reactionary act with a subversive gloss.

When I peer into this hip-hop shadow box where the stock characters of seventies' blaxploitation are revisited—how poignant this swan song, how funny this compulsive reenactment of a sexist past—I consume the performance of sexism, thereby assuring myself that the reality of sexism depicted in the lyrics is happening to an imaginary woman, not a real one. Unlike white hip-hop fans who confirm and celebrate their own perceived distance from racism by identifying with the purveyor of explicit antiracist, even antiwhite lyrics, I think there's a new woman on the dance floor who can chant "Bitch Betta Have My Money" and identify with neither the lyricist nor the sexual object, discovering instead a humor in sexist lyrics whose possible truth removes rather than implicates her. She realizes that AMG can't really be talking to her or anyone else, and if he is, he's got to be kidding.

There are also women out on the dance floor who accept these lyrics as truths about themselves—sometimes playing the bitch or ho role in the same spiteful way that the men explode the stereotype of criminalization. Or sometimes there's a recognition that a woman who dares to step out of her place, a woman who is willful or sexually uninhibited, may be called a bitch or ho, respectively. These women not only have a sense of humor about being called bitches and hoes, they have a sense of pride that they are finally being spoken to. The hip-hop ode to women has evolved from L.L. Cool J's "Around the Way Girl" to Sir Mix-A-Lot's "Baby Got Back" to Apache's "Gangsta Bitch," giving the ideal woman a rare multiplicity. These songs reveal how male hip-hop artists actually have provided public acceptance, not just degradation, for women who would never receive it elsewhere in popular culture.

Whether women respond with pride, a sense of humor, or righteous anger upon hearing sexist lyrics—or if they don't pay attention to the lyrics at all—there is and always has been a strong public dialogue between male and female rappers, between black men and women. That's another reason why I can croon along with Nate Dogg on "Ain't No Fun (If The Homies Can't Have None)" because I know that I and every other woman are always talking back. Call this dialogue the racist legacy of Moynihan's matriarchal pathology or the retention of an African mother goddess; it doesn't matter. We all know that if we'd ever been blessed with a blaxploitation sequel entitled *Coffy v. Dolemite,* Pam Grier and Fred Williamson would kill each other before letting the other win. More likely, they'd call it a draw and join forces against evil. In the same way, female and male rappers battle each other within or between songs, with neither sex ever having the final word. Hip-hop dialogue has a male advantage by sheer number and by male privilege in the language, genre, and social custom, but just one female who gets the crowd hype can rebut all the men if her style is identical to none. With dis artists like Shante and Bytches With

Problems, with spirits like Mecca of Digable Planets, Nefertiti, Medusa and Koko of Sin, T-Love, Lauryn from the Fugees, 99, and Rage, and with mainstream presences like Latifah, Lyte, Yo Yo, and Salt-N-Pepa, the burden of representation is spread wide on strong shoulders. And the mainstream media's strategy of coopting this dialogue for racist purposes, restaging black women and men's struggle against racialized sexism as a bloody cockfight, can be reappropriated as an opportunity to truly resolve the conflicts we have with one another and with the larger hegemony.

Recognizing that there is an uncut umbilical cord between hip hop's art and life as well as an infinite amount of exaggeration and fantasy only leads me to want to change the reality of sexism off of wax. Who would these rappers be, I wonder, if no ladies wanted to get with them? If all women, like the Athenian and Spartan coalition of Aristophanes' *Lysistrata,* agreed to abstain from sex with all rappers, could we end sexism in hip hop? Why is there so little space for public, artistic declaration of meaningful relationships? (Method Man's "All I Need" is a wonderful exception to the rule.) And aren't the women who do have recreational sex with hip-hop artists or who put on a thong bikini to play a "video ho" just searching for that place where we women can celebrate our bodies, where we can express our eroticism freely, where we can have sexual agency?

I had a dream in which TLC members Left Eye and Chili were sitting on a couch on the beach (embarrassingly, this is a real dream, hardly invented for the purposes of this piece). I sat on the couch and told Left Eye that the (real) *ViBe* cover with the trio in fireman's slickers might have been in bad taste since she'd just burned down her abusive boyfriend's mansion, and that the new (dreamworld) cover *ViBe* had replaced it with after recalling the original was even worse because it featured T-Boz by herself draped in white and discussed only her in the cover story. I wanted to share how incensed I was by *ViBe*'s mistreatment of them. Looking at T-Boz dipping her toes in the water, Left Eye and Chili said, "No, you're wrong." Left Eye explained in dreamy, lush language how T-Boz had enlightened her and Chili about feminist practice. How T-Boz had this amazing mind and was using her corporeality as a tool to free women, not to entice men. Elegy complete, Left Eye had tears in her eyes as she gazed toward her latter-day saint. I woke up and wondered if she could be right.

When sexist lyrics are not self-conscious but instead are full of vitriol and anger, they do still hurt, they still feel real. This pain only helps me diagnose the problem; it does nothing to solve it. And I don't have to throw away all the old words and the people who say them in order to have a new conversation. I can't have a vision of political practice anymore that makes no space for pleasure, conflict, personal and collective responsibility to cohabitate simultaneously. I have to genuflect to Dr. Dre for his genius as a producer and an artist while I lacerate him for his physical violence toward women. I commend and criticize. I speak not from the vengeful state I was in when I heard he'd beaten "Pump It Up" host Dee Barnes, but from the place where I want to be when sexism is all over.

I often think about these issues through the lens of humor because it often provides freedom, creativity, and a language that dispenses with blame and guilt, precisely what we need in our work toward transcending sexism. When I hear self-conscious sexism in rap and laugh at it, I am releasing a painful past and garnering power to shape a new future. For example, I love the two-syllable variation of "bitch" pronounced "bee-otch," because the word is distorted explicitly for humor, making light of the namer as well as the named, ridiculing the term itself. "We don't love them hoes," goes the misogynistic, faintly homoerotic Dogg Pound refrain, and damnit, the shit is funny. Admittedly, it's a humor that still operates on an uneven playground, where hoes and bitches get bullied much more than the niggaz. "Sexist hoes, they wanna get with this," flows Snoop, but since I've had Latifah's "U.N.I.T.Y." in my back pocket since long before she recorded it, I don't even have to let him know that I ain't a "bitch" or a "ho," because I know for myself.

An organic act of laughter upon hearing a lyric reminds me that the present manifestations of sexism in hip hop have a value for me: they are simply a tradition, like a woman wearing white when she marries, that I recognize and enjoy as such precisely because I know I am not bound to it. Although Snoop is talking to me, he isn't defining me, and this position spawns a new politics that protects our identities as women without sentencing us to life in a prison of identity we didn't choose. I want to infuse some of the necessary energy we spend fighting men's rules into working on a new extinction agenda, to sample Organized Konfusion, that will render sexism, racism, homophobia, and classism old sitcoms that we watch in syndication only to see how much we've changed.

When women no longer feel bound by sexist representations, when we initiate a dialogue that doesn't turn on the axis of anger, blame, or victimology, then artists who should attend Ism Anonymous meetings (treating compulsive sexism, nihilism, and marijuana use in lyrics) are finally recognized as valuable people who can become even stronger by assuming self-worth through constructing themselves rather than destroying others. I would love to see hip-hop battles, conference panels, and articles and essays like this one that talk about issues of sexism in hip hop supplemented by other formats for dialogue. While I have some drafty ideas for in-store listening stations with hardware for immediate on-line responses, the most effective formats are informal: relationships between artists and critics (in the loosest sense of that term) which probe these issues honestly, over time, are probably the best and most difficult way to get anything done. I am encouraged by relationships such as the one fostered between Harvard professor and novelist Carolivia Herron and Public Enemy, coinciding with Chuck D.'s lyrics moving from the misogyny of "She Watch Channel Zero" to the womanism of "Revolutionary Generation."

Even considering growth like Chuck D.'s, I don't look to hip-hop artists with the same religious zeal for The Answers that I once did, because I know those answers only pose more questions; I'm a big ho now and I don't depend on hip hop to tell me that I'm not or that I am or that I'm just joking. Since I no longer need hip hop to provide me with a fixed identity, I have no need to control hip hop's representation of women. I just want to continue talking to and hearing from the artists who do control these representations, as I have in the past through interviews, and in the future within these valuable long-term relationships I mentioned above.

More important to me than my conversations with artists is the conversation between Ice Cube and a woman who wants to produce a track for his next album, the conversation between a male higher-up and a woman marketing executive at a record label who wants to try something other than bikini and booty art on an album cover, the conversation between a woman and a man in a club who's called her a stanky bitch for not dancing with him. We must make a world outside of hip hop in which we and our daughters are equals in these conversations—and we can't make it with only guns, money, and tears to choose from.

In my personal/political upbringing, I got my theory at home and my praxis from hip hop. And I think I've grown up enough to know where else I need to grow. Latifah in all her avatars— Afrocentric, introspective, and relationship-hungry; plain old Dana; Khadijah on "Living Single"—isn't a model that was once useful for me and then thrown out; instead she has given me a foundation of bedrock to build upon. She and all women artists, mainstream and underground, get props for relentlessly transforming the taboo into the cool because we all privilege from the truth. My grandmother's version of black womanhood isn't a tradition that restricts me, either; rather it has allowed me to break those patterns that confine my growth, yet remains a home for me to return to and feed my spirit. Grandma continues to inform my choices, values, and dreams. Her lifelong work as an educator makes me want to make time for the children who are being raised by hip hop and Sega to sit down and actively analyze and filter what they learn. And I would love to see a public hip-hop library and studio to give access to anybody who wants to learn about and make music, because is there anything more joyful, more weary, more expressive of our humanity than hip hop, ever transforming, encompassing the universe of all music?

Fighting sexism isn't only about being offended by the

forty-five bitches and twenty-three hoes on someone's record. I hope that the strength we gain from realizing that we women —and men—are not bound to hip hop's representations can help to dismantle the sexism we've internalized, and empowers us to combat the sexism outside of us.

Identity Politics

jennifer allyn and david allyn

jennifer

My mother desperately wanted her first child to be a boy. She yearned to erase the disappointment her own father felt at having only daughters. He was saddened by the end of his lineage; there was no male heir to pass on his name. Throughout her adolescence my mother tried to fulfill this missing son's role. She went to every baseball game and spent hours watching trains. But no matter what she did, her developing body revealed to the world that she was a fraud. When I was born she felt like she had failed twice. But with time the feeling of inadequacy subsided. My brother's birth three years later did not bring the hoped-for sense of satisfaction or vindication. She was not more loved by this random event, and my grandfather died before he and Christopher could ever play ball. Ultimately the intensity of her feelings, the devastation, and the guilt were all for naught. She vowed that I would never regret being female, or know that she had felt anything other than absolute joy at the moment of my birth.

I have been a feminist for as long as I can remember. My background as a bossy little girl was the perfect training for an activist. College was my first opportunity to work with a community of women on feminist issues. As a volunteer for the campus women's center, I started questioning things I had previously taken for granted and struggled to integrate my political beliefs into my personal life. Like most of the women I worked with, I felt part of a new generation of feminists. We wanted to make room for play in our lives—dyeing our hair, shaving our legs, dressing in ways that made us happy—without sacrificing a commitment to political activism. Each of us struggled to decide which choices were personally liberating and which oppressive. For me, marriage seemed like something I might never be able to choose in good conscience. Aware of the poverty women often suffer after divorce, the risk of domestic abuse, and the unequal division of household labor that many women face, I could not see myself upholding the institution of marriage. Yet while being a part of the feminist community helped me to see the oppressive aspects of matrimony, it also enabled me to appreciate the spiritual freedom that marriage can offer.

One spring, I was invited by two friends to attend a formal ceremony honoring their commitment to each other. It was my first wedding and one I shall never forget. The service was held in an old New England church; the sun shone warmly on Angela and Carolyn as they walked hand in hand down the aisle. For them, a wedding was an opportunity to make their declaration of devotion out loud and in public, defying a society that would close its ears to such sentiments and legislate against "unnatural" love. Sitting in the wooden pews, pews that had seen the same ritual performed for hundreds of years, I witnessed all the promise and hope that marriage embodies. I discovered that two people could claim an ancient custom as their own and in doing so transform it. To change the institution of marriage, I felt strongly that I would have to challenge the first symbol of women's inequality: I would never give up my own name in order to take my husband's. The more decisions I reached, however, the more questions I had about how to achieve equality in intimate relationships.

Then one April evening, at an art opening held by the college women's center, I was introduced to a tall, dark-haired man. I asked him his name. "Now that's a long story," he replied. Intrigued, I pressed for a full explanation. Later, I asked him out for ice cream. Sharing a carton of vanilla fudge swirl, we talked passionately about politics and ideals and identity. Within a few weeks we had begun to study together, to write together, to fall in love.

From the first, David and I were explicit about our desire to have a balanced partnership. We knew we did not yet face any of the major obstacles to equality—negotiating two careers, raising children jointly, dividing the domestic responsibilities of adulthood—but we shared a deep commitment to the ideals of feminism.

Five years later, we decided to get married. And the first problem we encountered, the problem that pointed to all the political problems inherent in merging two identities, was what to do about our last name. Originally I wanted each of us to keep our own names. I certainly was not going to change mine to Smith (for both feminist and aesthetic reasons), nor did I feel comfortable with the idea of David taking my last name, Wilcha. While that might have been a powerful gesture on one level, it would also have represented a mere reversal of traditional gender roles. It would not have pointed to a more equal social arrangement. It seemed wrong for either person to be pushed into taking the name of the other, regardless of gender. Neither of us deserved anonymity. So keeping our own individual names seemed like the best answer.

But maintaining our own names posed another problem. What would we name our children? I knew too many women who kept their own name for professional purposes, but allowed their husband's name to represent the family. In many ways it has become the feminist path of least resistance. Although Hillary Rodham Clinton has fought many political battles to keep her "maiden" name, Chelsea Clinton's last name is simply that of her father's. I felt that such a choice would ultimately mean sacrificing my politics for convenience. As I struggled with this dilemma I stumbled upon a book that suggested "bilineality" as a solution. To achieve bilineality, daughters are given the last name of their mother and sons are given the last name of their father. While I did find something appealing about this concept, I also found it troubling. I wanted to raise a feminist son as much as a feminist daughter. Segregating children according to gender would mean highlighting difference based on sex, not challenging it. I wanted to encourage my children to transcend gender roles; bilineality seemed only to reinforce them.

Although we strongly believed in individuality, David and I also yearned for belonging. Hyphenation seemed like a logical option. If both of us changed our names to Wilcha-Smith or Smith-Wilcha and passed on the combination to the next generation, we would be making our feminist politics clear to the world while still honoring both family legacies. But David did not feel this was practical or fair. Ultimately our children would be forced to choose one name over the other, especially if a Wilcha-Smith ever fell in love with a Swift-Weinberg. We would be leaving our children without any model to follow. Would they then become Wilcha-Weinbergs or Smith-Swifts? David was adamant that he did not want to put our children through his own experience of having to choose to keep the name of one parent over the other, not to mention having to decide which name would come first in any hyphenated pair. I thought that our children, if they were ever confronted with such a dilemma, would simply make their decision as a matter of taste. If they thought Weinberg-Smith happened to sound better than Wilcha-Swift, the choice would be up to them. But finally I acknowledged that any such decision would be inextricably bound up with family loyalty, ego, and guilt. Hyphenating would mean we were passing our own indecision on to the next generation.

As our options diminished, we began to consider the possibility of merging our two different names. Wilcha and Smith could become With or Wilith. (Smilcha was quickly rejected.) Neither seemed right, however. Wilith. We practiced it on our friends. We tried accenting different syllables. Yet no matter what, it sounded like we had both developed a lisp. Frustrated, we suddenly asked ourselves why we were trying so hard to salvage the name Smith when it was chosen as a denial of ethnic heritage. Furthermore, the name Wilcha represented a tradition of patriarchy that I did not want to continue. Wilcha may be my name, but like all last names, it is also a whitewashed canvas beneath which lie innumerable other names no longer visible.

Slowly we began to realize that it might be better to start afresh. We decided to choose an entirely new name, one that was not burdened by any historical deception. We tried Providence, the city where fate allowed us to meet. But David thought it sounded too gentile—that others might question his motives—while friends thought I would sound like a stripper. Then we moved to names of things that we loved: authors, restaurants, streets. We thought of all the people we knew with names that meant other things: Strawberry, Pebble, Sparkle. In a tribute to matriarchy, we considered each of our mother's maiden names. With so many possibilities to choose from, our standards got higher. We wanted a beautiful, meaningful, and poetic name that would perfectly capture our relationship. What name could live up to such expectations? The freedom was paralyzing.

So we waited. We waited for something to leap out at us from a newspaper. We waited for a dream to tell us the perfect name. We asked all of our friends. I even asked a psychic (he told me to hyphenate). We weren't getting anywhere.

Without a last name, we felt like our lives were hanging. David Alan and Jennifer Lynn, two individuals with no sense of finality or closure. In times of boredom, instead of doodling, we would constantly rearrange the letters of our six first, middle, and last names. We kept expecting to have a moment of realization when the perfect name would appear in a flash of insight. Slowly we realized that names don't work that way. Names take time to get used to, they must be whispered and shouted and mulled over for hours before they can be adequately judged. And as we toyed with all the infinite possibilities, we felt a quiet desire to return to our own names, the names closest to our personal selves, names that belonged to no one but us. Jennifer Lynn and David Alan. Those were the names that we could be sure of. They had been given to us by our parents out of love, not ownership or obligation. And then we did have that flash of insight. The most obvious choice had been with us all along, and it took years of reflection to stumble upon it. Together we could be Allyn, our middle names united. It sounded good. It looked nice written on the page. It sounded either Jewish or Catholic, and it was still rooted in some sense of who we were. At last we decided: we would become Jennifer and David Allyn.

Traditions help to build stability, continuity, community. But sometimes following tradition feels a bit like sleepwalking. As we build a new family, David and I want to choose our traditions carefully and ask what each one says about who we are. We do not want to plunge blindly into something as significant as marriage. It is true that the meaning of marriage has changed dramatically in the last twenty years. It is no longer the promise of permanence that it once was. But for us, this new instability is all the more reason to reaffirm the meaning of commitment. Not just our commitment to each other, but to our shared values, personal and political.

My mother was recently asked where she thought my political convictions originated. Had she ever been involved in the women's rights movement? She answered by telling the story about her own father's sense of failure in having only daughters. "I was never directly political," she said, "but I taught Jennifer that she could accomplish anything. She was truly loved."

David and I hope to continue that family tradition.

david

I considered myself a feminist years before I met Jennifer. I attended a progressive high school, with a female principal, which was committed to teaching a multicultural, nonsexist curriculum. Later, at Brown University, I studied feminist literary and political theory, discovering the richness and diversity of thought within feminism itself. I learned how the second wave of feminism introduced the notion that "the personal is political," and I quickly saw the connections in my own life. My experiences—as a Jew, a white man, a son, a lover—have profoundly shaped how I view the world. But while it is easy to stand up for one's own personal and political interests, I have always believed that the true struggle is to draw upon one's own experience in order to empathize with, and defend, the interests of others. Although I am a man, I can empathize with feminist concerns about the importance of identity and selfhood. My parents' divorce taught me that names are extremely significant, and that they involve questions of loyalty, family, history, and identity. As an adult, I have come to learn that these questions can have political meaning, especially for women.

I was four years old when my parents separated. My mother remarried shortly thereafter. She felt that it was in my best interest for me to drop my birth name, Smith, and take the name of my new father, Wallach. She wanted me to have the sense of closeness and family unity that comes from a common last name. When my biological father discovered that my mother had made this switch, he was furious. He felt cut out, forcibly distanced from his son. For years, my parents and I fought about my last name. And for years I tried to determine what my name "should" be.

When I look back on old paintings and drawings I did in nursery school and kindergarten I see a bizarre evolution, like some sort of Darwinian struggle of identity, in the signatures that are laboriously scrawled in finger-paint and crayon. If one were to study only those early fossils of childhood looking for clues to the development of my sense of self, one would see no clear pattern or direction. For a while, at least, I wasn't quite sure what my name was. Sometimes I would sign paintings David S., other times David W., sometimes a joint D. S. W. and once in a while simply David. The memory of my confusion and anxiety is still painful.

I honestly believe that both of my parents were concerned with what was best for me. I was fortunate enough to have parents who were eager to raise me as their own. But the conflict over my last name produced a battle over loyalty and possession that ultimately tore apart the very relationships each of my parents was trying to protect. Compassion turned into contest, contest into conflict, and the result was unhappiness and disappointment on all sides. Ironically, my father and I are so estranged today because of the dispute over my name, that I do not even know how he feels about Jennifer's and my decision to rename ourselves.

As an adult I look back on that childhood struggle and see parallels with the politics of feminism. Feminists assert that names are important to each of us, and the demand that a person sacrifice his or her name is unfair. Critics charge that feminists are overreacting to a small, symbolic problem for women. But I know that there was nothing symbolic about my name. As far as my parents were concerned, and therefore as far as I was concerned, my name meant everything. It signified loyalty and alignment. The dispute over my name involved lawyers, therapists, and educators; in other words, it went from being a private matter to a public one. I know from my own experience that names are not trivial; no person—woman or man—should be forced by legal or social pressure to give up his or her name. A society that does not respect each person's name is a society that does not respect the autonomy and uniqueness of every individual.

When Jennifer and I first broached the subject of marriage I assumed that she would keep her own name. Throughout our subsequent discussions about children and family I never expected her to take my name. It might have been easier, but I knew we could find a more creative approach that would reflect our values. Now we hope our willingness to stray from the path of tradition encourages others to challenge social norms as well. Jennifer and I made a particular choice; I would not expect every couple to make a similar choice (not every couple shares middle names that would merge nicely!). I don't think that a true feminist politics would put pressure on anyone to make a major life decision that did not accord with one's own views and beliefs. What I feel is most important is that each of us approaches the decisions about marriage, identity, and equality self-consciously and critically, not complacently or blindly. In the attempt to be self-conscious and critical in our decision, we have had to struggle with several questions about the meaning of our choice.

What, for example, is the impact of our decision on our relationship to the past? Our surnames are one of our last remaining connections to our family history. As Americans, we live almost without links to our past. Geographic mobility, social mobility, ethnic amalgamation, and acculturation contribute to an "amnemonic" culture, that is, a culture virtually without memory. As someone training to be a professional historian, history is not just an abstract quantity but something very real and important to me. As a Jew, it is even more so, because Judaism has always been a religion that stresses the role of history in defining Jewish identity. So abandoning our last names was not an easy decision, it was one fraught with dilemma. What if everyone in society abandoned his or her last name? Wouldn't we lose our vital connections to the past?

I think that the idea that a name can serve as a bond of historical continuity has diminished the very meaning of historical tradition. A common last name has come to substitute for rich discussion about family history and bonds. I know that when I sit down with my children some day and explain the origins of their last name, I will have to go into detail about the history of our family: their grandparents, great-grandparents, and as far back as I can remember. When I explain how the name "Allyn" came to be, I imagine it will make them more curious about their own roots, and they may even challenge me on my decision. I hope it will give us an opportunity to talk honestly about what it means to start a family, to carry on traditions, and to create one's own. I also know that teaching my children about the name Allyn will afford the opportunity to teach them about historical discontinuity: how some cultures have lost or been deprived of their past. African-Americans, for example, were deprived of their African names and traditions in the process of being enslaved. Today they must make sense of this historical discontinuity in their own lives. As a Jew, my own father severed his connection with his Jewish ancestry by abandoning his Jewish name for the nonethnic name Smith. This too is part of the story of American history. It is important for all children to learn about these significant elements of American history and life.

Like our relationship to the past, Jennifer and I are also concerned about our relationship to the future. Do we expect our children to keep the name Allyn or do we plan on encouraging them to name themselves as we did? What sort of precedent do we hope to establish?

As I said earlier, I do not think that feminist politics can dictate the choices one should make. If our children want to rename themselves when they marry, Jennifer and I would be proud of their decision. More likely than not, our children will be disgusted with their parents' politics and somehow rebel by being dramatically conservative. In that case, Jennifer and I will have to come to terms with the real meaning of tolerance and diversity. But most important, we intend to instill in each of our children the sense that they can define themselves and make their own choices in life. Just as we are fighting a society that demands women to subordinate their own identities to their husbands', we would not want to impose our own vision of freedom on others.

In addition to examining our thoughts about the past and the future, Jennifer and I have also had to consider the meaning of our decision for the present. Rejecting the traditional approach to the married last name has been our way of contending with the legacy of patriarchy and discrimination on the basis of sex. But what does merging our middle names—and thereby choosing a single common name—say about our conception of identity and individuality?

Together Jennifer and I look forward to a world in which individuality and relationship are viewed not as opposites but as interdependent qualities. True individuality is really an expression of personal identity as it is manifested in various relationships. One cannot have a sense of self wholly independent from others. Likewise, every relationship is an expression of the unique individuals who compose it. No true relationship can suppress the subjectivity of a human being. Viewing individuality and relationship as interconnected allows us to balance individualism and feminism, competitive ideals and more cooperative ones.

So far, reactions to our decision have been overwhelmingly positive. Most people we know admit that they have thought about the "name issue," but interestingly we know only one other couple who have made a nontraditional choice (they merged their last names). Perhaps the obstacles seem too imposing. Or the mere principle doesn't seem worth the effort. But we have found that the legal process is not that intimidating, the bureaucracy can be navigated, and everyone from family to friends to professional colleagues have supported our decision. The second wave of feminism opened our eyes to the problem of gender inequity rooted deep in social traditions. It is the opportunity of the third wave to act on this knowledge.

Our daily lives have changed little as a result of getting married. However, our new names remind us that we have formed an emotional and political bond that transcends companionship. During our wedding ceremony, the priest described his own transformation when he changed his name to join the Church. The rabbi spoke about how Jews do not name their God because to do so would be limiting. As the Allyns we are trying to figure out how to live meaningful lives; to be transformed but not limited, united but not subsumed, self-aware but not selfish. Our new name is not so much an answer, as a question: what does it mean to build a family, a community, a society? We may never know the full answers, but at least we have given the question a name.

Beauty Laid Bare: Aesthetics in the Ordinary

bell hooks

growing up in conservative working-class and poor Southern black communities, I had no notion that black folks were inherently more radical or "cool" than any other marginalized or oppressed group. While the folks I lived amongst were often militant in their condemnation of racism, they were pretty much in agreement with many of the other values that trickled down from the worlds of the conservative ruling classes, from the white or black bourgeois world. When it came to materialism, across class it was clear that success in diverse black communities was measured by having nice things. Whether or not something was perceived as "nice" depended on one's social environment.

One of the intense pressures I experienced as an adolescent was caused by my longing to cultivate my own style and taste, clashing with the pressure to conform to set bourgeois standards. Sarah Oldham, my mother's mother, was the "style radical." Her aesthetic sensibility was grounded in a more traditional appreciation for the natural world, for color and harmony. As a quilt maker she was constantly creating new worlds, discovering new patterns, different shapes. To her it was the uniqueness of the individual body, look, and soul that mattered. From her I learned the appropriateness of being myself.

The example of personal freedom and creative courage set by my grandmother was constantly challenged by the bourgeois aspirations of my mother, whereby she insisted on conformity, on imitating acceptable appearance and styles. To my mother, "nice things" were not the earth, the sky, the eggs in the henhouse, a fishing worm uncovered in dark, moist dirt, the sight of a tomato growing on a vine; "nice things" were the objects seen in advertisements, on the screen, and in catalogues.

My grandmother and her daughter, my mother, did agree on the basic principle that beautiful objects enhanced life, even if their aesthetic standards differed. Although we came from a poor and working-class background, from a history of squatting, sharecropping, and working in white folks' houses, among the traditional Southern black folks I grew up around there was a shared belief in the idea that beautiful things, objects that could be considered luxurious, that were expensive and difficult to own, were necessary for the spirit. The more downtrodden and unfortunate the circumstances, the more "beauty" was needed to uplift, offer a vision of hope, to transform. When it came to the issue of desiring and longing for the beautiful object, whether it was a house, car, furniture, clothing, or shoes, everyone agreed, across class, that folks needed to be in touch with beauty. When I was a child, this did not seem to be a radical idea. It was such a common way of thinking about life it seemed "natural." There was never a need to make someone feel guilty when he or she did without the basic necessities of life in order to acquire an object deemed beautiful, healing to the spirit. At times those objects were luxury items, not intrinsically aesthetically beautiful, but desired because the culture of consumerism had deemed them lovely symbols of power and possibility. Even though folks sometimes laughed at the individual who bought a shiny car bigger than the wood frame shack in which he or she lived, underneath the mockery was the understanding that this symbol of luxury was a balm to a depressed and wounded spirit. This stance was in every way oppositional.

The black elders in our community, like my grandmother Sarah and my grandfather Gus, believed it was better to seek beauty in a world that was not subject to monetary exchange. For Sarah beauty was there in the growing of flowers in her elaborate garden, or in the making of her quilts. Alice Walker, in her insightful essay "In Search of Our Mother's Garden," acknowledges the way poor black women expressed their concern with beauty in the growing and arranging of flower gardens. Offering the example of her mother, Walker declares: "Her face, as she prepared the Art that is her gift, is a legacy of respect she leaves to me, for all that illuminates and cherishes life. She has handed down respect of the responsibilities—and the will to grasp them." This legacy had been handed down through generations in traditional Southern black folk culture.

These were notions of beauty and wealth grounded in a worldview that was in opposition to excessive materialism.

Southern black males who had an oppositional aesthetic were often economically deprived but rich in spirit. When the forces of white supremacy and capitalism denied them access to meaningful work, they cultivated ways to care for the soul that sustained them. For my grandfather, Daddy Gus, the will to create was life sustaining. To him beauty was present in found objects, discarded objects that he rescued and restored because, as he put it, "spirits lived there." His room was full of "treasures." Entering that sanctuary of precious "beautiful" objects, we were embraced by an atmosphere of peace and serenity. In *Shambala: The Sacred Path of the Warrior,* Buddhist monk Chogyam Trungpa teaches that we create this atmosphere by expressing gentleness and precision in our environment: "You may live in a dirt hut with no floor and only one window, but if you regard that space as sacred, if you care for it with your heart and mind, then it will be a palace." This caretaking promotes "awareness and attention to detail." There can be a sacred place in everyone's life where beauty can be laid bare, where our spirits can be moved and lifted up by the creation and presence of a beautiful object.

When I first began to travel to different continents, I was fascinated by how, in most parts of the world, especially in places the United States designates as "Third World," no matter how poor the surroundings, individuals create beautiful objects. In the deserts of North Africa, beautiful woven rugs were present in every abode, no matter how humble. In countries where folks are ravished by genocidal war and famine, suffering, anguished bodies shroud themselves in beautiful cloth. Indians in Mexico and the United States, living in various states of impoverishment, make clay pots that reveal artistic skill and vision.

In contrast, in the United States, contemporary African-Americans have been increasingly socialized by the mass media to leave behind attachments to the oppositional worldviews of our elders, especially to those having to do with beauty, and to better assimilate into the mainstream. Hedonistic consumerism is offered as a replacement for healing and life-sustaining beauty. Unlike the global nonwhite poor, who manage to retain an awareness of the need for beauty despite imperialist devastation, the vast majority of the black poor in the United States do not harbor uplifting cultural objects in their homes. This group has been overwhelmingly encouraged to abandon, destroy, or sell artifacts from the past. And this destruction has brought in its wake the loss of an aesthetic sensibility that is redemptive. For example, today's concrete state-designed-and-operated public housing for the poor takes away the opportunity for creativity that was characteristic of the rural shack, its porch and gardens.

Black liberation movement has not addressed the issues of aesthetics in everyday life. Militant black power movement in the 1960s and 1970s did not encourage a reclamation of attitudes about beauty common in traditional black folk culture. While obsessive materialism has been consistently critiqued in antiracist movements, as well as by radicals on the left, the issue of aesthetics has not received much attention, nor has the relationship between the desire for beauty and the longing for material goods.

At the onset of contemporary feminist movement there was significant interrogation of consumerism, of women's addiction to materialism, and of the issue of money, both its distribution along gendered lines and its use. Early feminist anthologies like *Women in Sexist Society,* edited by Vivian Gornick and Barbara Moran, included discussions of consumerism and beauty in relation to appearances. An anonymous "Redstocking sister" made the useful point that feminist discussions of female obsession with consumerism would be useful if they began from a standpoint that depicted Americans as mere dupes of patriarchal advertising culture, "oppressed" by an infatuation with goods. She suggested:

> The consumerism theory is the outgrowth of an aristocratic, European-oriented antimaterialism based on upper-class *ressentiment* against the rise of the vulgar bourgeois. Radical intellectuals have been attracted to this essentially reactionary position . . . because it appeals to both their dislike of capitalism and their feeling of superiority to the working class. . . . Oddly, no one claims that the ruling class is oppressed by commodity choices; it seems that rich people consume out of free choice.

As was the case in black liberation struggle, there was no discussion of aesthetics, of the place of beauty in everyday life, within feminist debates about materialism, money, etcetera. Progressive feminist thinkers are more likely to critique the dangers of excessive materialism without discussing in a concrete way how we can balance a desire for beauty or luxury within an anticapitalist, antisexist agenda.

As revolutionary and radical feminism becomes less visible, and as more reformist thinking, such as Naomi Wolf's *Fire with Fire,* prevails as the feminist order of the day, there is hardly any discussion among feminists about the politics of materialism or money. Contemporary feminists, myself included, can receive more financial rewards for feminist work than has ever been possible, yet we remain relatively silent about these issues. Wolf is not silent. She advocates a brand of "power feminism" that sees nothing problematic about both pursuing and achieving wealth and opposing patriarchal domination. Certainly there is a distinction to be made between the processes by which material privilege can be acquired and wealth accumulated.

Most radical and/or revolutionary feminists continue to believe that living simply, the equitable distribution of resources, and communalism are necessary to the progressive struggle to end sexism while ending class exploitation. All too often in the past, living simply was made synonymous with a vulgar anti-materialism or antiaestheticism that privileged living without attention to beauty, to decoration, either of one's person or one's space. Although nowadays the tendency seems to move toward the other extreme, toward indulging to excess, some radical feminists, myself included, grapple with the place of beauty in revolutionary struggle, with our materialism and with our longing for luxury. Just as my Southern black ancestors recognized that in the midst of exploitation and oppression suffering could be endured if transforming encounters with beauty took place, many revolutionary feminists recognize that we need these same values within progressive feminist movement. Since it is so easy for those of us with material privilege to hoard resources, to have an attachment to wealth or privileged class power, we need to be vigilant in creating an ethical approach to consumerism that sustains and affirms radical agendas for social change.

Rather than surrendering our passion for the beautiful, for luxury, we need to envision ways those passions can be fulfilled that do not reinforce the structures of domination we seek to change. Hopefully, feminist thinkers will begin to engage in more discussions and theorizing about the place of beauty in revolutionary struggle. Many of us who have a degree of material privilege find that sharing resources, sharing objects we find beautiful that enhance our lives, is one way to resist falling into a privatized, hedonistic consumerism that is self-serving. Those of us who engage in barter, conscious gift-giving, tithing, sharing of living space and money, celebrate the luxurious if that which we deem luxurious is not acquired by harming others.

Females in white supremacist patriarchal society are socialized to consume in an unmindful manner, encouraged to value goods, especially luxury goods, over our well-being and safety. Many women remain in domestic situations where we are being hurt and even abused by sexist men because of an attachment to material wealth and privilege. While there are many poor women who remain in abusive households because they plainly lack the economic means to leave, there are also women who remain in such settings because they fear leaving behind material abundance. This kind of attachment to luxury is life-threatening and must be challenged.

Beauty can be and is present in our lives irrespective of our class status. Learning to see and appreciate the presence of beauty is an act of resistance in a culture of domination that recognizes the production of a pervasive feeling of lack, both materially and spiritually, is a useful colonizing strategy. Individuals who feel constant lack will consume more, will submit more readily. As feminist thinkers construct feminist theory and practice to guide us into a revolutionary, revitalized feminist future, we need to place aesthetics on our agenda. We need to theorize the meaning of beauty in our lives so that we can educate for critical consciousness, talking through the issues: how we acquire and spend money, how we feel about beauty, what the place of beauty is in our lives when we lack material privilege and basic resources for living, the meaning and significance of luxury, and the politics of envy. Interrogating these issues will enable feminist thinkers to share certain strategies of resistance that will illuminate the ways we can create a balanced, harmonious life where we know the joy of collective, progressive struggle, where the presence of beauty uplifts and renews the spirit.

Close, But No Banana

anna bondoc

I am a dancer. I believe we learn by practice. Whether it means to learn to dance by practicing dancing or learn to live by practicing living, the principles are all the same. In each it is the performance of a dedicated, precise set of acts, physical or intellectual, from which comes shapes of achievement, a sense of one's being, a satisfaction of spirit. One becomes in some area an athlete of God—practice means to perform, over and over again in the face of all obstacles, some act of vision, of faith, of desires. Practice means inviting the perfection desired.

—Martha Graham

Since the self, like the work you produce, is not so much a core as a process, one finds oneself . . . always pushing one's questioning of oneself of the limit of what one is and what one is not. When am I Vietnamese? When am I American? When am I Asian and when am I Asian-American or Asian-European? . . . The question . . . is no longer: Who am I? but When, where, how am I [my emphasis].

Trinh T. Minh-ha

if you grew up catholic like me, you were made to go
to confession starting in second grade. I explain to non-Catholic friends that it was basically a feminist's notion of the seventh circle of hell. You stepped into a dark booth, knelt down, heard the priest from behind a curtain saying, "I'm ready." This was your cue to say, "Forgive me, Father, for I have sinned. It's been (insert number) weeks since my last confession." After an awkward pause, you listed your sins, ranging from bad to very bad: from "I stole my sister's pocket change," to "I lied to Mom about my homework," to "I drank myself into oblivion last night," to "I thought about having sex the other night." (And later, you'd have to confess about lying to a priest because you really *did* have sex the other night.) Then the faceless man told you that absolution was yours for the low price of ten Hail Marys and one Our Father. I stopped going to confession in sixth grade after a priest yelled at me for saying it had been a year since my last confession. "Would you not bathe in a year?" he barked. No, I managed to whimper. What was my problem, then, he wanted to know. I ran out of the confessional with my

tail between my legs, vowing never again to share my sins with an unknown man. Not unless he shared his, too.

It wasn't until after I moved away from home to the University of Michigan and eventually to New York City that I officially left the Catholic Church behind me. I awakened to left politics, involved myself in reproductive rights, feminist and antiracism causes, and encountered people from all walks of life, seeking salvation in environmental justice, abortion rights, single-payer health care, and lesbian and gay rights, to name a few. I soon discovered, though, that I had jumped out of the Catholic frying pan and into the fire of the Church of Progressive Politics. In meetings and social occasions in political circles, I noticed a tendency for people to ferret out information about each other—anything from yearly income, love lives, fashion sense, preferred reading—to pick at and tear apart. Certain personalities would designate themselves as judges of us sinners not "down enough" with the politics. Frustratingly, this ritual was more intense among the younger twenty-somethings and middle-class people of color. Sometimes, I thought I'd have a T-shirt printed with these words on it: "Hi. I'm Anna. I'm Asian-American, heterosexual, middle class, pro-choice, feminist. Slot me where you will."

Don't get me wrong—I'm not denigrating commitment to social change. Just some of the more torturous routes we progressive people can take getting there. Both directly to my face or behind my back, I soon became aware of the ways in which I had sinned politically. Below, I've listed the five which have kept me up at night the most:

1. I come from an upper-middle-class family.
2. I'm not a full-time activist.

3. I don't identify exclusively with an Asian-American community.
4. I love a white man.
5. I'm not angry enough.

Certain progressive people whom I've both met and, at times, emulated, focus so sharply on shaping themselves into perfect beings: color-blind, well-read, articulate people who can organize rallies, volunteer in soup kitchens, raise thousands of dollars for the good fight, and leap tall buildings in a single bound. We don't want to hear about or face others' shy, hesitant admissions of struggling with anger, fear, homophobia, racism, and classism. It's easier and faster to point the finger than to encourage or, worse yet, face our own dirty little secrets.

I don't believe in confession anymore. I believe in honesty and struggle. In the Catholic confessional, I wanted to tell the priest that a) I didn't actually believe sex was sinful, and b) I was still working on things like being fully honest with my mother. But he always seemed less interested in debating Catholic dogma and more concerned with my quick and dirty attainment of sin-free perfection. In the same vein, I wanted to remind finger-pointers from the Church of Progressive Politics that my expensive college education no more doomed me to elitist snobbery, than the fact that I had taught at a predominantly Black elementary school made me an expert on African-American issues. In the following pages, I examine items 1 through 5 and come to shed the "sin" label, instead claiming each as a talisman—a comforting and enlightening touchstone of my identity. Enlightening, because they remind me that I am an evolving political person with a capacity to change.

Comforting, because I come to accept myself as a reality, not an ideal.

1. i come from an upper-middle-class family.

Until college, my nickname was "Anna Banana." Then I learned what the term *banana* meant in the world of identity politics: yellow on the outside, white on the inside. It is to Asian-Americans what *Oreo* is to African-Americans and *apple* to Native Americans. These terms are much more than just about race. They're about life-style and class. Here, they say, is a privileged person of color who hasn't suffered and is comfortable in white circles and doesn't have an accent—in a word, a sell-out.

At first glance, I *am* Anna, a Banana. My father is a physician. I grew up among mostly white people in Cincinnati, Ohio, a homogeneous city of German and Irish Catholics. I played in the large backyard of my suburban home, wore uniform skirts in a private day school, then went on to spend my days fretting over my grade point average and blue book exams at a prestigious university. People have been both upfront and backhanded about using their assumptions about my class background to discount me. As a volunteer in a low-income elementary school in Detroit, a teacher reprimanded me after seeing that one of my students had given me a hug. Didn't I know that I could get sued by parents for inappropriate behavior? Furthermore, how dare college students like me waltz into this school from sheltered Ann Arbor two days out of the week and try to make all these kids love me? On another occasion, I accidentally discovered that certain people I worked with in an activist group had been discussing my tendency to "always look put together" and how it meant I was "still so trapped in the middle class."

I used to think that the only way to convince these people that my politics were legit was by telling them a small detail about myself: my parents disowned me after my sophomore year in college after discovering I wasn't going to mass anymore, I was seeing someone, I'd made appointments with a gynecologist for birth control, and, worst of all, I was going to Washington to march in NOW's Pro-Choice Demonstration. Five years later, my mother still refuses to acknowledge my politics and my father has told me my actions are immoral and abnormal. My older sister hasn't spoken a full sentence to me in three years because, according to my mother, I've embarrassed the family beyond repair. I was sure that if I shared my sense of loss—I gave up creature comforts and an allowance, not to mention my family—to pursue my ideology, they could never doubt my commitment to social change.

Or so I thought. I told my story to a group of Reproductive Rights activists at a conference in Chicago. Gloria Steinem and I had held an intergenerational dialogue in which I spoke about building a political family when the biological one rejects you. An Asian-American woman was critical of my remarks and disappointed by the dialogue. Ending my talk on an unreconciled, estranged note with my mother, she said, made it seem as though I was unreconciled with my [Filipino] community. Couldn't I have ended in a way which showed I was still loyal to my roots? My political identity—no matter how honest I had been about it, didn't fit her ideal. I woke up in my hotel room at 4 A.M. that morning, sweating. It was the second time I discovered that being myself didn't guarantee unconditional acceptance, this time, from a woman who looked like my mom and dad to the rest of the world, but whose politics were apples to their oranges.

Why, then, did I insist on thinking of my upper-middle-class privilege as a transgression to feel guilty about? Because I hated the barrier it placed between myself and the students in that school in Detroit in whose lives I was trying to make a difference. What I learned from the Chicago conference, though, is that barriers exist based on anything from political ideology, to class, to race, to religion. The question is, do you commit yourself to struggling to tear down that wall, and why? I am slowly breaking down the wall between my family and me, brick by brick because of the countless things we share: relatives, the Philippines, instilled sense of discipline, Filipino food, and, yes, appreciation of a nice home and good education. By the same token, the woman at the conference and I may not have agreed about my speech, but I committed to engaging in discussion with her because she joins me as a fellow traveler and colleague in the fight for Asian-American causes and reproductive rights. With all the barriers thrown up between human beings, I figure it's wiser to form alliances for the struggles ahead.

2. i'm not a full-time activist.

When I left my job at a young women's advocacy organization and entered the world of television, I seesawed between relief that I could finally pursue my fascination with the media and children, and tremendous guilt for not doing the political thing on a full-time basis. Some colleagues wondered aloud if I was "leaving the movement." Be careful, they warned, you'll sell your soul working in the for-profit world! Some were sterner, telling me, "You're kidding yourself if you think you'll stay committed to politics!" So I began to devise all kinds of litmus tests to see if I was a true-blue activist, capital "A." One goes like this: in the name of reproductive rights, would I be willing to a) get arrested in an act of civil disobedience (like my friend who blocked the Holland Tunnel in 1992 to protest the restrictions on *Roe* v. *Wade);* b) serve as a clinic escort; or c) sit in the waiting room of an abortion clinic holding a friend's hand? Some voice inside me whispered that the *real* activist would make time to do all three things.

Saying "I'm an activist" is like saying "I'm an artist" or a writer. People don't believe you, think it's an arrogant statement, and have a vague, typecast view of you (an Abbie Hoffman radical, covered in "statement" buttons, attending protests, waving banners—the kind they'd put on "Murphy Brown"). My problem with the term is: who defines it? The Queen dubs knights, the Pope canonizes saints, a panel of judges crowns Miss America, but who pronounces us activists? I almost wish we could come up with a new definition or dispense with it altogether, letting our actions and work speak for themselves.

I used to think that my resistance to being an in-your-face activist came from constantly being shamed as the only member of my family for asserting, even as a teenager, that people on welfare weren't lazy and immoral or that it was stupid to wear fur coats. The more left I got, the more I had to abandon my family. More recently, though, my reasons have shifted after seeing activists, particularly women (many who have been my mentors, teachers, heroes, friends, and mothers) martyring themselves for a political cause. Some have become threadbare rugs, having given over their time, energy, lives, and homes to their work, drying up their physical and emotional wells in the process. Yes, they say, I'll let anyone sleep in my house at all times of the day or night. Yes, I'll work sixteen hours a day for weeks on end. Yes, I'll spend most of my savings on a cause. I've sat next to them in meetings watching them chew off their fingernails, scream at anyone who disagreed with their point of view, and even smelled the alcohol on their breath. At first, I thought no one could find fault with them because of their boundless loyalty. Secretly, though, I started to get irritated.

Somewhere in the continuum of activism, between burnt-out and bitter feminist matriarchs and women who hide copies of *Ms.* under their mattresses, lies me, a second-generation Filipina who recently left a job writing grant proposals for a reproductive rights organization and now spends her time writing children's books. I've taken the time I used to waste feeling guilty about not performing some of the more in-your-face type of activism and used it to pursue my passions—writing, learning to cook a great sugar-free chocolate cake, saving up money for my vacation in Belize, learning Japanese. Luxuries, you say? No. Living out what we're struggling for and then being a whole enough person to share the wealth by writing this essay, illustrating a children's book, teaching a class, and, yes, eventually helping organize a march.

Saying one qualifies as an activist if she participates in x number of rallies or protests, gives x number of dollars, is like saying there's one way to paint or sing or write a book. In this whole world of fucked-up things, I have got to believe that each one of us can pick one small or large thing to change which nourishes our souls while nourishing the world. And it need not consume all of our time, either. Reading about the civil rights movement, I learned that any overturning of hei-nous law and every major rally or demonstration required a menagerie of people, including those with the chutzpah to stand at the podium shouting eloquence and spitfire, and the quieter ones with the patience to hang coats in the meeting hall.

3. i don't identify exclusively with an asian-american community.

So far, in these few twenty-five years of my life, I've been a nomad, having fled Cincinnati, lived the transient student life in Ann Arbor, and entered the fragmented neighborhoods of New York City. As I've searched out a community, I began to confront this resistance I have to hanging out *exclusively* with Asian-Americans, with whom society, or at least, affirmative-action questionnaires, would have me grouped. In some ways, this resistance is a function of my pro-assimilation upbringing, having spent my adolescence in the white middle-class world of prep school and college, and my father telling me not to waste college tuition taking Tagalog classes. Some Asian-Americans have looked askance on my mixed group of friends, clucked their tongues at mention of my Jewish boyfriend, and asked me why I don't belong to the local Filipino American Association. An angry Filipino told me I was out of touch with my culture and settling for an Americanized, whitewashed identity.

Although I take comfort in the bonds I share with Filipinos and other Asian-Americans, my definition of individual empowerment hasn't always meshed with theirs. My parents' circle of first-generation Filipinos were, like them, doctors, nurses, and engineers. Most had the mentality of, "I came over to this country for a better education for you. Don't make waves and waste your education by being a troublemaker—for God's sake, make some money!" The comfort of going to Filipino parties was the respite from having to explain to my predominantly German, Irish Catholic friends what *lumpia* and *pancit* tasted like and why my parents had funny accents. The tradeoff was being milled about like prize cattle in front of our parents' friends and spoken about in the third person: "Her grade point average is going up again. She's taking a Kaplan course to do well on her SATs. She's applying to Harvard and Columbia." Being a "smart girl" made me eligible for living up to the apex of my community's potential for me: doctor, lawyer, engineer.

I thought maybe I'd have an easier time with the progressive community of Asian-American writers and artists in New York. Like so many other communities of color, though, it can fracture along lines of class, nationality, sexual orientation, and political bent. You can't just walk into a room and say, "Hey, I'm Asian, too! Let's all go bowling!" The divisions make themselves clear immediately. Recently, for example, I read a magazine column entitled "Asian-American Victories," proclaiming that *Playboy* magazine had chosen some lucky Asian-American woman as Playmate of the Month. When I complained about it to an Asian-American male colleague, his response was, "Well, that's so [white] feminist of you."

It hasn't always been easy to connect with Asian-American women, either. While it's true that my closest friends are Asian women, at one time or another we have lamented the fact that, while Black women on campus would often nod to acknowledge each other on the street, Asian women actively avoided eye contact or gave each other the "competitive Asian woman look." Some Black women would add an affectionate "sistah" when addressing each other, while we groped clumsily around for our own terminology. I worried that, in an honest effort to be unique, exceptional, and to have an identity which wasn't tied to the world's tiresomely trite stereotypes of Asian-

American women, we resisted making contact. We were declaring to the world, "Hey! I'm not the Vietnamese prostitute you saw in those Brian DePalma and Stanley Kubrick movies." "That girl you hated in fourth grade because she beat you in math? I'm not her." "Wrong, I'm not Chinese, Malaysian, Vietnamese, or Japanese. We're not all related!" If we did come together we might be forced to confront the shared experience of having been called gook, chink, slant, and model minorities.

So here was the root of my so-called sin: while I wanted to ally myself in solidarity with Asian-Americans, what was I to do with my outright disgust with the politics of some and the machismo of others? And what was I to do with my feelings of isolation from the vast majority of Asian women? (Not to mention the fact that most of my female mentors were Black or Jewish!) But enough with biological essentialism. Having slanted eyes didn't make us all fiendish or good at math, so why should it make us united in our commitment to social change? Why should I be shocked at hearing racist slurs against blacks, whites, and Latinos coming out of Asian mouths? Society groups us together on the basis of our lowest common denominators—the slope of our eyes, black hair, golden skin, and country of origin located in the same general longitude. We check off the box marked "Asian" or "Oriental" or "Asian-American" or "Pacific Islander" on countless application forms, but we may have completely different languages, religions, reasons for immigration, etcetera.

Here's the flip side. Just as we aren't immune from the "isms" and insecurities, nor are we exempt from building bridges to each other because of shared visions which have everything and nothing to do with race. Now I find myself building a mixed, eclectic community of friends and colleagues based on our shared social consciousness and life passions.

Like my friend writing an anthology about lesbians and straight women. And another helping to build a school curriculum in Ghana. And another teaching social ethics and leadership classes to disadvantaged students. Not all are Asian-American. Not all would necessarily even call themselves political people. Yes, there's my Korean friend with whom I enjoy talking about our cravings for sticky white rice and parents who made us study extra hard and play a musical instrument. In the long run, though, our friendship has deepened over seven years and we remain true compatriots and allies because of our dreams and perceptions, which match much more closely than our skin and hair.

4. i love a white man.

In a color-conscious society, there's no escaping coming to terms with being an Asian woman in a relationship with a white man. Don't think I haven't tried. Saying things to myself like, "He and I love each other for the person underneath." "We've been together for five and a half years, it's no passing thing." "He's Jewish—he understands discrimination, too." They all sound like excuses or apologies, falling short of something much more real and painful to deal with: no matter how much you trust the love between the two of you, there's an outside world to contend with. A world which produces people who have actually spit at me (not my partner, but me) walking down the street. Or a Black friend who told me I was "settling" by being with a white man. Or an Asian-American man teasing me that I was trying to marry "up." Or Spike Lee telling us we have "Jungle Fever."

What does a relationship have to do with being an activist or politically progressive person? A hell of a lot more than I thought. I've been in formal and casual discussions with political people of color who, clearly in the context of trashing another activist have said, "Did you know that s/he's with a white wo/man?" On another occasion, a woman asked me in that unspecific but insinuating tone, "Is your boyfriend white?" When I said yes, there was a pregnant pause, then she nodded knowingly. The implication in these two examples was that someone isn't fully antiracist or completely loyal if they love a white person. I began to wonder if they were right and that my not dating a Filipino person meant I hated myself or had internalized my own racism.

At my most insecure, when political people told me they didn't believe in interracial relationships, I started to wonder if they were right. White people, they said, could never empathize with racism. How could you build a lifelong relationship with someone who could never share this pain? Our kids, I was told, would lose their Filipino-ness and have a screwed-up identity. What's wrong, I was pressed, don't you like Filipino men? With horror, I realized that, the times I allowed myself to start to buy into these theories, I had turned my partner, someone I knew intimately, into a vague generalization: insensitive, privileged white guy. But loving someone, friend, lover, or family member alike, is a highly specific act. It means taking the vast amount of time necessary to discern the complexities of another human being, their specific fears, assets, and shortcomings. It also means committing to struggling with political obstacles. Yes, my boyfriend and I have argued about white male privilege, sexism. But these struggles are private property and, as I mentioned before, I don't believe in confession anymore.

If I were in a relationship with another person of color, I might be better accepted by my critics. But in the private world of two, the color of our skin wouldn't keep us immune from struggles over everything from stressful jobs, to fights over money, to being scared of codependence, to psychological abuse. And if these people I've told you about really looked closely and asked around Asian-American circles, they'd see that, for example, it's apparently cool for me to date a Japanese person (because we're both Asian-American and Pacific Islanders). But my grandfather, who nearly died during the Japanese attack on the Philippines, would turn over in his grave before seeing me date a Japanese man (or woman, for that matter). I didn't choose to love my Asian friends just so I could parade them around like emblems of being down with people of color causes. And I'm not going to trash or even question a seven-year nourishing relationship just so a few people who think there's a gene for intimacy will sleep easier at night.

5. i'm not angry enough.

In a room full of angry political people harping on a point, I'm likely to try to diffuse the anger by asking how we might take steps toward righting the matter. It's gotten me into trouble. I'm thinking of the times I've sat around a table where a meeting is going poorly and someone decides it would feel good to criticize another person or organization. "That organization's executive director has hired only white people." "So and so isn't voting for single-payer health care." "Have you seen their offices? They spend all their money on nice furniture and not on their programs." "They don't have a woman of color on their board." I'd open up my big mouth and say, "Well, those complaints are legitimate, but how are we going to spend our time—denigrating other people or trying to make some action plans of our own?" I unleashed the wrath of some who told me

I needed to take off my Pollyanna glasses and see the world as it is—ugly and brutal. I was too afraid of confrontation, I'd better grow up. If everyone thought like me, we'd all be right wing Democrats. Someone has to push the envelope—not everyone is moderate and accommodating.

Anger can be healthy—the fire that sparks social change. It also induces clarity, providing a distinct enemy and rallying cry, the way nationalism increases when a war is declared. It's true that my specific experiences of indignation have determined my politics. I became a feminist after I got pissed off about men trying to make legislation which restricted women's right to have legal abortions. I became angry about class issues in a course on Marxism when I found out that 5 percent of the population owns the vast majority of the wealth. But anger can also be a fire that consumes, lays waste, and turns everything to ash. It's like the toxic therapist who wants you to point the finger outward at everything that causes you pain but doesn't want you to heal because he or she gets $100 for every hour that you cling to it. Anger brings us together around the table like the knights of the round table, united against a common enemy or fighting for a cause. The problem is, if we're lucky enough to slay the dragon, we're left staring at each other, not knowing what to do next.

Have we come to the point where the angriest people are those best cut out to work for human rights? I think the easy part is feeling angry. But clinging to that anger is a crutch that lets you stay in the position of critic pronouncing sentence. But to get that job done, to really serve the community you're supposedly committed to improving, you need to shelve the sugar high your ego feels bitching (righteously, perhaps) about the bastards at city council and metabolize that anger into problem solving, getting the job done. If the health-care legislation gets passed, if your school gets new textbooks you've been lobbying for, congratulations, move on to the next dragon.

I can turn angry and feel guilty about my expensive college education and sit in a café and brood about it (which I've done). Or I could take that education and teach ESL courses to immigrants (which I've also done). But it comes down to this, to paraphrase Martha Graham: practice living, get the words on the page, take the first dance steps, fall on your face. But perform anyway, in the face of all obstacles, toward a better way of living.

I've been told I have a sympathetic ear, which has brought people wanting to confess their own sins and political demons to me. Like mine, theirs are either self-imposed or inflicted by others, ranging from the serious to the more ridiculous: "I'm having a hard time dealing with my friend coming out to me." "I have a trust fund." "I like to have my nails done." "I want to make a lot of money." What bothers me most about the (Catholic) notion of confession was having to ask someone else to absolve you and take the burden away from you. To escape. My hope (or prayer or mantra, or whatever you want to call it) is that we all stop confessing to or indicting each other and learn to claim ourselves, warts and all, and pursue what it is that we really want.

My biggest ally in my short twenty-five years of living has been Change. Capital "C." I have gone from wide-eyed Catholic schoolgirl volunteer, to raging newfound feminist, to political fundraiser, to wanna-be writer. This comforts me as I fantasize about being a mother coloring with my kid, a television producer, and, yes, a noisy participant in a demonstration against inadequate health care. I don't think we can afford to emulate the beauty editors of fashion magazines, airbrushing out blemishes and hawking a political ideal in which progressive people have no acne, no stupid remarks. If the small-waisted, big-chested, white-capped tooth, porcelain-skinned woman is the unattainable ideal of modeldom, then the progressive ideal is equally unattainable: racist-free, classist-free, 100 percent antihomophobic, angry, and able to fully articulate every political issue.

To make the quantum leap from private angst to generating positive change in one's community or even the world requires a tremendous amount of courage and a wallop of self-esteem. So I want to help develop a politics of wholeness and three-dimensionality in which it's expected that people put their feet in their mouth, down their throat, and out their ass again (recall Jesse Jackson's "Hymietown" comment) and be forgiven because they're working and open to changing themselves as much as the rest of the world. Uncompassionate activists are, to me, the ultimate hypocrites. How, after all, can you make things right if you're addicted to pointing out everything that's wrong? I hope never to be the perfect political person. They exist in fairy tales. I'm happy in the real world down with the rest of the sinners and fools where we can get down to some serious work.

Motherhood

allison abner

"is it pink? or do you think it's gonna fade? do you think it's fading? 'Cause if it's not . . . I think this is it."

"I can't tell yet," he says, knowing damn well he can.

"Oh, my fucking Jesus Christ. This is it. It's not fading. It's not going away. The pink is staying. This is it."

My breath gets shallow and my palms sweat even though my hands are ice cold—Nixon hands, he calls them. Now what do I do?

"We could get married?"

I turn from staring at the tin ceiling and look, dazed, into his face. He's talking to me, saying things, but I only catch snatches of what he says because the blood has filled my ears and all I hear is my own pulse. Swish thump, ". . . up to you . . ." Swish thump, ". . . could work . . ." Swish thump, ". . . if you wanted . . ." His nose grows and his eyes soften the longer I stare at him. All I can think of is Saturn Return, that astrological milestone that's supposed to hit when you're thirty that my friends kept warning me would seal my fate for years to come. I know I'm standing at a crossroads in my life so enormous I can't fathom it. Inside, I keep thinking I should have somehow known this is how it would all happen; I should have been able to predict my future would be with this man. I wish I had more preparation. But such is a decision: it only takes a second to say "yes" or "no."

So I say, "Let's do nothing for five days. Let's think about it without telling anyone else. Either way, we'll know the right thing to do."

These are the oddest five days of my life. From this moment on, every time I look in the mirror I mouth the word countless times, trying to make it match the image I've held of myself for twenty-eight years. Dragging out each syllable, I stand naked and mesmerized, saying over and over, "Mm-moooommmyyyy." Then I immediately run to the shower and bathe with my eyes closed, trying to accept it all.

After day three, it becomes a game. I say it like a child: "Mommy, I want some milk." Then as if I were talking to a teacher on parents' night: "I'm her mother. Yes, nice to meet you, too." Then admonishingly: "Because I'm your mother, that's why." The whole thing starts to crack me up, like I'm wearing an invisible Halloween costume. How did I get here?

I had always envisioned myself becoming a mother before I hit thirty. Not too early, so that I've had enough time to mature, sow my wild oats, and launch a career. Not too late, so that I have to run after an infant without much energy, stop my career momentum midstream, and enter my twilight years when he or she hits college.

I even told a friend that I wouldn't be able to make the decision consciously because it was too immense: "I'd have to put myself in the situation. With my back against the wall, I'd make up my mind." It was a roundabout way of saying I was beginning to have maternal feelings that I couldn't easily acknowledge, especially considering I never had a burning desire to have a child, never baby-sat, never cooed over infants. But something in my subconscious must have been brewing, because there I was fulfilling my own prophesy.

By day five, we have already decided that we want each other—and that we want this baby. We discuss abortion and the fact that I have a manuscript due around the same time as the baby; we tell each other that there's never a "perfect" time. We go down the can-we-really-do-it checklist: there'll be enough money; we own a loft that has plenty of room; his job is secure and my freelance work is flexible enough to easily accommodate a baby; we're in good health; we have a solid relationship that has withstood some profound tests over the past year we've been together; our families will be overwhelmed but excited to have the first grandchild. All the practicalities seem in order.

The big questions for me are how being a mother/wife fits into my self-concept, and whether I have the emotional capacity to care for a child. About the former, I've always had reservations. I hate the term "wife" but feel I want a solidly committed relationship within which to raise a child. No way am I brave enough to go it alone. I want a partner, not a friend or a breadwinner. In fact, I have always felt marriage to be superfluous unless kids are involved because the legal ramifications make getting out too sticky. But "wife" always sounds like the losing side of an equation where x is greater than y, x being "husband."

Socially, legally, and experientially, wives have been the underdogs. I grew up in a traditional nuclear family with a devoted mother who did a hell of a job but had no alternative security away from my father. She made a point to raise her daughter to have a good education and a viable skill so I'd always have choices. Though my parents are still together, I'm sure there were compelling moments when my mother wished she had options that would allow her to walk if she so desired. Dad held all the power because he made all the dough, despite the dedicated hours Mom put in to her career as a mother/wife.

But I accept the title of "wife," believing that I don't have to repeat everything in my parents' relationship and that I can pioneer a new version for myself, incorporating those stellar qualities I admire in my mother. Her respect for children as individuals, her willingness to educate herself and adapt to changing circumstances, her desire to face her shortcomings as a process of growth, her understanding of the patience it takes to raise a healthy child, her ability to maintain a sense of humor —all these qualities will make my life as a mother rich and as a wife evolving.

So "wife" reinvented doesn't sound so bad anymore. I share my new vision of "wife" with my new husband. We have no strict division of labor in our home: we agree to assume equal responsibility for child care, given the circumstances of our jobs, and to participate equally in the daily raising of our child. More important than the household responsibilities is the balance of power, to which we are hypersensitive. We joke constantly about who's more controlling and who would be sadder if the other died. The most honorable quality in our relationship is fessing up when wrong. Moreover, Mark and I have worked out a comfortable blend of sexual passion and intimate friendship with a little sibling rivalry tossed in.

Since my idea of wife goes hand-in-hand with the role of mother, I have to question my ability to rise to the occasion of motherhood. Like most of my peers who had a protracted adolescence—attending pampering colleges, seeing the world, switching jobs at whim, living with one lover this year and another the next—adulthood seems elusive even as I round my late twenties. But something is catching up, otherwise why else would I have moved in with a forty-year-old man who is eager to start a family . . . with *me?*

Nonetheless, thinking about kids in the abstract future is different from having one growing inside my uterus. Until recently, kids scared me because their needs are so great. I feared that so many of my own needs had not been met, that I required almost as much attention as a child would. I wanted to be held and babied, to do what I want when I want. After shelling out good money to some good therapists, I have forgiven myself for having been a child with so many needs. I have come to accept my innocence and vulnerabilities as a creative force to try to recapture rather than squash. Having a baby will lead me down that road because he or she will be a great reflector from which I learn about myself.

Day five arrives and the answer is "yes." My fears are vanishing, as is the woman in the mirror. My whole identity has changed and it seems even harder to change it back.

I try to explain this to one of my friends when I tell her I'm pregnant and planning to get married. Her first reaction is, "Do you know how much that's going to change your life?" The next time I see her she gives me *Of Woman Born* by

Adrienne Rich. I read it in college but think I could get new meaning out of it this time. After the third chapter, I hide it in a drawer under some magazines. I fear that Rich's strong resentment of her children and husband will rise up and haunt me, like a Kewpie doll. At the same time, I feel as alienated from her and angry as when I attempt to read books by many white male writers. I just can't connect to the experience.

Like many feminists of the 1960s and 1970s, Rich saw her life as wife/mother as an impediment to her essential development as a woman. The social pressures that led her to enter into an unhappy marriage and have child after child imprisoned her, she believed. Luckily, through her honesty and that of other feminist foremothers who have related their misery and resentment and fought for change, we've moved into the Age of Choice. Unfortunately, with this choice has come the worship of a false idol: work.

Work is the one option that has compelled young women of my generation to postpone motherhood or abandon it all together. We're forever chasing the ideal job in the hopes of attaining the money, prestige, accolades, and challenges that our male counterparts have. We believe familyhood is contrary to these ambitions; it is a goal that attracted our square acquaintances right after college. And since the Newt Gingriches of the public world have coopted the definition of family to mean that women stay home with Junior while Dad brings in the bacon, and that we only have sex to procreate, no one with an ounce of feminist self-respect would want any part of a "traditional" family (as if there ever were such a thing).

Though I don't want any part of the Christian Right's idea of family, I do want to create something like it. I plan on staying home, preparing for the baby, and working lightly, while my husband pulls in the real paycheck. During my third trimester, the impact of this arrangement on our individual lives comes up. We discover we're both envious of the other's situation. I admit to strong feelings of loss at having to postpone my career ambition; he laments not being home to witness the daily changes the baby will go through. His solution is to take family leave the first month after I deliver. Mine is to wait and see how I'll feel a few months into it.

I have the rest of my life to work, but only a limited time to mother an infant. I honestly believe I can do both well, but not at the same time. Besides, as far as I'm concerned, work is overrated and most people only have jobs, not careers, and even those of us with "successful" jobs are still looking for "something more." I think to myself, What could be "something more" more than caring for a little soul?

For the first sixteen weeks, my husband and I are convinced that we're having a girl and think of all the girl-worldly ways we'll raise her. Then, during my ultrasound, we discover she is actually a he—and we are shocked. We ask the technician to "prove" he's a boy. She obliges by hovering over a floating appendage with her cursor, then taking a still photograph using the machine. The cursor is pointing to his floating penis. He is definitely a boy. Thus we learn our first parental lesson: accept your child for who he is.

Our concern isn't that we will love him any less as a boy, but that his life will be more difficult as an African-American boy born in the antiminority nineties. My husband knows first-hand how cruel life can be for a light-skinned black male who gets scapegoated, taunted, and labeled. Growing up, I witnessed the hardships my own brother faced as he confronted deep-seated mistrust and envy from white males who went out of their way to demean him.

The scars that have healed over these significant wounds in both men are endemic within the community. African-American males are the fastest-growing group of suicide victims, the primary targets for sexual harassment in school, and are dying at younger ages in far greater numbers than their European-American counterparts. Though my child won't grow up in the ghetto, inside or outside of the 'hood, we can't protect him all the time. Growing up in Los Angeles, I often witnessed cops pass over bad-ass white boys to arrest the one black boy who was just tagging along. Will Miles, my son, end up another brother with a record?

It's hard to imagine what difficulties Miles is likely to confront, what rejecting experiences are waiting to test his dignity. Nowadays, the topic of girls' self-esteem is all the rage, but the level of hostility that awaits all African-American males—that undermines their competency and erodes their vulnerability—is just as damaging. How does a young male preserve his sensitivity and openness in the face of these attacks?

My challenge, not just as a mother but as a feminist, is to raise a son who can rise above the clamor to maintain his true spirit. I must teach him to trust his instincts, must tell him that his perceptions are real, and must answer the questions before he can ask "Am I okay? Am I deserving?" Sadly, too many men go underground with their self-doubt, turning it into aggression, rage, and Ruff Neck manners. I have a chance to influence his life as no other person can. What a monumental power, and yet one that many women often forget they have.

Raising a son with feminist values has just as much significance as raising a daughter with such philosophies. The world can definitely use another conscious man. One who understands the meaning of "no," who cries when he's pained, who loves other men without fear, and who respects powerful women. Seeing him give to the world what I want to give him —a sense of decency, honesty, and fairness—will mean more to me than any of his singular achievements. These are the qualities that create community and preserve life. They prove that there is "something more."

For me, that "something more" means being part of another tradition, the eternally connective tradition of motherhood. For me, having this child won't be an impediment, but a channel through which I feel connected to other women, other mothers, other wives who have placed family at the heart of their self-concept without feeling they've lost themselves.

Gestation ends with one final episode: the suffering of giving life. One last push and he leaves my body to share the outside world with us. He comes to us with his eyes wide open, intensely staring even while in the birth canal. This is how we meet, finally, with a mother-to-son gaze that will never leave my memory.

For an hour, we lie chest to chest, quietly studying each other's hair, face, breathing, gestures. I hadn't expected him to be able to focus his eyes yet, so I feel a slight chill and instant familiarity looking back at those eyes that so resemble my own. This stare, I hope, will come to mean that he is constantly assessing his situation.

As he yawns, I catch his sweet, milky breath through my nose. It fills me with devotion. Learning new ways to love him and teach him to live with his eyes open will surely be my greatest creative achievement. Letting him see the world in all its cruelty will surely be my greatest pain. I am his mother.

Born to Dyke

greg tate

some of his best friends are black lesbians. some of his best friends insist that he's a Black Lesbian in disguise. As in his personal manager, the Black Lesbian entrepreneur, who invites him to a girl-party thrown by two Black Lesbian promoters and quickly assuages his anxiety about bum-rushin' with "How could it not be cool for you to come? You're the dyke of the century." As in his ex-lover the creative director who tells him, "You were my great lesbian love affair, the man who solved the mystery of what making love to a woman would be like." As in his buddy, the ex-Crip Yale NYU Law–grad public defender and Black Lesbian mack of the century who often cites him as her twin. While he finds these comments perversely flattering, he also finds them bewildering. Even given his self-mocking paraphrase of the *Goodfellas* line: "All my life for as long as I can remember I've wanted to be a Black Lesbian feminist."

Well, maybe not all of his life. He can trace this desire back to the tender age of nineteen when he developed a mad crush on the brilliant Black Lesbian filmmaker and poet Michelle Parkerson. Before he could declare his love, he deflatedly learned from her coming-out poem that she was a "Shopping Bag Dyke." As queer and mysterious as all women seemed to him then, Parkerson's moment of revelation made the distaff side exponentially enigmatic. As professed in his response-poem "the x-girl factor," which began "Black Lesbians Unknown/These the eyed and these the unseen women in the room."

Over the years, enchantment with Black Lesbians became a pronounced feature of his persona, his circle of friends, his writing and his music. This is why he formed a band called Women In Love to perform songs like "Just Another Flybutch in a Black Leather Jacket," written after lustily observing two sistas mack each other out on Christopher and Barrow. He claims he's not interested in what Black Lesbians do in the bed —though he'll cop to being startled by the strap-on-dick concept—eschewing the mundane male gaze agape at the vision of two women doing it. In this sense and several others, like his inability to derive stimulation from pornography or fellatio, he believes he is truly the brother from another planet.

By his reckoning he is a voyeur of Black Lesbian style, Black Lesbian cool, and Black Lesbian constructions of femininity. How Black Lesbians dress, converse, and play has always seemed as magical to him as what jazz musicians do, and as smoothly coded. In his mythifying eyes Black Lesbians carry themselves with more relaxed sensuality than their straight, or "het" (to use the parlance), sisters. A willing tool of Black Lesbian mesmerism, he perceives their world as one where gender boundaries are collapsed and personal agency is like the universe, forever expanding. Black Lesbians seem to exist in a more fluid realm of black humanity, having liberated themselves from repressive notions of gender and erotica.

And of esthetics too. Not long after Parkerson came out to him, he attended a black writers conference at Howard University where Barbara Smith, a Black Lesbian belle lettrist was pilloried by a straight sister for offering a pro-lesbian interpretation of Sula and Nel's friendship in Toni Morrison's *Sula*. When Smith was accused of sullying a good book with her "perversion," his now lesbian-sensitized skin began to crawl. Parkerson's influence also affected his experience of Fellini's festival of androgyny, *Satyricon*, and of Isaac Asimov's *The Gods Themselves*, a gift from her, which imagines a genderless race of extraterrestrials. Gradually he realized that being a Black Lesbian allowed girlfriends a vantage on gender which privileged black female eroticism and fetishized polymorphous perversity. His ease in exploring human sexual possibility in his fictional (as opposed to his journalistic) writing dates back to Parkerson opening his eyes to the world of The Other. And further explains his compulsion to place black women protagonists at the center of a science fiction novel, a dream-play and two suspense screenplays.

Out of the romance with Black Lesbians Parkerson inculcated in his late teens and early twenties, have evolved friendships in his thirties that find him engaged with Black Lesbians emotionally, intellectually, artistically, and financially. (For the record, he has white lesbian colleagues and acquaintances but no white lesbian friends—hardly surprising considering that there's only been three white women he's ever considered close friends.) Due to anti-sexist positions he's taken in various essays over the years, and the pro-feminist stance he's taken in certain songs performed by his band, he feels he is sometimes misidentified as a Feminist Man. He has often wondered whether he embraces feminism (and feminists per se) to the same degree he embraces the ruffneck Black Lesbian gals who now run his life.

As he once confided to fellow butch-hag Arthur Jafa, "I'm probably too sexist to be a real feminist man. Too much of a dog, you know?" Meaning he believed himself too compromised by his interpersonal dealings to deserve true feminist ranking—"unless you can be a feminist and a dick too. What I'm struggling to be is anti-oppressive toward the women who enter my cipher. I don't know if anti-oppressive and antisexist are the same thing."

He believes he's never harassed, stalked, or physically abused any woman in his life. He will cop however to leaving a fair share of emotional and psychological wreckage in his wake. He wonders whether the absence of sex (though not intimacy) from his Black Lesbian friendships allows those to blossom minus the melodrama usually afflicting his relations with straight women. (Though not all his women friends are ex-lovers, note that his white women friends have evaded his trauma ward due to his anxiety about interracial sex, a phobia that may require therapy.)

To paraphrase Wim Wenders, Black Lesbians have colonized his imagination, and he loves it. If his Black Lesbian friends don't absolutely love him as a genre, he loves them as a genre. Yet this realization begs the question: why does he feel more comfortable receiving love from his Black Lesbian friends than he does receiving emotional support from his lovers? Why does he expect more emotional and economic stability from his Black Lesbian girlfriends than his het ones?

He might answer that since Black Lesbians demolish categories of masculinity and femininity, he sees them as human and capable before he sees them as "girls," or worse, as sexual prey. He might also answer that since he is not a "guy's guy," the "manly" aspect of Black Lesbians stimulates the woman in him. Or that Black Lesbians appeal to the science-fiction nut in him, proposing we dream a world where black women and men can interact without tripping over who's the man and who's a bitch. Black Lesbians have also enabled him to foresee a time when black folk will find revolutionary solidarity by celebrating rather than chastising one another's differences.

Over and above political correctness, he's come to recognize that his attraction to Black Lesbians owes something to them being women he can have raunchy sexual conversations with without swinging from Clarence Thomas's nutsac, or his hairy Coke bottle, as the case may be. Once he discovered that Black Lesbians could be more carnivorous sexual players than any brother this side of Wilt Chamberlain, he recognized them as his compatriots in the consumption arena. This was a terrifying thought in one respect, since it suggested that what was most alluring about Black Lesbians was their doggish side. Did he love Black Lesbians for the same qualities he'd found loathsome among the locker-room cadres? Had he gravitated to Black Lesbians because they were women who could dog out other women without penis guilt? This may be too hard a read on his affection for the Black Lesbian coven. He'll say he loves his Afro-Sapphic sisters because they are so fierce and "flava-ful," like he wants all his niggas to be. Still the question remains: how does his lesbo-philia explain his inability to sustain relationships with sisters who ain't gay beyond a New York minute? Could his Black Lesbian affinities run so deep that he has little love for women still under the sway of Dick, even when it's his own?

Before we answer that, however, I need to say, funk him who is me, and his tired old literary distancing devices. That's all good, but right now I need to talk to I & I about something that happened on the way to this forum. As stated above, my manager Angel got vocalist Helga Davis and I on the bill at a girl-party. I'm expecting this small and intimate affair and it turns out to be a muhfunkin' warehouse jam. So check it out: one-thirty in the morning on a Sunday night and boatloads of sisters are lined up around the block from the Jacob Javits Convention Center dropping fifteen dollars a head to party 'til thabreakadawn with about 1500 other black women (some of whom I discovered had flown in from Los Angeles, Atlanta, and D.C.). I gots to say, seeing platoons of pleasure-seeking sistas arrive on the Manhattan shore to thoroughly enjoy one another's company did mess with my head a little. Yes, even mine.

For as I stood in the hallway awaiting clearance I came to a Gadzookesean epiphany, not unlike Charlton Heston's upon sighting the Statue of Liberty at the end of *Planet of the Apes,* or Einstein's when he glimpsed the speed of light. To wit: there are no more straight black women in New York City between the ages of eighteen and twenty-five. And as unlikely and ludicrous as that might sound, it forced me to recognize that we have come to a crossroads, if not a full-blown paradigm shift where lesbian exploration is concerned in The Hood. Cause see, this wasn't no academic-boho-lesbian-feminist crowd, y'all. (For one thing, there were next to no white women at this gig, a statistical signifier that this was an event sparsely attended by your academic-feminist-boho Black Lesbians.) This was predominantly a working-class black girl affair where style, complexion, and beauty standards ran the fly ghetto-goddess gamut: from ruffnecks to babyface killers, from backward baseball-cap-sporting hip-hop butches to plastic miniskirted video vamps, from dreads to fades to fried dyed crucified and laid-to-the-side Brooklyn posse girls, all my sisters, every kind of black woman you see every day coming straight outta Bed-Stuy, Fort Greene, Jamaica Queens, and the Bronx wuz representin' out that piece yo. And they were all, to a woman, fine, bumpin' in fact, not because I say so but because they thought so, moving through the club with a graceful, frolicsome ease that said, Ain't we black women bad, the joint, the haps, the dopest, hippest, happiest thing on the face of God's creation right here, right now, up in here?

We don't have to assume all these women were gay, or bi, or even testing the waters to cull that hell of fine sisters of all sexual persuasions just want to have fun without The Black Man being much in evidence. And while I found myself a lonely corner booth to hole up in with my het-girl and did not trip when she went off to the dance floor, I realized my anxieties about occupying womanspace were moot since the sisters did not look upon me or the four other aimless Negroes up in there with disdain. They didn't track us as if we were interlopers or invaders; we were more like irrelevant, invisible men.

As a Jessica Rabbit–waisted, cleavaged-out Latina waitress offered tequila from a spray-cannon tubed up to plastic tanks strapped across her back, one thing crossed my mind: obviously there is a lot more acceptance of lesbian sexuality among young working-class black women than anybody's talking about.

If 1 out of 4 people in the population are assumed to be

gay, for black women between eighteen and twenty-five in New York that figure should probably be revised to more like 3 out of 4. Like greatness, we can assume that some sisters are born Black Lesbians, some choose to have Black Lesbianism thrust upon them, and others are just making up their sexuality as they go along. Whatever brought these 1500 sisters to party that night, I couldn't help feeling that the attraction to a space where male members were at a minimum was provoked by the alienation and antipathy black men are producing in Today's Black Woman, or more bluntly, how tired the superwomen are of putting up with black macho bullshit. I don't think women start loving women only in reaction to male abuse. I do think sistas are gravitating toward and creating spaces, domestic and public, where the power of black love can be free.

In discussions about this movement, straight black women friends have admitted to feeling like they are now a dying breed. My ace boon dream hampton, a wannabe lesbian if there ever was one, confesses, "I'd be a lesbian if I could get over my fear of eatin' pussy. I'd be one bad bitch. I feel like I'm out of the loop. My lesbian friends say things to me like, 'You still into boys? You funny.' Like I'm being cute or corny."

"When I hang out with my gay women friends," says Miss Ards, "I say, 'Damn, they look happy. I wonder if I've made the right choice.'" Miss Ards doesn't think all black-woman bonding is in pursuit of the pleasure principle, however. "I went to Abyssynian Baptist Church for a meeting of black women and made the mistake of asking, 'How can we bring black men's voices into this discussion?' They just dismissed me and my question." The political ramifications of black women creating exclusive support groups in The Hood suggest that Black Lesbians aren't the only ones that are too-thru with The Black Man.

Now comes the hard part. With these kinds of numbers and this kind of money to spend, we are talking a demographic here, a market share. If all these black women were out the closet, even the straight ones, in their support for Black Lesbianism, they could probably own their own damn Barney's or Bloomingdales or WBLS even. Leading me to wonder that if this many sisters are down, then why don't they rally behind their own red, black, and green flag? Why is there no Black Lesbian movement for empowerment?

For answers to these questions I went to my three card-carrying black feminist friends: the notorious bell hooks; the homegirls' Simone de Beauvoir, Ms. Rebecca Walker; and my aforementioned manager, the born-to-dyke Angel Rhyan. As far as brand names go, hooks is a self-described sex radical, Walker an avowed bisexual, and Rhyan a devout homosexual. Rhyan, twenty-five, shares the class background of the sisters who were up in the party. Having been "in the life" since she was sixteen, it's her belief that few of the women there would "claim 'lesbian' as the identity that they are proud of." She recounted that when Helga sang "Flybutch in Black Leather Jacket" at the club a friend heard a sister crack, "So what's she gonna do, sing about dykes all night?" A book-party I went to for *Afrekete: An Anthology of Black Lesbian Writing* (edited by Catherine E. McKinley and L. Joyce DeLaney) confirmed this. I counted as many white women and black men among the thirty or so folk there as black women. Subtract the editors and the three women who read from the anthology, and it would seem that the surest way to get Black Lesbians to avoid a Black Lesbian event is to raise the Black Lesbian flag.

We do need to consider the spectre of homophobia when questioning why the butches didn't flock to jock the book-party the way they did the girl-jam. As Walker pointed out, we don't know what forms of personal resistance Black Lesbians who may seem apolitical wage in the course of their everyday lives. These women, she says, could be engaged in antipatriarchal acts that we have no awareness of. I agreed, but asked how these individual acts of resistance could ever coalesce into a mass movement if nobody wants to grip the Black Lesbian label. Walker countered in that New Age peace-love-and-power way I find more naive and more revolutionary than I'll ever be, that "we have to recognize that their brand of feminism may be valid too, and as potentially transformative."

I then proposed a hypothetical scenario wherein a gay black woman is bashed and in the fracas slaughters her attackers, only to be charged with murder. Would Black Lesbians make her a cause celebre? Rebecca found my example extreme. Angel believed some of these apolitical clubhead lesbians might support my heroine as a victim of racism or sexism but not of homophobia.

We turn now to bell hooks for an opinion on undeclared lesbianism among these young women and older black feminist icons. In her opinion, "they're just greedy." Not for the dollars but for a variety of life-style options. She saw this as cutting two ways: living sexually undeclared spares you homophobic assault if you're already in that high-risk black woman category, but it also spares you the burden of heroic lesbian representation. She went on to say that she was surprised no well-known Black Lesbian intellectual had taken up Audre Lorde's mantle, since Lorde's position presented tremendous critical freedoms as well as restraints. She feels sexual conservatism is another reason otherwise fear-defying black women warriors don't come out. As hip-hop has proven, foul language can provoke as much of a ruckus in the middle-class black psyche as white violence. Where sex talk is concerned, I know black folks who blush and blanch at the mention of words like dick and pussy in polite discourse, but who relish putting their lips on the very genitalia those vulgar terms describe.

For years we've known that many black women look upon *feminism* as a nasty word, too. Even though folk like Alice Walker, bell hooks, and Ntozake Shange have all made critical and inclusive interventions in the Feminist Discourse, we can conjecture that many black women continue to find the Discourse alienating. But what if Black Feminism thrives in silence? What if, á la jazz, the practice of Black Lesbianism in The Hood is the real Black Feminist theory? What if, to build on KRS-One's cipher, real bad girls also move in silence? Perhaps there's more of a political statement to be found in Black Lesbians quietly boosting their ranks instead of walking around with big L's on their chests. Though Angel is proud to be a Dyke with a capital D, she envies the women she calls "post-lesbians." "They are who I want to be when I grow up," she muses. "They're comfortable in completely straight scenes. I've always thought of myself as post-race in that way. I can be the only black person in a room full of white people and not notice. But I just can't let my lesbian identity go in the same way."

Just so no one thinks the irony or the outrageousness of a man writing this essay escapes me, yes I do feel weird and conflicted. Though I generally despise white writers who apologize for being white when they write on black subjects, I've developed some empathy for them writing this joint here. On the other hand, several Black Lesbian writers have told me, I might as well go ahead and put their stuff out there, since they ain't about to. They're not interested in being consumed or on display. (It seems that Black Lesbian filmmakers, and not essayists and activists, are more interested in publicly probing contemporary Black Lesbian life, erotica, and politics. Perhaps there's something in the power dynamic of film that attracts or encourages Black Lesbian exhibitionists. (See the work of Jocelyn Taylor, Dawn Suggs, and Cheryl Dunye.)

When I presented my conundrum to Lisa Jones she said, "well I can't write about that scene because I'm too much of an outsider." And like, I'm not? To which she replied, "you're an insider by virtue of your desire to be inside of it." You think I got a snappy answer for that rape-inflected colonialist reading, you got another think coming. In considering my desire to be one of the girls, however, I'm reminded of a rhyme by Q-Tip: "The thing that men and women need to do is stick together/ Progressions can't be made if we're separate forever" and of this passage from André Breton's 1944 book on Woman and War, *Arcanum 17:* "After so many female saints and national heroines fanning the combativeness of this or that camp, when will we see a different miracle extending her arms between those who are about to grapple to say: you are brothers. Is it because the yoke is crushing womankind that she definitively abdicates before forces that are obviously opposed to her? I see only one solution. The time has come to value the ideas of Woman at the expense of those of Man. It is artists in particular who must maximize the importance of everything that stands out in the feminist world view in contrast to the masculine, to build only on women's resources, to exalt, or even better *appropriate to the point of jealousy making it one's own.*" [Italics mine].

In ways that I am only beginning to understand, my dialogues with Black Lesbian friends, and black feminists in general, are providing me with insights critical to my becoming a nonoppressive and non-self-destructive Black Male.

Perhaps this outing of my own Black Lesbophilia is my way of returning an embrace I see as essential to black folks surviving the twenty-first century, of shouting out to progressive brothers and sisters alike, à la James Brown (and Rodney King): Can we still take it to the bridge, y'all? Can we even locate that muthafunka?

How Does a Supermodel Do Feminism?

an interview with veronica webb

REBECCA WALKER: do you consider yourself a feminist?

VERONICA WEBB: Yes, I consider myself a feminist, but not in the fist-in-the-air kind of way. It's kind of hard to define, because so much is taken for granted by our generation. We just assume women are supposed to be paid equally and all the rest. I mean, I march for reproductive freedom, and I raise money for breast cancer research, and I am definitely concerned about women getting what they need in order to be in control of their lives.

You know, I was sitting on the couch crossed legged on a cold night a few weeks ago, and it was just one of those nights where nothing was going on, and I was flipping through the channels on TV and Vanessa Redgrave was on PBS doing this dramatic reading of Virginia Woolf's *A Room of One's Own*. There she was, in this dark oak corridor of some university somewhere and she starts reading Virginia's essay about going to this university and being shut out of the library and shut out of knowledge because she is a woman. You know, the beetles chase her off the grass, and she tries to go into the library and they tell her she can't because she is not a male student. Woolf is really talking about women's lack of access and where access comes from: knowledge and money. And not just money, but money that comes with no strings attached. And I found myself really moved, because what she was talking about is something I so relate to, a need for access and privacy, a need for sovereignty. And I think all women need that, sovereignty. And by sovereignty I mean having the freedom to be self-governed. And by self-governed I mean that there's nobody up in your house standing over you telling you what to do because they control the purse strings.

RW: Do you feel there's any conflict between being a "feminist" and working in a profession that many feminists say objectifies women?

VW: Well, first let me say that I think that all people are judged by their looks, especially women, and that we cannot escape it. I'm not saying it's right or wrong, it's just what it is: a part of human nature, the same way we have certain associations, both positive and negative, about people because of what race they are. I personally don't feel objectified, because I control the way my looks are used, not the other way around. There is a lot more self-expression involved than people realize. I mean, people always ask models, do they make you cut your hair? Do they make you pose nude? And it's like, no, models *choose* what they want to do. Everyone at the top of their profession has looked at themselves and said this is who I am naturally, or this is the persona that I want to create, this is how I want to use my looks to create an enterprise. That's why Cindy Crawford chose to do *Playboy*, because that's what she is naturally, she is very very very very sexy, and that was her springboard to a professional empire.

And that's on a grand scale, but on an everyday scale, the way I look gives me power in different situations, and this is nothing new. There's something about being pulled together and in control that makes people want to emulate you, which makes people begin to have certain associations about how you run your business and how you run your life, it's a very persuasive thing. When you are in a meeting you can be well spoken, but when you are well spoken *and* pulled together you have a whole other kind of power.

RW: What do you think about the whole debate about the standard of beauty—that models create a standard of beauty that most women can't attain and which ends up making women dissatisfied with themselves?

VW: Well, I did a lecture at Vanderbilt University and there was a girl there who was very upset because she said I set an impossible standard and was participating in an industry that makes impossible standards. And that made me think of this Kurt Vonnegut story about a society where everyone has to be equal. So there's a musician who has to wear lead earmuffs all the time, and there is an artist who has to wear these gloves that make him clumsy, so that anything special about people is muted so that everyone can be equal.

Anyway, at one point she just blew up at me and she screamed, "You're just a piece of meat, you have absolutely no power!"

RW: And what did you say?

VW: I said, "Well, first of all, for you to get that upset at me already tells me that I have emotional power over you." And then I began to tell her about different work I'd done to raise public awareness about different issues, not to pat myself on the back, but just to say this is an influential and powerful business and it could be used to our advantage. She walked out, but a lot of women started to raise their hands, and they were saying, "Well, my boyfriend loves you and he has your picture on the wall and I feel that I could never ever look like you." And I said, "No one can ever look like anybody else, sorry! I can't look like you either, but if it makes you feel really bad, if it makes you feel inferior, either ask him to take it down, or put your own icon up and tell him to live up to it."

Listen, no woman can be an air-brushed photograph. Just like most men cannot be a Arnold Schwarzenegger, they just can't, yet men are not held back by the fact they don't have movie-star looks, and women are. There is obviously something else going on there that I am not so sure you can blame on modeling.

I mean, I'm sure the fashion industry is culpable on some level for causing women to have feelings of desperation or inadequacy, but you know, I have friends who have a daughter who is physically deformed. She has a very big head and is very odd looking. She is not unconscious and can process almost everything that goes on around her. Her mother and father and brothers gave her almost perfect love and worked very hard on accepting her, and she actually has more self-confidence than I do. She has really made me see that how much self-confidence and self-esteem you have comes from how you were raised and how much attention and value people placed on you as a child.

It has to do with other things you are exposed to, but a lot of it has to do with how much you were loved for being you.

RW: What was your mother like?

VW: Well, my mother was born in 1922 and in her time you had to do what you were told to do, and being black there were two things you could do professionally: you could be a schoolteacher or a nurse. So my mother's parents made sure she became a nurse even though she wanted to go to an ivy league school and become a concert pianist.

My mother worked really really really really hard to make sure I was educated in a way that would teach me to think and which would allow me to compete on a lot of different levels and to have entrée into a lot of different places. She would tell me, I don't care what you do with you life, I can't tell you what to do or how to spend it, just make sure you do what you want.

You know, all through my upbringing if I did something right or discovered something new my mother would clap her hands over her head and shake them in the air to cheer me on, and you know, any lesson I wanted to take she would make sure I had it, and she was always there with information but never there with too much direction because she wanted me to find my own way. And I'm really lucky that I got put on that track because there were no other examples for me really, and it wasn't until much later in life that intellectually it clicked, and it was because of *A Room of One's Own*. I realized that without any rhetoric or expectation of payback, my mother had basically set up a room of my own for me. Pushing me to find my own way was what my mother gave me.

RW: Have you ever felt guilty about what you are doing? Do you ever feel like you are playing into stereotypes of women, or creating them?

VW: I felt a lot of the guilt in the beginning of my career, and certainly it comes back every once in a while, from what people from Naomi Wolf to Gloria Steinem have said about models presenting negative images to young girls, images which hold all women back, and all that. But you know, being black and growing up, I went through school in the sixties and the seventies, and there were not a lot of images out in popular culture for me to relate to. I felt almost invisible. I mean, the world was going on. There was Angela Davis, Barbara Jordan, and all those people, but they were far from my age range, and they were doing things that, as a child, I couldn't really understand. That's not to knock or diminish them, but in terms of there being some kind of intermediary professional image of a black woman that I could relate to, there just wasn't one. So, on some level I feel that the fact that I'm there visually and I'm represented is helpful to young black women looking out into the culture and trying to see themselves.

RW: I was at a Third Wave board meeting last week and we were naming people for our advisory board, and I suggested you and one of the other board members said, "Oh—I just hate models, they're just like little dolls, not in control, and I don't think that's the right image." Another member then said, "I wouldn't want to participate in an industry that makes women spend billions of dollars trying to improve the way they look." What do you think about these responses?

VW: I think sometimes people think that if women use and manipulate their sexuality in any way it makes them a prostitute, which leads to that whole question of being in control. As for the second question, the industry doesn't *make* women spend billions of dollars, people *want* to. We're a nation of consumers, people want to go out and have something new, a new dress, a new shade of lipstick or nail polish, or a new cream because it makes you feel renewed, it brings something new into your life. I do think the industry is at fault when it makes false promises. Like when women read ads and magazines and things are presented in a very real way, promising that if you do this you will get "x" results, rather than saying this is an idea, this is a suggestion. You can't let yourself believe that there is a plastic surgeon or a genie in the bottle, cosmetics are just a little pick-me-up.

RW: What kind of role model would you say you are?

VW: I put emphasis on thinking, on being outspoken. I mean I'm certainly not an ivy league scholar or anything like that, but I just think it's really important to be self-educated and self-determined. I also think that if you are a woman, any way that you can amass power and money you have to do it as long as it's ethical, because it's just something that we don't have. And you know, it's funny, because you go back to when people say well, women trading off their looks strips them of their power, but it has empowered a lot of women. If you look at me, Cindy Crawford, Claudia Schiffer, Naomi Campbell, Elle McPherson, and many others, we've become phenomenally empowered by trading off our looks, the same with Hollywood actresses. The bottom line is how you do or don't use your power.

I am not saying that you have to create some kind of colony or alternative life-style, that's not what I'm suggesting at all. I mean, I feel that I can use my power to really do something to educate young black people, I can set up a foundation or a school. And hopefully I can amass enough capital at some point to give my life over to a charitable enterprise.

You know, some people say that what models get paid devalues other women in the workplace, and I don't think that is true. What making money does allow me to do is hire other black people and other women, because I'm an enterprise and

how does a supermodel do feminism?   215

I can create jobs, and certainly if there are women in my employ we can have a better working environment and get farther in general than if someone has to go into a huge corporate system, or be at the mercy of a Newt Gingrich.

RW: Speaking of Newtie, what do you think about the welfare debate?

VW: Well, first of all, I think welfare is the code word for black.

RW: Black women.

VW: No, welfare means nigger, that's what welfare means. I think that during elections, when it's time for us to make important decisions, that is when the racial debate gets thrown up. Do you remember when the welfare debate started there was a cover story in the *New York Times* with a photograph of an overweight dark-skinned black woman getting ready to put these two chickens in the oven, did you read that story?

RW: Umm, I might have missed it.

VW: Well anyway, the story was this: she has three kids, she gets off welfare and she finds a job where she can make $7 an hour and at the end of the week she makes something like $300. But she has to wake up every morning at three, get her two infants dressed, and take them to her grandmother's house, drive her son to school by six, and get herself to work. She can't receive phone calls at her job, and if her mother has a heart attack they won't put the phone call through for her to know, and if one of her kids gets sick or her car breaks down, then she is totally back in the hole again, in debt, and her life goes back into a tailspin. It was very manipulative because here she is being used as the poster child for welfare—see, if she can do it, then anybody can do it—and anybody who isn't willing to live a life that is so totally distorted is lazy and someone who is working this hard shouldn't be, quote, humiliated, by any help.

RW: Yeah, no one seems to be talking about the cost of child care, the unavailability of birth control and information, instead they're talking about the woman who's getting over on the system. And what about the sixteen-year-olds in my neighborhood pushing baby carriages who know about birth control, but who live in a culture that says you don't become a real woman until you have a baby?

vw: Maybe I'll write about the welfare debate in my next column for *PAPER*.

rw: Where do you find strength?

vw: First of all, from my mother, from knowing how much she loved me, knowing that she would lay down her life for me. I also get a lot of strength from knowing that I am the object of love from a Divine Being.

rw: How do you know that?

vw: I know that from growing up in the Church, from reading the Bible, and from looking around myself and seeing how many blessings I have. I consider myself very lucky that God does not test me very often.

rw: Did you always believe in God as defined by the Bible?

vw: Not at all. I grew up having different relationships with God my whole life. Like, I have always thought that Jesus was really cool and really sexy, and that God is like the Prince symbol: both sexes at once. But that's really obvious.

rw: Do you feel connected to other models? Is there any kind of sisterhood?

vw: Well, certainly Karen Alexander, Cindy Crawford, Tyra Banks, and Elle McPherson are friends of mine, they're all people I turn to for comradeship and advice in the business. And Cindy especially, she will always help you. She is a very firm believer that we have to be really open about what kind of commission structures we have and how much money we make, so that we don't get ripped off. I think most of us work hard to eliminate any feelings that we're fighting against each other.

RW: Are there any principles you live by?

VW: Don't do anything you can't own up to. And always be grateful.

Testimony of a Naked Woman

jocelyn taylor

combining responsibility for my body and my desire for political representation has been a continuous learning process. My survival instincts have always surfaced through the more physical side of my self, maneuvering, twisting, and contorting my way through to the other side of whatever problem I was facing.

This sensibility kicked in strongly when I first moved to New York City. I had come out as a lesbian just months before. When the first opportunity presented itself, I left the comfort and security of my native Washington, D.C., a predominantly Black town with close, nurturing community ties, to move to the Queer Capital of the East Coast. I left in hopes of validating and creatively expressing this emerging aspect of my identity—one that was coming out kicking, determined, and increasingly radical.

When I first arrived in New York, I worked several low-paying, time-intensive jobs. I was attending meetings of the AIDS Coalition to Unleash Power (ACT-UP) regularly and had become involved in its media affinity group, DIVA-TV (Damned Interfering Video Activists). We hit the streets with meager equipment in hand, ready to document demonstrations and to protect protesting civilians from dirty dealings by the police. Six months later, I joined House of Color, a multiracial group of video beginners who developed a video project incorporating dialogues about exoticism, marginality, and homophobia. I discovered the link between media activism, representation, and creative expression as a member of that collective. Video was working for me. Cameras weren't too hard to come by; those who had equipment lent it to those who didn't. The thought that I could actually make my own television imagery was appealing.

The more I became involved in the alternative media community, the more I felt resentful that I didn't have the money to spend greater time developing myself as an artist and activist. I could barely support myself. A 9-to-5 job was out of the question. I felt that joining the labor force would consume my time and energy and become a form of enslavement.

The promise of fast cash and more freedom led me into the world of sex work. I started working as a stripper in hustle joints. I bought a dark pageboy wig, some fishnet stockings, a cheap pair of heels, and a tight hairnet. I wore the wig so that my new dreadlocks, which were short yet "radical," didn't show.

I got my first job as a stripper through my roommate at the time, who worked at the Hustle Joint and is now a well-known performance artist. Hanging out with her fueled my exhibitionism, a posture I was increasingly acknowledging. She had a girlfriend, a photographer, who was putting together a series of nude women in public. So, at 8:30 one Saturday morning, the three of us drove up to 42nd Street. My roommate held my coat while her girlfriend took pictures of me standing stark naked in front of the Roxy Theater. The whole thing took about thirty seconds. A couple of guys stood with their mouths agape, unable to believe their eyes. Another man walked by mumbling, "Fuckin' dykes." I guess they weren't used to seeing a naked woman in steel-toe boots getting her picture taken. I pushed back feelings of vulnerability and the voice that served a "racial reminder" on notions and images of Black women as sexual beings. I focused on the belligerence of the act—which I saw as speaking against censures from both within my community and without—and at that moment, I felt liberated.

As far as we knew, my roommate and I were the only lesbians working at the Hustle Joint. Listening to the hetero dancers discuss which men they were attracted to made me ill. It seemed that the straight women had a lot invested in the "Pretty Woman" fairy tale. They were looking for wealthy, benevolent sugar daddies to take them out of their economic misery. Some men *had* come to the bar hoping to meet women. The exchange was always the same: "I'll give you money if you make me feel like I'm in control of my life in a world of chaos." Being detached from the heterosexual-power-fuck relationship between money and sex, I maintained another fantasy. I thought that I would earn enough money to put me on easy street and beat the whole game. Money, in my mind, became the solution to all my problems. Once, a man offered me $300 to have dinner. Of course there was the specter of a larger expectation. Yet, for a lousy three hundred bucks I actually considered spending the evening with him.

I was one of only two Black women who worked at the Hustle Joint. I never really got to know the other Black woman. She was darker complected than I and well tipped as a result of that "exoticism." In the Hustle Joint, "Black girl" is a fetish category just like bearded ladies or tattooed women. We were clearly novelty items. Occasionally, the owner of the bar would tell us to approach some dusty, old white patron who was a regular customer. The owner would say to us, with a gleam in his eye, "He *likes* Black girls." We "Black girls," however, didn't make nearly as much money as the white women who worked there.

We were all, Black, white, and other women, referred to as "girls." We called each other "girls" ("How many girls are working this shift?"). When I walked through the entrance of the Hustle Joint I left my politics at the door. I was most worried about how I was going to pay bills and buy tape for video projects. I was worried about how I was going to *continue* as a radical Black woman if I didn't have the money to survive. I knew that stripping was a means to an end. I knew I wouldn't and couldn't do it forever. Somehow I just found it to be much more palatable than waiting tables or working an office job. Stripping was easier. The Hustle Joint was another world: working there was an exercise in detachment that I performed very successfully. I could slip into my exhibitionist mode, and imagine that I was really in control and, in fact, taking advantage of the situation. I also thought that I was experimenting with an aspect of my erotic self. There was part of me that liked performing, liked having a captive audience who would only watch me.

At this time, I had already started the Clit Club, a lesbian party night for women, but still had big financial struggles. The club started in the summer of 1990, during a dry spell of activities for women in New York City. At the Clit Club, women of all shapes, colors, and sizes were encouraged to stretch their sexual boundaries and to explore lesbian sensuality in the safety of an all-women's space. It was important for those who walked through Clit's door to feel comfortable enough to shed any barriers that might inhibit their desire. It was the first place to unapologetically *emphasize* sexual pleasure for dykes in a club atmosphere. Videos, erotic slides, and dancers were employed to punctuate the club's "sex-positive" vision. The Clit Club was going on strong then and, as I was just beginning my experiment with exhibitionism, erotic power, and representation, I believed that stripping (even though I was stripping for men) was allowing me to discover more of my own sexual agency.

Unfortunately, the money trip obscured the part of me that was seriously questioning whether or not I was trading away my power or perpetuating negative stereotypes; I was too busy trying to sell an overpriced glass of juice. In New York City, hustle bars are restricted from selling sex and booze, but that didn't eliminate the hard sell. The juice was $30 to be exact. We dancers got 20 percent of everything sold. If the customer was really hungry, he was enticed to buy a $300 bottle of nonalcoholic champagne. The $300 also paid for the company of a dancer in a more private area toward the back of the bar. Lots of things happened in those private $300 quarters.

I was reluctant to go that far. Besides, it was really hard to get someone to pay that kind of money. I was almost sure that I wouldn't have to deal with it. I tried to find out what went on behind the curtains. All the answers were incredibly vague: "Well, I dance completely nude for a while, then I give him a little massage." As the question "What do you mean massage?" would begin to form in my throat, my inquiries would be cut off ("Oops, it's showtime, sorry"). I couldn't get a straight answer out of anybody. I packed a few condoms in my purse just in case. I wasn't at ease with the thought of getting fucked, but realistically, I wasn't sure how far I was willing to go with this experiment. I was aware that women received extra tips from the big spenders. My fear was that someone might make me a crazy offer that would be difficult to refuse. I kept thinking, "What if I haven't made enough money to pay bills and rent this month and somebody lays out $1,000 for me to sit on his dick?" I packed a dildo in my purse as well: perhaps I could work it into a situation where I could fuck myself, the customer could watch, and I could still get paid. Eventually, I was able to coax someone into buying the pseudo-champagne, but once he paid for it, I realized that I had made at least $60, and I wasn't willing to negotiate for anything else. I went into the room, did a little dance, moved the toe of my spiked heel in a circular motion on his groin (my special massage technique), sipped some phony champagne, and left. At one point, he tried to stick his finger in my anus. He barely made it in, but my asshole was on fire for the next week. He had put something on the tip of his finger. I was totally freaked out. I was fired shortly afterward. It turned out that I wasn't bringing in my quota of "champagne" buys, and besides, they already had one Black girl there.

In the sex industry, you don't feel, you perform. It's striking to me how removed I was from myself and what I determined was political resolve at the time. I was mildly concerned when objectifying, racist remarks were tossed my way by customers and coworkers. Hell, I was only in it for the money. A bunch of rowdy white college boys came into the bar one day and hooted about getting to stare up into my Black vulva. I showed it to them as long as they were shelling out dollars, but when the money ran out, I walked off the stage. It was the only way for me to assert myself and exercise the little control I had. My favorite thing to do after a day's work was to remove my wig, makeup, and fishnets and don the most butch clothes I could find. Somehow I needed to balance the stripper performance with a shedding ritual (like butching out) to try to ground myself.

On one hand, I was struggling, trying to pull my Black lesbian identity away from the societal fringe. Meanwhile, my concerns about freeing the Black female body and starting the Clit Club were what enabled me to see sex work as a possibility. At the Clit, fierce lesbian women acted out a variety of sexual postures. That was encouraged. I often walked around the bar with next to nothing on. I thought, "Something is so right here. I'm able to be a sexual Black woman in a way that I've never experienced before." I had gained a certain amount of ground in how I was able to celebrate my erotic power. I relied on that power to protect and affirm me while I stripped for men.

I left Washington in 1989 and made frequent trips back to a lesbian community I barely knew. Once, during some casual banter at a lesbo bar, a woman said to me, "You're from New York, aren't you?" I explained that I was born in D.C. and grew up in D.C. I reminded her that she had a sister who used to go to my elementary school ("Oh, you're that Jocelyn Taylor!"). The gap was widening between the hometown and home girl. Close friends became the closest connection I had to Washington. Teresa, my friend and witness forever who helped me to get to New York, came up often to check up on me. I was thrilled when she told me that she would be spending the New York Pride weekend with me. It was my first Pride ever, in fact.

Pride in New York was a lot different than the relatively smaller scale events at Dupont Circle and P Street Beach in D.C. In New York we were strutting down Fifth Avenue topless. I had accented my breasts with Silence = Death decals. Teresa said she felt rejuvenated by the feel of her chest in the open air yet saddened, too, by the fact that this would never happen at home. The lesbian community in D.C. didn't feel safe enough to experience this during any queer celebration. Even in the "safe spaces" for women, lesbians were unlikely to go bare-breasted in public. Inspired by the visibility and fearlessness of New York dykes, I proposed to Teresa that we do a topless "action" at one of the few women's bars in Washington. We encouraged other D.C. friends to join us in what we thought would be a strong statement toward personal power and self-affirmation.

It was Ladies Night in July 1990, and the women were out in droves. This monthly soiree for lesbians was an anxiously awaited event that attracted predominantly Black women from the city and suburbs. And thirty days was just enough time for the dyke community to heat up enough sexual energy to turn the club into a pressure cooker of desire. Women danced nipple-to-nipple and cheek-to-cheek; the music was happening and the place was packed. Couples were linked in an intimate grind on the outside dance patio. I stopped to watch women's bodies curve into each other and undulate to the DJ's choice of a "slow jam." Folks were touching, grabbing, squeezing, feeling, and feeling "it." I snapped out of voyeur mode when a house tune kicked in and switched into a frenzied dance any exhibitionist would be proud of. "It" began to possess me, and my body became a six-foot-tall erotic nerve ending. The dance floor was writhing. Teresa gave me a nudge to remind me of our mission, and the next thing you know, our shirts were off. Then more shirts came off, but nobody stopped dancing. I could have been on a granola-girl campground shaking my boobs toward the shooting stars; I could have been dancing in front of the mirror at home; I could have been marching down Fifth Avenue. I looked to the sidelines to see a row of Black women snickering, pointing, and jabbing each other in the ribs in disbelief. Hadn't they ever seen tits before? Seeing folks nude in public is surprising, but the reaction of these sisters surprised me. I could tell they were embarrassed, but why did they behave like men watching a girlie show? These women were so uncomfortable they could only impersonate a male "gaze." In their view, our action was not about erotic expression or liberation. It seems they had learned too well that sexualized body parts (like breasts) were to be hidden unless someone was ready to "get down." When some women began to comment on breast sizes, I finally spoke up:

"What's up with you guys?" I asked.

"Why do you have to take your shirts off? Don't you know that's nasty?"

"Well," I said, "it's not about what other people think is decent for me to do. This is about individual freedom."

"Y'all are freaks," she said.

Being called a freak made me stop in my tracks for a moment, so I scrambled for a controlled textbook-like response.

"Freaks? Freaks are individuals"—the term mostly refers

to women—"who have no sexual boundaries and who are 'indiscriminate' about their sexual encounters. Women who enjoy many relations are considered freaks, as are sex workers and lesbians. Isn't there something *wrong* with that?" I demanded.

Actually, the real attention-getter was a Black woman in the middle of the dance floor who had already bared her upper torso and was about to remove her blue jeans and panties. When the jeans came off, I felt myself panic. Here I was—bare-breasted—and suddenly forced to confront the fact that I had prescribed limits as well. I feared for that jeanless woman more than I feared for myself. I could see her curly black pubic hair as she inched the panty line further and further south.

The breast issue has long been at the forefront of the women's movement as an example of what female body parts have been appropriated, tortured, and idealized as measures to control women. Likewise, the vagina has been high stakes in the reproductive rights and abortion battles. However, there's been no organized feminist agenda protecting women's right to public nudity, much less one that specifically protects Black women's right to explore alternative erotic possibilities. Of course there are places where public nudity is not a threat and there is a sense of safety, even if illusory. I was again reminded of my fear and internal contradictions in the face of what I meant as an act of political belligerence.

By this point, the nightclub SWAT team was on the roof shining high-powered flashlights onto the crowd in an effort to locate the perpetrators. Minutes later a security guard approached me and told me to put my shirt back on ("Put your shirt back on or I'll have to escort you out of the bar"). I could only smile, catch my breath, and offer my simple response ("No, thanks anyway"). The guard figured the cards were stacked in her favor so she attempted to call my bluff ("Put your shirt back on or I'll call the cops and have you arrested"). In a perfect world I would have reminded the guard that girls just want to have fun too, and doesn't she remember that on the boys' nights many gentlemen are wearing next to nothing? We would have a laugh, buy each other a beer, and the party would continue. Under the jurisdiction of reality I could only tell her that I wouldn't leave willingly. I laid my bare back on the dance floor and prepared myself for the repercussions ("If you want me out you'll have to carry me out"). As effortlessly as I lay prone beneath her, she hoisted me over her shoulder and marched toward the exit sign.

Setting me down barely inside the club's doors, the guard continued her reproach. She asked that I put my shirt back on for the sake of my "sisters." Her tone implied that I was not conducting myself in a way that was appropriate for a Black woman. She was embarrassed and ashamed, and obviously disapproved of my insistence that a woman should be permitted to be topless in a lesbian bar if she chooses. Yet, despite my pushy affront, I understood how she felt. My beliefs—the "politically correct" framework which had initially instigated the action—became inconsequential because I was acting out of both self-centeredness and exhibitionism. What my sisters were reacting out of was age-old fear and self-censure in the name of counteracting negative stereotypes of Black women.

Our bodies—our tits, asses, pussies, et al.—have been sewn into an image of the "wild thang"; the different, dark, and mysterious body that is fetishized and exploited. To expose myself in public in front of men (even if they were gay), unfamiliar women, and white folk was to revive a painful image that our female elders taught us to revoke, often to the point of self-abnegation. Though I honestly believe that parents, grandparents, extended family, etc., want to teach us how to "act" in order to survive in a Black-hostile, woman-hating environment, the lessons are often transmitted in the form of policing. We're taught to modify our behavior to an antierotic standard so that we can feel safe in our own bodies. Meanwhile, darker berries provide sweeter juice and I am the "exotic" even with my clothes *on*—still the target of nonconsensual eroticized desire.

I wanted to take my eroticism back, but when the guard said, "Put your shirt back on for your sisters," I put my shirt on, wiped my face, which was moist with tears, mumbled something like, "I'll be back," and ran out the door. I bumped right into the white owner of the club who shook his finger in my face and said that he wouldn't have called the police if we had asked his permission to remove our clothing. Ask permission? The words still ring in my ears. I told him that I thought I was in a lesbian and gay dance club, a phenomenon that exists only precariously in states where same-sex love is against the law. Lucky for him, Washington, D.C., legislation permits him to operate without fear or retribution. At that time the club had one night a month that was for women only. I wanted to know whose side he was on. Exactly who and what was he defending? Ultimately, he was most concerned with defending his investment and didn't want any publicity that might tarnish his profitable relationship with the queer community or his ability to operate the club. When the cops had left, he surprised me when he decreed that we were "allowed" to take our shirts off inside the bar. Fine. The cops left, women shimmied barebreasted to the music, and I sat, paused at the bar, with my shirt on.

I felt less than triumphant about that evening. I felt discouraged because it seemed that few understood the political impetus for my actions. Before the guard had removed me, a close friend came up to me and said, "Jocelyn, girl, you are so

230   jocelyn taylor

crazy!" She was half-serious. She said that she would never take off her shirt in public because her breasts are too big. Too big for what? I wanted to ask her how she learned that her breasts were too big. I wanted to change the rules. I wanted to change the meaning of publicly condoned behavior; behavior that is expressed through the human body and therefore is an expression of the human spirit.

I understand that walking down the street topless in the wrong context is dangerous for my health. I don't want to do it. But I thought that a homo club full of lesbians might be an appropriate spot to explore erotic possibilities. Not! Why couldn't large/medium/small-breasted women be topless in a gay bar? I knew that legislation existed that forbade women to be topless in public (except in places with cabaret licenses, i.e., strip joints), but everyone in the club was already living unprotected from many forms of abuse and discrimination—essentially living outside the law. I was outraged by the contradictions that were operating. I was also deeply troubled that I hadn't resolved the conflict between myself and the group of women who felt uncomfortable with what happened and a Black sister's role in it. I was overcome by a gnawing sense that I was using strategies that didn't translate honestly into the realities of Black women's lives. Of all the women in the club, about 70 percent were Black. Of the thirty or so women who went topless, over twenty were white. My direct action became a reaction rather than an interaction. Direct action as a form of activism is not foreign to the Black community. As a kid, I watched endless newsreels of the Civil Rights and Black Power movements. Although I had attended the March on Washington led by Martin Luther King in 1968 with my mother, I had no other physical memories of the struggle. The newsreels graphically depicted the resilience of Black people and our fervent drive to achieve social equality. That worked for me. That's why I joined ACT-UP, even though it was a predominantly white gay male organization. I was attracted to the group's use of direct action—demonstrations, phone zaps, "die-ins," etc.—which recalled the fervor of that struggle in some way. Eventually, however, race and class divisions undercut coalition building. The AIDS crisis was our focus, some argued, not whether or not signs and placards got translated into Creole or Spanish. Applying what I learned in ACT-UP about in-your-face activism to the action in the club that night was both admirable and naive. The action caused a mild stir in the lesbian community of D.C., but I didn't talk to anyone there about what happened. I didn't approach any of the women in the bar who were not my friends about what they thought, how they felt, or what they wanted to do next. A little dialogue and a little organizing could have gone a long way in creating a forum where Black women could talk about owning their bodies whether they're in public or private or wherever they may be in the world.

While trying to understand the D.C. action, I had to painfully confront that I am an exhibitionist. As someone who likes to be "out there," I'm always negotiating spaces and actions. I do it partly because I want to be assured that I will get the attention I'm looking for and partly because I want to be sure that I'm safe. Rarely do I perform some outrageous stunt without knowing that I won't get hurt. (Walking down Fifth Avenue topless surrounded by thousands of queers is one example.) The ability to make decisions about my safety and whom I'm performing for is how I place controls on my immediate environment. It's all a mental exercise, though, because some variables can't be accounted for. I never really know how people will respond. I like to pretend that it doesn't matter how people do, because I'm busy trying not to make myself vulnerable enough to care. I often ask myself if I do things just to get attention. I don't know. I think I act out more because I don't want to be forgotten. I want to be seen and remembered. However, the action at the club in D.C. was too close to home. My shield of ambivalence dissolved into uncertainty because I knew a lot of the women there. We had similar experiences, had gone to the same high schools, and had mastered the same task of maneuvering—with varying strategies—in a society that was anti-Black, anti-female, anti-gay, and therefore anti-us.

And then I like the way my body looks. My mother persistently affirmed my Blackness by offering her descriptive personal narrative of learning to love herself as a Black woman. She told me stories of wearing clothespins on her nose to make it look thinner and of special bleaching creams used by her friends to look lighter. Later, when she had gained a stronger sense of self-identity, she, like many Black women in the late sixties and early seventies, wore a large Afro. Then, in the late seventies, she cut her hair very close to her scalp. Hair texture, facial features, and skin color still remain indicators of self-worth for Black women. I was learning that the power to resist and motivate politically can be connected to seeing yourself as beautiful and deserving of love. It took me a long time to get angry about the specific cruelty that women of color are subjected to, but once I figured out that it was *my image* that was oppressed, I set out to use my own body as a political tool to challenge and defy institutionalized self-hatred.

I consider the mere Black female form a source of power and a symbol of resistance. When I think about the worldwide prevalence of the fear of women and the fear of Blackness, and the subsequent frenzy to control these entities, I think about being in a Black female body and how powerful that is. I have fantasies about riding with an army of naked women on horse-back down Constitution Avenue in Washington, D.C. The nudity is an important part of the fantasy because it's a strong and fearless image that says we do not believe that our bodies are inferior or ugly, or open to assault of any kind. An army of women is a force that will not lie on its back passively while others eroticize and differentiate. I dream about armies because it's scary to stand up alone and in small numbers. I need a haven where I know that I'm okay and protected. In this war, I will watch your back if you will watch mine.

I took my shirt off that night because I was fed up with the limitations that are imposed on me through my body. My anger leads me to the third truth about myself, which is that I believe in radical politics. Governmental and local authority as it pertains to women, queers, and Black folk has caused me to develop a healthy disrespect for this nation's generic brand of morality thinly masked by the law. Too much legislation has been created by hypocrites and individuals who are more interested in acquiring and wielding power than instigating radical change that serves all people. Living in New York opened my eyes again to activism and taught me important lessons about direct-action strategies. My struggle now was to integrate the truths and contain the contradictions to which I was becoming more fully conscious.

The Clit Club opened two weeks after that experience in Washington. I was anxious to find erotic imagery that reflected Blackness as a desirous entity separate from stereotypical, exoticized expectations. The most difficult task in pulling together the visuals for the club was finding erotic videos of darker women made by lesbians, or made by anyone for that matter. The absence of presentations of Black lesbian desire made me understand very clearly that I was never meant to feel passionate for myself or anyone who looks like me. I set out on a mission to "see" myself even if it was a mirror reflection; even if it was just a picture of me. I participated as the darker sister in photo shoot after photo shoot, hoping to create some parity for a lesbian subculture that is greatly underserved. Many times I was nondiscriminating. Often my exhibitionist-ego side was functioning at full force, but I was determined to get all the attention that I didn't get every time I opened a magazine or turned on the television. I was battling erasure, asserting my sexuality, and getting my kicks all at the same time. No wonder I thought I could handle being a stripper; I was always dealing with racism and misogyny, so what if I did it for money? A few times I discovered a fine line between "being out there" and selling yourself short.

While working on a video about the connections between sexuality and spirituality, a cast member was required to don traditional makeup from some unrecognized East African culture, then scream into the camera. This particular section of the video was about opening your throat in order to tap into your sexual energy. The voice-over instructed viewers to feel free to expose a more "primitive" or "wild" side of themselves. The Black woman chosen to play the part walked off the set. I supported her in her actions, but chose to stay on. I talked to folks on the set about how the suggestion that sexual liberation through the appropriation of East African traditional customs was more than problematic, it was offensive. The implication of a culture and tradition as wild and primitive exposed the producers (a combination of white lesbians, sex workers, and heterosexual women) as racist and Eurocentric. Great pains had been taken to assure the "authenticity" of the makeup (the makeup artist had purchased a book about Sudanese cultures), but there was no effort to clarify any ceremonial, religious, or sexual symbolism behind the image. To this day I'm not sure if the producers understood how disturbing the African simulation was. I'm afraid that we were all suffering from the psychological effects of having worked in the sex industry; it's a mentality that allows you to take, borrow, or appropriate anything for the sake of "sexual freedom," "artistic expression," and of course money. The producers were "sympathetic," and some changes were made. I experienced other unsatisfactory interactions where I allowed my image to be used in situations that still cast me as the "exotic" or token other. I gave up stripping because my illusions of financial gain were rooted in a pornographic sense of self-denial. Every time I stripped for men I was stripping myself of emotional response. Yeah, I could get off on dancing, on just feeling my body move to the music, but I realize that I was marionetting, performing for an audience from which I maintained considerable distance. When I thought my body was being appreciated, it was actually performing for someone else's pleasure. When I thought I was making money, I was selling part of myself to the nonerotic: trading cold cash for true emotion and feeling. I don't know how long it took me to realize that a Black woman is not likely to find her liberation in a Mafia-owned strip joint.

I approached another crossroads in late 1992. I retired from stripping after working at it on and off for about two years. Ironically, I retired from the Clit Club around the same time. The bar scene had become a tremendous drain on my creative process. My body became a secondary resource as I began using video more exclusively as the medium to collect and proliferate images of me and my sisters. Now my life is all about making videos that emphatically celebrate Black lesbian sexuality. Bold, sensual, funny, and powerful, they draw from the lessons of these experiences and provide looks that are beginning to fill the erotic void that has been present in my heart and the hearts of others for such a long time. There's so much pain in invisibility. It took me a while to learn that I don't have to be the one in front of a camera feeling uncomfortable and thinking that something is better than nothing. No one does. I've been in New York for such a short time. Somehow it feels like forever. At every juncture, I learn how I can affect the future without compromise; without altering my political beliefs, my connection to my community or my physical self. The locks I started at the beginning of this journey are below my shoulders now, long and with beautiful specks of gray. Too long to hide under a wig.

Virtual Identity

mocha jean herrup

when i came out as a lesbian at nineteen, i wasn't looking for an ambiguous support group. Filled with self-hatred and revulsion, what I really needed, sadly, was to feel normal. I needed to believe that being a lesbian was okay, and I got that affirmation not by thinking about my sexuality as anything uncertain, unstable, or ambiguous, but by thinking about my sexuality as a fixed identity with a community of people "just like me" included in the deal. I soon became an activist—joined ACTUP, then Queer Nation, and pursued an active social life. I learned to dance from a gay boy, got to "know" the women's community, and for the first time that I can remember, I enjoyed being a girl. I had an identity, and with that, a social life and a cause—the key to my power and pleasure. After years of not even being able to say the word *lesbian,* I learned to love my label.

And then things got a little queer. My lesbian identity didn't always make sense. I mean, how could I call myself a lesbian when the woman I once had a crush on continued to make my knees wobble when she turned up later as a man. Or what did it mean when my lover stroked my hair, told me I was such a good boy, and let me suck her cock? Equating my identity with my sexuality, despite all the political power and social support it brought, presented a problem when my fixed "lesbian" sexuality no longer seemed to exist. I mean, what kind of power and pleasure come from an ambiguous identity?

I started to realize that sexual liberation isn't a simple matter of asserting that a particular sexuality is okay. Liberation has to do with challenging the very forces that categorize sexuality in the first place. That is why in the last year or so I have moved from identity politics to a new domain of ambiguity. "Accept the ambiguities" has become my personal mantra. I repeat these words not to invoke their action, but to cast their spell and release the magic that comes from engagement with uncertainty.

My current desire to embrace ambiguity has a lot to do with my recent immersion in new technology. What began as an attempt to dial into an on-line women's activist network has brought an entirely new texture to my daily life. Now, I am wired. My most intimate community is an electronic one; every day I speak passionately with friends and colleagues I have never seen. I live and work—form friendships, send love letters, exchange research—in cyberspace. For me, the on-line world has become anything but virtual.

In cyberspace, a realm in which the body is not physically present, where confirmable identity markers such as anatomy and skin color are no longer visible, the fluidity of identity is thrown into high relief. Though it is possible to think about identity in this way in what we call "real life," it was in cyberspace that *I* discovered an on-line sexuality that questioned my "predilections" and asked me to rethink my identity. In this world of keystroke come-ons and ergonomically induced orgasm, I found a place to appreciate my own ambiguity.

In cyberspace, simulated environments called MUDs and MOOs provide a unique sphere for interactive communication, role-playing scenarios, and the joys of cybersex. MUDs (or Multi-User Dungeons) and MOOs (Multi-User Dungeons, Object-Oriented) can best be described as text-based role-playing games. The acronyms are really a misnomer, though, as many MUDs don't involve dungeons at all and have nothing to do with killing or winning. Rather, they are social spaces in which participants may contribute to the community by programming the database to include objects of their own design.

The two most important commands on any MUD are "say" and "emote." When you type "say," followed by the text of your speech, all participants in the "room" you are in read your words on their screens. The "emote" command works in the same way, only you type what it is you want to do. So if I am logged into a MOO as Mojo and I type "say let's head over toward that cottage" followed by "emote winks suggestively," this is what appears on people's screens:

Mojo says let's head over toward that cottage.
Mojo winks suggestively.

At which time, another player could type in a response, which might look something like this:

Paks notices the cottage in the distance and grins knowingly.

Once inside the cottage, Paks and I begin to act upon the desires we have expressed for each other. I kiss her hand, gently, and glide up her arm. With the stroke of a key, she strips slowly and seductively. As battle cries and paging requests methodically appear on screen, Paks and I roll around on the four-poster bed that appears out of mutual consent. My body gives in to this interactive, text-based arousal, and it is all I can do to keep my fingers on the keyboard. Paks unzips her pants; my tongue meets her breasts. When we finally sign off, I am astounded by the "aftersex glow" that meets me in the bathroom mirror.

In this text-based realm, participants must write the self. No longer a matter of physical attributes, identity is made intelligible through the art of self-performance. And "self" in this realm is anything but fixed; it is as multiple as the imagination, unstable and infinitely "morphable." A simple "change description" command puts identity reconfigurement at your fingertips.

To doubt the intensity of experience on a MUD is simply not to have ever been on one. I recall one of my early MUD experiences when I happened across a participant named Trance. Trance was hanging out on the Terrain of Postmodernism and I decided to teleport there directly. We struck up a conversation, "So how's the weather here on the terrain?" and shortly thereafter, teleported to Trance's own corner of the MUD, a replica of California's Bay Area.

Upon arrival, Trance and I were presented with several directional choices. I chose to go north, up to the Berkeley Hills. I may have been sitting in my shabby New York City apartment at the time, but that night I was consciously in California. It felt so nice to be outside on a cool, autumn evening, listening to Trance tell me all about growing up in Berkeley. Things were very lucid. I became chilled and hugged my sweatshirt tightly, glad that I had remembered to bring it along. Trance shivered, too, and I moved closer to this strangely familiar figure sitting next to me.

On another occasion, a friend and I decide to stretch our sexual imaginations. Both of us share a certain fascination with gay men, a curiosity I have found to occur among more and more lesbians that I know. We want to experience gay male sex, and set off for a MUD to do so. Logging on as Jamie and Mr. Benson, we travel around on another MUD, donning leather, chains, and a dog collar for me. My description reads:

> A small, frail boy whose unbuttoned shirt reveals a shiny chest. His moves are tentative, and he coughs slightly as you gaze at him.

I enjoy being a helpless boy being led around by an older, stronger, demanding master. When I first log on to this unfamiliar MUD, greetings and directions buzz across my screen, causing an alphabet of chaos. I attempt to find Mr. Benson but keep getting lost in empty rooms with no obvious exits. I send out a page command. It works and I receive a message from Mr. Benson telling me that he is on his way to get his boy. I feel safe, about to be rescued from my confusion. Our cybersexplay, which takes place in an old woodshed, is an exploration of newfound needs and desires engendered by our gay male personas. The sex is about blow-jobs, erections, anal stimulation, none of which have ever been a part of my sex life before. Such acts either hadn't occurred to me or weren't anatomically conducive. But in cyberspace, I really feel like a gay man: the desire is "instinctual," the performance "natural."

My cybersex encounters aren't always an extension of a real-life erotic encounter, nor do they always fit into a gay or lesbian sensibility. When I meet Trance again (whose "real-life gender" I do not know), we decide to buy some X on Telegraph Avenue and teleport back to Trance's home, a tripper's pad complete with shaggy rug and lots of candles. We take the drug, and the words that appear on my screen tell me that things are beginning to take on a very tactile quality. Trance puts on techno-beat, and I feel the undulating rhythm, matched by the flickering disco lights that now appear. Trance has programmed a beautiful rave, and I decide then that I want Trance to be a man. I type my desires, "Mojo places a hand on your broad chest, just to see what it feels like," and he bends down and kisses my lips.

The success of this encounter with Trance inspired me to pose as "Sassy Chick" on the lookout for "hot guys." I love to cruise around in cyberspace wearing a tight-fitting striped T-shirt, hip-hugger jeans, and platform Pumas. I am assailed with friendly greetings and choose to answer only those whose descriptions meet my aesthetic qualifications: those who match the "Patrick Swayze type." As Sassy Chick, I am young and spontaneous, unaware of my own seductive powers. I love to picture myself in the arms of some big muscled, sensitive type, and it's the ones who look sweetly into my eyes that get my blood racing.

Cyberspace is different from other kinds of erotically charged mediums because it is interactive. In order to engage in cyber-sex, you must actively write, create, and present a self. And when this cyberspace self becomes the vehicle for real-life arousal, what you think of as your "real-life self" becomes im-plicated in whatever sexuality you experience on-line. Even if this cyberspace self is entirely fantastical, such as my *Sassy* Chick persona, there is always some kind of "real self" that is implicated insofar as you believe you had a role in deciding which fantasy persona to take on—which fantasy self would enable the typing self to get aroused. As the sites and sources of erotic stimulation stretch beyond the confines of your famil-iar sexuality, you begin to question, what is sexuality, and who am I?

From these on-line exploits, I have learned that my sexual-ity has much less to do with the sex of my partner and much more to do with the art of desire itself. Cyberspace is a non-physical realm; nothing can be seen, felt, or heard. Erotics, then, is a matter of words, not bodies. I am turned on by mere descriptions—"a well-worn leather belt," "a sharp jawline that accentuates her firm lips"—and by text that signifies actions, intentions, feelings, and physiques, not by actions, intentions, feelings, and physiques themselves. When Mr. Benson whacked me with a wooden spoon, it was not an actual spoon which got me off, but indeed, the representation of a spoon.

There has been much discussion about honesty and moral-ity in connection with "gender passing" on-line, about the need to know people for "who they are." But had my friend Trance lied about being from the Bay Area, would there have been any cause for concern? Trance talked like someone from Berkeley, and the replica felt like the Bay Area to me. My time spent with him had a great deal of meaning to me, which simply would not be lost if Trance turned out to be what some cyberspace participants call an "identity predator."

I think that the hype about gender deceit, framed as genuine concern about being lied to, is largely about the fear of being confronted with the fact that one's sexuality is not as well-defined and unambiguous as one may have thought. There is a fear of being lulled into a "false sexuality"—of falling for someone whose "real gender" turns out to be the same as someone who considers himself or herself to be strictly heterosexual, or the opposite of someone who considers himself or herself to be homosexual. Gender play on-line, whether intentional or a matter of an inaccurate assumption, is not just a matter of crossing over from one gender to the other. Given the possibility for participants to experience very real sexual feelings that supposedly contradict one's gender, cybersex questions the very *idea* that gender and sexuality are physically grounded in the first place.

Thus, it is absurd not only to think of gender as true or false, but to think of gender at all or to assume that there exists a set of stable characteristics that are determined by one's anatomy and that in turn determine one's sexuality. Indeed, the anxiety of gender bending on-line is not simply about the fear of deception, it is also about the fear of chaos and ambiguity.

There has never been a place for ambiguity when it comes to politics. My friend Mary Beijan was not thinking about ambiguity when she became my first feminist hero by chucking a raw chicken leg into the lap of the *Playboy* representative in search of women for the "Girls of the Big 10" edition. "Here," she screamed at the rep, after going through the entire selection process. "Because it's raw meat you want, you bastard!" There was nothing ambiguous about marching in Washington to demand my right to choose, or confronting that horrible man in the shopping mall whose T-shirt rejoiced that "AIDS kills fags . . . Dead."

But when it comes to identity politics, certainty has had a frustrating, if not dooming, effect. What happens when the identity politics that bring about effective, issue-oriented struggle begin to break down? When we realize that not all women think alike, and that differences such as class and race can no longer be sutured over by the "certainty" of a common gender? That any kind of identity, no matter if it is an identity of resistance, is also a creation of boundaries? How to act when we realize that to fight AIDS we must fight homophobia, and to fight homophobia we must fight racism, and so on. We face a choice between focusing our energies on one issue or acting with the knowledge that oppression is interrelated and pursuing a more broad-based, but perhaps more indirect, approach. And (here's where it really gets difficult) how to fight those underlying power structures once we've learned that we too are *part* of those structures?

Can there be such a thing as a politics of ambiguity—a politics that recognizes we must learn how to negotiate ourselves on a terrain in which, as Cornel West articulates, everything is ungrounded, even the notion that everything is ungrounded? What would this kind of politics have to offer someone whose experience of pain and discrimination is very well grounded indeed, as mine was as a self-loathing nineteen-year-old? How does this understanding of the constructedness of identity help when, artificial or not, these identity distinctions are in fact imposed and used as a means to oppress and discriminate?

An encounter I had on an airplane with a career military officer shed unexpected light on these questions. After inquiring about the paperback she was reading, our conversation drifted into the ever-popular subject of gays in the military. I'm somewhat ambivalent about the issue: I'm against the discrimination, but not willing to devote a great deal of energy fighting for access to an institution whose activities I usually condemn. In high school, I had dreamed of being in ROTC. That was before I came out, and when I still believed in things like absolute good and evil. Despite my ideological differences, my fascination with the military was still intact, and I really enjoyed talking with the lieutenant. She told me that West Point had given her a top-notch free education and a good career. I was very impressed, and she had my respect. West Point, wow, she must be a really good athlete, too.

Then we started to talk politics. The lieutenant believed that the rigid environment necessary for an effective military would be disrupted by the presence of homosexuals. Sexual tension and sexual activities would break up the discipline, she argued. "Yeah, but how do you ever know for sure who's a homosexual?" I asked. "And anyway, all of those men and women having sex in the Gulf weren't given dishonorable discharges. If we lived in a society in which we were comfortable with all kinds of sexual relationships, would same-sex attraction still be a disruption?"

"Maybe not," she replied, "but right now, society isn't comfortable with it and so it is a disruption."

"But wasn't that the same argument for excluding black people from the military?"

As an African-American in the military herself, she thought that was an interesting point. "Yes, there is a similarity there," she acknowledged.

I said that as a white person, when I first came out, it had never occurred to me that gay people could be black too. "Isn't that weird? I mean, there I was in college and I totally equated gayness with whiteness. I guess because I had never met or seen a black person that I knew to be gay. I saw a sign up in one of the dorms for a black lesbian support group and it really took me by surprise. I wondered whether there could be more than one woman like this on campus, or whether the woman who put up the poster was just looking for a date."

The lieutenant laughed and looked startled. "You know," she said, "I completely understand what you just said. Up until this moment, gay people were always white to me too. But that makes no sense."

Somehow, during the course of this interaction, we identified with each other. Though I find myself politically at odds with the military, that didn't prevent me from admiring the lieutenant's poise and the power of her stripes. And she told me it was fascinating to talk with someone like me who had spent so much time "thinking about things." I think we could talk because, for a moment, we let go of the contours between us, the identities that had always kept us apart, and just let things be a little fuzzy.

A politics of ambiguity requires that the fronts of activism be rethought to broaden the definition of social change. Improved standards of living, freedom, liberation—these causes need not be fought for, demanded, and expressed in the form of one kind of politics. Social change is not just about the kind of political action brought about by group action. Politics is also interpersonal—about how we talk to each other and how we relate to one another when there is no group to call out our names.

There will always be a need to label—categorization is fundamental to our understanding of our world. But if we understand that such categories are dynamic ones, based not on transcendental truths but on the cultural forces of a particular place and time, then perhaps we can acquire the agility and flexibility needed to keep those categories fluid and open to future articulations.

There are differences among those we think of as the same, and similarities among those we think of as different. When we speak to each other, it is not as simple as a clash of identities. Just like on the MUD, we do in fact know each other in many ways. To embrace this complexity, to accept the ambiguity of the human experience, is to understand that what we think of as "self" and what we think of as "other" actually need one another to exist. To understand this is to look at "difference" and not judge.

Cyberspace, with its anonymity and nonphysical presence, no more masks the "truth" of identities like race or gender than visible signs like skin color and anatomy prove it. Identity, no matter how concrete the experience, is always constructed, never innate. To realize this fluidity is to understand that we are all different and the same. Accepting this ambiguity is not a political end in itself, but it may be a precondition to long-standing liberation. Accepting ambiguity can provide the agility to make sense of a chaotic world without relying on an oppressive system of static categories, and it may also provide the faith to connect.

The author would like to thank Rachel Gold and Kate Griffin for their contributions, and would like to acknowledge the work of Sandy Stone, which has greatly influenced this article.

She Came with the Rodeo (an excerpt)

lisa jones

i come with a dowry. four boxes of props, most nota-
bly a construction hat, plastic pork chops, and several unused
diaphragms poked with holes. Two boxes of costumes, among
them a half-dozen pairs of black leggings well worn at the
crotch. One box of faded press releases announcing the Rodeo
Caldonia High-Fidelity Performance Theater. An album of
photographs showing young women outfitted as urban witch
doctors in faux-leopard skirts, lace veils, and the occasional
cowrie-shell ankle bracelet. A black leather motorcycle jacket
bought brand new for twenty dollars from a junkie on Astor
Place—its side pockets now caked with bits of Jolly Rancher

watermelon candy and missed birth control pills, its breast pocket permanent home to a small tin of rum raisin lip gloss, a New York City subway token from 1986, and a crumbled copy of the last page of Shange's *Spell #7*. The play's final line is circled in red: "crackers are born with the right to be alive/I'm making ours up right here in your face/& we gonna be colored & love it."

I am a Caldonia and these are some of my personal effects.

We decided against the Warm Leatherettes and took Caldonia, fancying the inheritance of B.B. King and sundry blues songs that told of "hardheaded" brown girls with pretty lips. Caldonia, B.B. sings, why is your big head so hard? A rodeo brought folks together to stir up dust. Shange herself had moved to Texas and was riding bareback. We were impressed. Rodeo Caldonia, it was. Twelve women, sometimes more, in our twenties and giddy with our own possibility. We were gonna do theater. Performance pieces we were calling them. We didn't care much about genres and structures and things. Our need was to get out in public and act up; to toss off the expectations laid by our genitals, our melanin count, and our college degrees. Rodeo heralded our arrival; young, gifted, black, and weird (so we thought), and in search of like souls.

We splurge on a cab to carry props. Me, Celina, Derin, and our caravan of shopping bags and backpacks. First stop at a drugstore to buy spray paint and Tampax, then to Sweetwaters to do "Carmella & King Kong" in the basement. We have nerve to knock egos with R&B supper-club legend Arthur Prysock. His people get mad at us for taking up too much dressing-room space. In the hallway we run lines as the guests arrive. Suited-up black folks from the upstairs, up-class Sweetwaters come watch our show, along with our dread and Lycra friends from downtown. The Uptowns snicker and squirm. But we are hardly studying them; this is for us. After the show Prysock's henchmen ban us from the dressing room, so we gather instead in the tiny ladies john. Wasn't Sandye's eye rolling absolutely brilliant? How did Candace manage to give La Josephine and valley girl all at once? We are the most beautiful women in the world. Art, says Nan Goldin, is about leaving a record no one can revise. We are not thinking of hereafters. Art is how we love ourselves now.

For such a grand name, Rodeo Caldonia High-Fidelity Performance Theater, we had a small repertoire: two theater pieces written by me, "Carmella & King Kong" and "Combination Skin," and one poetry revue, "Welcome to the Black Aesthetic," that never made it to the stage, though was quite the out-of-body spiritual experience to rehearse. Probably our most significant contribution to the world of performing arts was us roaming the streets as a pack, showing up at parties, and talking race, sex, and hair into the night over Celina's barbecue wings and Donna's guacamole. A kind of traveling conceptual art piece on black female representation, in which Diana Ross's whine matters as much as Mary McLeod Bethune's institution building.

We are smart-ass girls with a sense of entitlement, who avail ourselves of the goods of two continents, delight in our sexual bravura, and live womanism as pleasure, not academic mandate. Ten years earlier, when most Caldonias were just graduating junior high, Shange had told black women to find

God in themselves. We are the prodigal daughters come home to roost. Lots of lip and shorter hemlines.

A cherished keepsake of Rodeo is that it was, without premeditation on our part, a walking tableau of diva complexity. Each eccentric self and artistic point of departure—from the composer of fabulist slow jams (Derin) to the collard Marilyn (Candace)—made possible one's own. We didn't come together around a rigid ideology or fixed notion of black identity. We came simply to break bread and share our yearnings. And in this common space, each found her own voice, her own funk.

With Rodeo I was able to dig out that voice my sister Kellie was so certain I had. It surprised me when I did find it. It is a laughing voice, impudent, at times even sinister. Not at all, some say when they meet me, like me: a short girl who is polite to old people and painfully shy. In the company of the Caldonias I become a rogue. Our call and response is lusty and loud. I begin to write thinking of Rodeo as my audience, not, as I had done before, the gray bosses at work, gray professors at university, gray poets of the textbooks. This frees me, I feel at the time, to say and do anything.

Talk about blue lights in the basement. We were witnesses tonight. Saw this power hovering above, we actually saw it. A blue magnetic field. Freaky-deaky. A visit from ancestresses or something. Alva, as Carmella, and Sandye, as Torch Singer, took the spirit and rocked. Had a table reserved for Gramma and Aunt Cora. They got stuck in Jersey traffic and missed the show. Sweetwaters agreed to let us do the entire thing all over again just for Gramma. Must've been her silver Afro and the way she strut into the joint like it was a meeting of the Phillis

Wheatley Literary Society. I did hide behind the bar while Derin and Amber, as Beautietta and the Twilights, set up the voodoo pyre with those diaphragms next to that Alice Walker datebook and those plastic watermelon harmonicas, but Gramma and Aunt Cora laughed for days. Those Sweetwaters people must think we're très *weird. Our boyfriends don't comb their hair. Derin's running around calling herself the reincarnation of Lieutenant Uhura. Alva mainly stays to herself munching on blue corn chips and reading* Black Women in Nineteenth-Century American Life. *And there's Candace, always trying to sell the bartenders antique jewelry or Jamaican cupcakes, then getting onstage as Princess Pamela the restauranteuse in those polka-dot spike heels, waving plastic pork chops around and talkin' 'bout the affair she's having with Idi Amin.*

The Rodeo got taken to task for our humor and enjoyment of it. One memorable occasion was on a late-night talk-radio show. How dare we, the host was anxious to know, call a black male character King Kong? Had we forgotten how scorned black men were in America? How could we, as we did in the slides that accompanied "Carmella & King Kong," show photos of bare black breasts alongside Fannie Lou Hamer trudging through the southern dust? Was Pam Grier worthy of being named in the same breath as Coretta Scott King? There was this assumption that being black and a woman carried with it a responsibility to be dire and remorseful. Or mystical and abandoned. Or issuing proverbs from the rocking chair. You-all are having too good a time, said the stares we got from the host, you don't want folks to think you girls are hoes. As if there was no identity between that of the girl who wanted the bluest eyes and that of the grandmother who had learned to love her brown ones, except that of a ho.

Growing up, the Caldonias inhaled the parody so evident in blaxploitation flicks and saw, through the rose-colored glass of childhood, the Black Arts movement's celebration of everything Afroed and black. The renaissance of fiction by black women that dawned in the seventies, we caught that too. These books made us feel less invisible, though their stories were far from our lives as big-city girls; girls who took ballet and were carted off to Planned Parenthood in high school so as not to risk that baby that Mom, not Mama, warned would have "ruined our lives." College was expected. The southern ghosts of popular black women's fiction, the hardships and abuse worn like purple hearts, the clipped wings were not ours. We had burdens of our own. Glass ceilings at the office and in the art world, media and beauty industries that saw us as substandard, the color and hair wars that continued to sap our energy. We wanted to hear about these.

I travel to New Orleans. For sale, for sale, get your mammy figurines, for sale. Stout blackened women with red bubbles for lips and starched white aprons. No resemblance to my grandmother or great-aunt. Women with width, but women whose mothers made sure their baby girls never had to step foot in the big house with a rag and Murphy's Oil Soap ever again. CONTEMPORARY REPLICAS OF A BELOVED AMERICAN CLASSIC, *says the sign in the curio shop. I buy two. Back home I chop off their heads and put the torso mammies in a performance piece.*

• • •

There was talk in 1986 of the arrival of a new way of looking at the world by young black artists. The new black aesthetic it was called by those who christened it, namely Trey Ellis and Greg Tate, and those who spread the word such as Michele Wallace and Henry Louis Gates, Jr. This aesthetic was described as being wide enough to contain everything from Spike Lee's Hollywood-financed dramedies, to Lorna Simpson's photo-text and its landscape of female symbols, to the revamping of the classics by Armani-clad jazzbos who had no use for the avant garde, to hip hop's deification of Malcolm. It was said to embrace, among other things, irreverence, profit-making, an elastic view of "black" art, ideas of integration and nationalism, a yen for tradition (or at least the apparel), and the usual questions about who we are and where is our home. Rodeo was named as one of the upstarts of this aesthetic. Such a lofty goal was the furthest thing from our minds back then, I can testify. Though reflecting on those performances of ours—really rites of self-discovery staged in supper-club basements, church sanctuaries, and bars—it's clear to me that our take on blackness and femaleness did trumpet the cultural explosion that followed.

Two photographs of Rodeo, one that appeared in *High Performance,* a magazine covering performance art, and one in *Interview,* scorched through the available portraits of black women and caused a stir at the time, this being 1987. In the *Interview* photo we pose in party dresses from the fifties and African-print lapas. Alva holds a flower. Lorna wears glasses. We are not selling sex or pain, but we are sensual. Our skin color variations make a lush fresco, and our jumble of hair textures and styles is throwing curveballs at correctness. There we are, breathing intelligence, mischievousness, and triumph. There's also something pampered about us and fancy-free. We're not career girls or call girls or Bess or Beulah. We seem to be urban intellectual bohemians or art-school grads or some such diva. Miles from naturalistic. In 1987 this was still a brand-new image. Had young black women been presented this way before in the mainstream? Apparently not.

Julie Dash called. She was in preproduction for a film called *Daughters of the Dust* and wanted Alva Rogers as her lead. Cinematographer Arthur Jaffa was equally spellbound. There were calls from Hollywood agents and production companies. Letters from young bohemians from Iowa to Teaneck. We become a metaphor for a new generation by standing in front of a camera and being ourselves, with a little stardust courtesy rags from Donna's bottomless closet. In the *Interview* photo, I am wearing a red silk bathrobe. A white baby doll is pinned to my temple like one of Billie's gardenias. (Who knows what look I was going for—Lady Day reincarnated as a womanist kitchen-table surrealist playwright?) I remember the day well. After the photo session the Caldonias walked around downtown, where we continued to act out and take photos of ourselves. Look at us, we were saying, acknowledge us, commit us to memory.

We help Derin move the rest of her stuff from her mom's place in Brooklyn to her new studio in Sugar Hill. She swears to us she lives underneath the legendary actress Butterfly McQueen, who may be mad and may zoom around her apartment all day on roller skates. Derin's man is up in the loft bed writing songs on acoustic guitar. Derin and I go stand in line for fish sand-

wiches. Fish "sangwiches" remind me of fried whiting in New-
ark. "Fried whitey," as it was called, which you ate with ice-
cold watermelon. While Rodeo rehearses, sometimes I think of
Papa B. of Sterling Street, Spirit House, and the Spirit House
Movers; of Papa B. rehearsing plays in the theater on the first
floor of his house, Spirit House. How a dozen of us, adults and
children, piled into a broom closet one night to record sound
effects for Slaveship. *Recreating the entire Middle Passage in a*
broom closet. I was not more than seven, but I remember
women crying and men moaning and someone holding me very
tight, as if the ship and the water that Papa B. had told us to
imagine were right here. I remember a flood of terror. The
shackles and chains. The heave of the ship. The rocking.

Rodeo connected with black men who knew our art was
women-centered and were drawn to it for just that reason. One
night at Sweetwaters Sandye Wilson, who played Torch Singer
in "Carmella & King Kong," thanked Greg Tate for hanging.
He had not come to lift props or lend some cliché version of
emotional support; he was there to dig the art. Tate came every
weekend of our run, along with other male artists-in-arms. It
meant a great deal to have black men respond to the work. I
was excited by the possibility of belonging to a community of
artists where women and men could engage each other's minds
with candor and the assumption of equality. Given the hostility
divide in black literary circles, stoked to boiling point by the
media, such an alliance seemed all the more meaningful.
Though Rodeo and the male artists we moved with never did
realize this community in any organized way, there was definitely an exchange of ideas going on, and a potent one.

The Caldonias were in relationships with men who were

anything but "sitcom brothers." Young schemers like us, they were conversant in black politics and culture and had passed on job security for creative freedom. They too were exploring "out" texts of blackness—from minstrelsy to the dread hard-core of Bad Brains. Though I chose woman as my primary subject, these brothers hit me with a challenge to make art that could also upend stock effigies of black men. Arguing, busting up, chowing down, and partying with these guys, I often felt during those days that the brother-sister thang glorified in black folk talk was a genuine, nourishing part of my life.

I squint at the mirror. All my life I felt I was too big down there. I always covered up. Now I have calf muscles from climbing flights of stairs to the subway, to my apartment on the fifth floor, to work, carrying props, journals, cameras, but still hips and still ass. Show that butt, wear tighter clothes, flaunt those hips, Donna says. It's Donna who dresses us and tells us how fab we look. Alva does our hair. These two roommates know all the beauty secrets for black girls. Use this. Don't use that. Their elaborate rituals at the quest of beauty amaze us. They take this very seriously. Like Madame C.J. inventing a wider-tooth hot comb. You will love yourselves by any means necessary.

The portrayal of feminism as some sort of game sport of man hating or pulpit of crunchy-granola correctness has always read to me like some impossibly cartoonist send-up. It remains so far from the feminism that I have lived, particularly the one I knew in Rodeo. I'd count Rodeo as my defining feminist experience, even though I've been calling myself the f-word since high school. In Rodeo, I learned that feminism was to me, stripped to its intimate essentials, a passion for the creative culture of women and a belief that communion with other women was a bread and water necessity. Outside of debates on employment rights, abortion, child care, and whether feminism serves women of color—and the other big politics of the movement—what has kept me interested in feminism and *identifying* is the pleasure. The pleasure in women's voices, our dozens, our ways of caring and getting mad, and above all, in the way we love deeply. As some call it, *hard*.

Give me a girl gang, a crew. A zillion sisters ain't enough. To be a girl among girls, I feel as if I am at the height of courage and creativity. As an adult I am continually trying to re-create these spaces of safety and unconditional love. Like my grandmother's house, where Gramma, Aunt Cora, and Mom addressed the world's ills with a little Johnnie Walker Red and a clean dishrag. Like Mom taking her daughters out of the city in her geriatric car, us three singing love songs from the forties like belles of the ball. Like the We Waz Girls Together Off-Campus Collective at Renee, Myra, and Maria's, where we took character names from black women's fiction and imagined ourselves divas of myth. Renee was Willy Chilly, after the Wild Child of *Meridian;* let Desdemona keep stepping. Like Rodeo.

Lorna Simpson's photographs are in museums across the country now. Amber Villanueva is a rap star. Pamala Tyson was an Ikette in *What's Love Got to Do with It?* The Jones twins' crossbreed of theater and music, "be-bop muzak," can be seen around New York. Derin Young just got back from Japan, touring with French pop star Vanessa Paradis. She's gigging now with her own band in Parisian nightclubs. Alva Rodgers is workshopping her play with music, *The Bride Who Became*

Frightened When She Saw Life Open, and studying toward a masters in musical theater. Raye Dowell is living and working in L.A. Donna Berwick designs costumes for film. Celina Davis is still directing. Kellie Jones' exhibition "Malcolm X: Man, Ideal, Icon" is touring the country. Candace Hamilton, the relentless romantic, found love, made a baby, and now runs a small press with her husband. Sandye Wilson is writing plays and acting in New York. We never officially disbanded, just moved on. I went off to film school, a trade mill that frowned on the word "art," a drastic change from the feel-it, do-it aesthetic of Rodeo. The trade mill succeeded in convincing me not to trust that voice of my own, so recently found. Eventually I did get her back and I don't plan on letting her go any time soon.

There are times when I mourn Rodeo's passing on. Our grand schemes still beg to be realized. Imagine if we had launched, as we dreamed, an institution or two: a center to finance and stage work by black women in the theater arts regardless of waves of commercial interest, a multimedia production complex devoted to collaborations between African-American women across disciplines. Or think of what we could have done just as a theater collective, touring the country as ambassadors of kitchen-table surrealism, hauling our conceptual art piece on black female representation around the world. If we had gone national, Greg Tate is sure we could have done for womanism what Public Enemy did for black nationalism—made it pop. The next generation of Caldonias will have to take up that flag. Perhaps the young women of hip-hop, groups like T.L.C., have already begun.

• • •

Tonight's our reunion. We sit around 'til late (not so late this time) talking about days present and past, over Donna's guacamole and Celina's wings. Everyone's radiant and full of gossip. I ask for old Rodeo stories. Celina, C. as we call her, goes first. Hers is about our gig at Blackbyrds, a little bar downtown that's long gone. Some young white gentlemen were using the stage as a chaise lounge. Our show was going up in an hour, but they weren't moving. I had arrived first and they flat ignored me. C. came next; they weren't having her either. The two of us sat there all frustrated with these white gentlemen. But soon the other Caldonias floated in. Just these women setting up slide projectors, throwing clothes, fixing hair, talking about last night's date and who would come to the show let loose a stream of energy that swept the white gentlemen off the stage; which is what spirit bound together should do, move mountains or, as here, molehills. After C.'s account, there's silence around the table. C. lets the silence lie. After a while she says, "That's my story."

My dowry: a motorcycle jacket and a mammy doll missing its head. Plastic pork chops and New Orleans amulets. Diane's whine, Josephine's wiggle, the roll of Nina Mae's eyes, Fredi's demons, Bessie's stomp, Billie's fruit, Adrienne's ghost, Julia's wig box, Pam Grier's gun, Shange's God. A Caldonia girl. Swollen with dreams, fearless and fine. I came with the Rodeo.

Congratulations, It's a Girl

amruta slee

some time ago i came across a photograph of my mother taken on her wedding day in Bombay, India. Jasmine blossoms trailed from the hair piled on top of her head, a heavily embroidered sari fluttered around her body. She looked very young, exotic, and a little unreal; a paradigm of compliant Asian womanhood. Beside her my father beamed, to her left my grandfather looked on with the kind of unconditional approval he would never display toward her again.

I take this photo out and stare at this earlier, foreign incarnation of someone I grew up with. When I remember my mother it is in active poses—reigning over parties in some impossibly glamorous outfit, her cigarette held aloft or striding purposefully through the living room when her eye lights on a stray sweater or book lying where it shouldn't: "Is that part of the decoration?" On warm afternoons she would arrive home from work, mix herself a Campari and orange juice, and energetically tell her half-listening family what was wrong with the state of the world.

Fragments of her history floated through our conversations. Her father was the principal of a secular all-male school in Poona and in her youth she had studied alongside boys as one of them. She was a cocky girl, able in math and good with homework. At school she had met my father, a lapsed Muslim, and they married, producing two children, my brother and me.

Somewhere along the line the reality of being a wife and mother hit, dissolving the bright expectations good grades and a middle-class upbringing bring. She met another man, an Australian student, they fell in love, and from there, the legend goes, it was a short step to divorce, scandal, and a mixture of experiences I never fully grasped. When he went back to Australia, she lived on (literally) peanuts, unwilling to ask for help, until finally landing a job in advertising. She had left me and my brother while doing all this.

Eventually she would marry the Australian, my stepfather, and later, we—they, me, and my new little sister—would all go to live in Sydney. Later still, she would decide marriage was not for her and leave again, refusing alimony in the sort of proud, stubborn gesture which characterized her life.

Her second divorce coincided with a long period of unemployment in which she would swing between elation when she landed some freelance journalism and black despair at the prospect of another week without a job. We were the single-mother-on-welfare family of stereotype. I saw it in terms of not having new clothes or not being able to go on as many holidays as other kids and reasoned we could always ask my father for money. She saw it as a bid for economic independence and clearly hoped to get us out of it herself, without reliance on the monetary transactions marriage symbolized for her. We could never understand each other.

She died when I was eighteen and we were beginning, at long last, to see each other as human beings, pulling against one another but inextricably linked. I missed my chance to ask all the crucial questions and so I look at the figure in the wedding photograph and wonder where it all came from—the instinctive chafing against female restriction—and what my life would have been if she had not taken the first step and then another and another.

At dinner parties people turn to me and ask about the Oppression of Third World women, their voices expressing proper concern and pity. Perhaps I'm wrong but I think what they envision is a series of snapshots; brown-skinned creatures kneel at the feet of the patriarch, shift a child from breast to hip, stir pots, smile and dance in contented, swaying movements. Part of me wants to acknowledge the truth in the image. The other part wants to say, "Forget it." Were I not a piece of a different trajectory maybe I too would look and see all women as the one woman accepting her fate without question, but as it is, that is not my story.

Childhood figures in my memory as a blur of sunny days and bales of hay ready to be leapt off. I ran barefoot around the mango farm my father owned in Bombay with a gang comprising mainly boys—the girls we knew were older. We were a restless lot, exploring the corners and nooks of the property, which dutifully yielded surprises—once I hit a shuttlecock into a hole in a tree and found it lying in the belly of a snake that had curled up there for a sunbath. To each other we displayed the wounds, scratches, and scars earned in the long-running mock battle that was our favorite game. We read voraciously of Viking and Greek myths and pored over a book called *Man Eaters of Bengal.* In the soothing light of day we ran about slaying the ferocious beasts of fiction. My father, a vague, smiling man, raised beautiful roses and mangoes and observed our activities from afar.

I was five when my mother reappeared in my life with a new family, an Australian husband and a baby sister. I had no recollection of her and understood hazily that she had been in some other country and was now going to take me with her. We weighed each other up, neither of us too impressed by what we saw. She decided I needed to begin wearing shoes, brushing my hair, and going to school. I suspected she was the wicked stepmother of countless fairy stories, come to distract me from my real goal as a world-famous adventurer.

We moved, soon after, to Sydney. Neighbors welcomed us, cooking up strangely lurid yellow curries in an attempt to alleviate homesickness, and the kids at my school asked why I didn't have a red dot on my forehead. We were "New Australians" in polite conversation, "wogs" in others, with the kind of benign racism middle-class comfort allows. No one could pronounce our names—my mother, Shubha, was addressed in the diminutive as "Shoob."

During my early teens my mother became obsessed by women's lib; she would hustle my sister and me off to marches where we shouted ourselves hoarse about liberation, and self-defense courses where we grappled with pretend rapists in the form of punching bags. The books that appeared on the shelves were by Kate Millett and Germaine Greer, the women coming to our house smoked feverishly and discussed divorce and men and jobs and money.

To me it was all common sense. I retained my pre-pubescent mistrust of girl-ness and had little patience with the vapid crap I saw women doing in the media compared with what I saw them doing in real life. In movies, women walked down dark alleyways into the arms of mass murderers. In advertisements, girlish Moms thrilled over their sparkling windows. I had begun as Thor, King of the Heavens, and wound up as this?

In social science class we drew women in India carrying pots of water on their heads home from the village well, and, alternatively, doe-eyed princesses lying on ruby-encrusted palanquins. Gazing at the pictures I decided I must be Australian since I had nothing in common with these things. Heroines came from the pages of books like *Gone with the Wind* and *Girls Own Annual* in which spunky women rescued their family from dire poverty, averted train crashes, and invented earth-changing gadgets all the while looking terrific. The only trouble was, they weren't Indian. This was a bind about which I spent considerable time thinking.

Boys were becoming strangers. It was unclear whether we wanted to kiss or wrestle. My boyfriend told me he no longer liked Suzi Quatro, the singer. I asked why, he said, "She says she's a feminist."

I felt like a foreigner in my sex. My sister, less of a tomboy, wriggled into skin-tight cocktail dresses and winkle-picker heels in a mean imitation of Diana Ross. She and her girl-friends giggled as they dressed and made up, then they would go out on the town with ferocious determination. The detritus of femininity, its fluff and floss, was fascinating, but it seemed safer cloaked behind jeans and sneakers where my looks met with less scrutiny. It took me years to trust lipstick, putting it on seemed like a betrayal of my former self, wearing it meant people would notice I was a girl. This meant I would have to act a certain way, to pout and look alluring, maybe to run my fingers through my hair, that was what girls did. I practiced these moves in front of the mirror and couldn't even convince myself.

On my first trip back to India at age fifteen, I hoped to find a country of people who looked like me, anonymity from the constant spotlight of living in a country of pink and gold skins. It wasn't quite like that. Everywhere I went with short hair, a sleeveless T-shirt, and a scathing contempt for caste systems, I created the effect of a Martian landing on earth. "Miss, you're English?" people asked in the street as I walked by. They confirmed what I had long believed, that despite the color of my skin and the race of my family, it was true I was not authentic in any sense.

I had a guilty feeling of being Westernized, not just by clothes and accent, but by some indefinable meshing of attitudes. The women I met were on their way to medical school or economics degrees. We would smile at each other and make small talk but we had little in common beyond having been born in the same country. The etiquette of another culture—mine—seemed at once close and out of reach. I felt loud and clumsy, stumbling about conversations, groping for points of departure.

My grandmother, sari-clad, walked about the school grounds she lived on. She was small and peppery, alternately reprimanding me in a theatrical way and bestowing affection via enormous meals—she watched me eat and complained how little it was no matter what. My accent reduced her to fits of laughter, and for entertainment, she would make me repeat the names of Australian friends, shrieking over Gretchen or Susie. I didn't think about her life, she was my grandmother; she couldn't make sense of mine. Sometimes, unexpectedly, we would click. When I was older I visited them with my then boyfriend, a medical student. She asked, unable to remember his name, "Will you marry the doctor?" I said I didn't think I'd get married, maybe even, (!), not have children. I waited for the usual barrage of warnings; instead she nodded in perfect understanding.

My family did not go in for sentiment. We talked about ourselves in sporadic bursts, unwilling to commit to any one thing, and avoided each other's lives. There was little time for conversation. My grandmother looked after other people; she went around the country visiting the old boys from my grandfather's school, read a lot, took tea with the teachers, and at night would rub the body lotion my mother sent her from Australia onto her feet. That is all I know about her, it never occurred to me to ask for more.

Back in Sydney, university held the promise of burgeoning women's groups. At one meeting the leaders declared we would bar all men except those who were black or Asian. I could not decide what to make of this statement and since there were no other Asians or blacks in the group, it went undiscussed.

Images of women were changing in magazines and on television, now they wore business suits and made important decisions, and it looked like the right direction to be going in. I started work and discovered a minefield. You could be aggressive but not too aggressive, if you thought someone was dumber than you it was a good idea not to show it, you curbed your irritation at the small slights and hostilities and learned your limitations quickly. Some of the constant anxiety was due to the kind of thing I had learned about and read from my mother and her friends; it came under headings like sexism and discrimination and racism but there was something else, too, and it was less easy to define. I felt the walls of the office in which I worked close in on me like a chicken coop—outside lay the lure of the unknown, but in here, here was what we had all fought for: a desk, a nameplate on the door, a chance to lunch with the big boys.

The options offered to me were a career and motherhood or marriage and motherhood, and there was no third road. The questions were perpetual—what to do with the legacies inherited in lives which were too short—but they had the feeling of having been decided for me a long time ago. In daydreams I craved experiences, I couldn't say what they were, but they had little to do with climbing to the top of corporate ladders. They hinged on boats floating seamlessly over still water, novels effortlessly written, or the tinkle of piano music in the background as I stepped onto a balcony, brilliant thoughts in my head, dressed in an outfit by . . .

Occasionally I feel my life careen and spin. Thoughts I don't want to think, fantasies I want no part of get inside my brain and make me long for a tradition to be part of, one that is safe and secure, a space I can fit safely into, a known destination. Words like *security* and *safety,* however, are tied up to terms like *wife* and *mother,* and the hard part is inventing a new picture. If I am not the person carrying water from the well, not the girl with a baby on her hip, not the woman with the briefcase and the portfolio, not quite this or quite that, then who am I?

My feminism is not the feminism of my mother—it starts from a different point and has traveled different routes. It is a bunch of circumstances in search of a shape and in its complex-ities it rejects the figures offered to it; the bland Superwoman, the babe with a gun, the vengeful bad girl, all of them too cartoonish to be of any value. I watch films, scan books and newspapers, looking always for the person I could be, looking for figures of Indian descent who lead messy lives, looking for women who tumble off the track, looking for reassurance and encouragement that things will work out to counteract a nig-gling uncertainty that they won't, looking for someone who looks a bit like me, thinks a bit like me.

This story is unlikely to be coming soon to my local Cineplex but there are signs it is a script in the process. In a New York newspaper I read about a woman from a village I'd never heard of in India. Her name is Phoolan Devi and she is a bandit queen who hid out in the forest with her band of ex-ploited laborers in an uprising against greedy landlords. Even-tually she turned herself in after negotiating a deal with the police in which she would be sent to jail but her gang went free. Once in prison, she decided her real mission was to win women their rightful place in society and she has become a crusader. She is in her twenties. A couple of years ago I inter-viewed an Indian novelist who created a sensation by writing pop books containing sex and greed and who fought with her editors for more money and fewer rewrites. She said she wanted to write about women she liked. In Bombay, a maga-zine profiled an uneducated woman who decided she was go-ing to take her husband to court for beating her. She defended herself, won, and became a national figurehead.

I follow these stories, their casual triumphs, their semi-happy endings, with giddy hopefulness. They function as a his-tory, reminding me where I came from and adding to my pan-theon of fictional and true-life heroines, a kind of family tree to which I belong. That these women broke out of their contexts is no less a part of their appeal than the fact that they did it out of an instinctual urge for freedom. Their lives fill in the blanks to all the lives I don't have—my mother's, my grandmother's—and they go some way toward explaining my own.

A Punjabi friend who grew up in London listened to me moan and groan about the lack of paths to follow, and after I'd finished she screwed up her face, tossed her hair, and said, "I don't need role models. I have myself." This is a phase I'd like to get to soon. But meanwhile I'm left to answer the questions that come up using a philosophy that is in itself a series of questions. My sister calls from Australia to announce she has given birth to a baby daughter, Della, and we argue about whether her child should have her last name or her boyfriend's or both, and finally, exasperated at what she sees as my rigid thinking on this, she points out that our last names, like every-one's, are handed down from fathers. I'm unconvinced, and she says snappily, "Should I call her Della X?" We both laugh. For a second the idea has appeal.

My mother's voice sounds in my head saying, "Yes, well that's quite enough about yourself." Simultaneously though, her voice urges me on to do all the things she and my grand-mother dreamed of doing, of self-definition and a chance to make stupid mistakes and change any rules which no longer apply. It doesn't clear everything up—there's still the worry of getting old too soon and of having spent too much time on the wrong things and of not being able to ever grow the perfect gardenia—but that voice helps in the moments when the road ahead looks wobbly.

Any day now I expect one of my nieces to bang on the front door, pint-size Doc Martens on her feet and a don't-mess-with-me attitude in her eyes. I picture her as calm and confident, unfazed by the past, prepared for the future, full of the breezy contradictions that make up her genealogy. Who knows what she'll be looking for, but when she arrives, I want to be ready for her.

Afterword

angela y. davis

i first learned that rebecca walker would be editing a new anthology on contemporary expressions of feminism shortly after she had organized a project that took a busload of 1990s freedom riders to the South to register people to vote and encourage their participation in the 1992 presidential election. Rebecca later told me about the intense discussions of the meaning and relevance of feminism that took place during the trip. I therefore assumed, without giving it further thought, that her book would deal more directly with possibilities of social activism in a period when activism seems to be a rarely trodden backroad obscured by a maze of crowded superhighways. She speaks directly to me in her introduction when she raises the questions, "What about the activism that people need to hear about? What about the expectations that this book will be an embodiment of what I seem to represent to the outside world: young feminist activism and organizing?"

I realize now that my preconceptions about the content of *To Be Real* . . . reflected my own need to have Rebecca identify the thinkers and organizers of her generation who would be able to furnish instant answers to questions many young people have posed to me as an "activist elder." When questions about the direction of contemporary social movements—or the lack thereof—are posed to me, my usual response is that such questions will have to be sorted out by young people, and not primarily on the level of contemplative theory but, rather, in the process of developing new strategies for political practices that weave together the last quarter-century's lessons about the intersections of gender, race, class, and sexuality. When young people have asked me about future prospects for youth activism—and long before I had seen any of the manuscript—I have on many occasions referred them to this book. "Some possible answers to your question(s) undoubtedly will be contained in Rebecca Walker's new book," I confidently assured them.

When I received the manuscript, my first instinct was to race through it in search of those answers I had promised others would find there. Once I slowed down and allowed the book to unfold in its own way, though, I began to realize that rather than providing answers to the usual questions, *To Be Real* . . . defiantly challenged the way certain questions are assumed to be the only possible—or the only important—ones.

Rebecca Walker has constructed a book that permits us to behold a mosaic of vastly different ways in which some of her generational peers attempt to come to terms with feminist consciousness. As she indicates in her introduction, this is not meant to be a book on contemporary feminist political theories and practices. Nor does it mean to carve out an agenda of struggle by identifying *the* issues that deserve the attention of political activists in the late 1990s. Rather, her book is a gathering of "introspective" voices examining their own personal histories for signs of feminist influence and evaluating the usefulness of what they identify as "feminism." Most of them forcefully resist what they consider to be obsolete and austere versions of feminism associated with preceding generations. (Of course, this sense of obsolescence and austerity is almost a necessary function of the passage of time.) Some of them lay claim to feminist consciousness even as they engage in rituals, careers, sexual practices, and cultural politics that they take to be decidedly "unfeminist" according to standards of second-wave feminism.

What I find most interesting about these stories is the way many of them imagine a feminist status quo. While their various imaginations often represent very different notions of what this feminist status quo might be, many of them agree that whatever it is, it establishes strict rules of conduct which effectively incarcerate individuality—desire, career aims, sexual practices, etc. Moreover, in seeking to dismantle this status quo and break free of its strictures, many of these writers attempt to work through their often complex relationships with the notion of social activism as responsibility by recalling embarrassing childhood experiences with radical mothers, or by rejecting the concept of "political correctness," which so often is assumed to be an activist posture.

As a member of an older generation associated with one or more versions of the feminist status quo under contestation, I feel obliged to try to understand these writers' positions, while simultaneously arguing for the same kind of nuanced vision of historical feminism that the anthology wants to apply to third-wave feminism. I want to join Danzy Senna in arguing for a vision of both historical and contemporary feminism(s) that recognizes the persistence of material conditions and power relations which privilege some feminisms while marginalizing or altogether dismissing others.

As one of many participants in earlier efforts to challenge a status quo based on class, gender, race, and sexuality, it is indeed exciting for me to witness the multiple transformations—at least in the realm of consciousness—that have occurred over the last quarter-century. Walker's anthology permits us a glimpse into the fragile institutionalization, for better or worse, of certain forms of feminist consciousness passionately fought for by women and men who hardly could have imagined that any version of feminism would ever be taken for granted by anyone. And while all of the contributors to this collection eagerly embrace feminism even as they contest it, many young people today would never openly associate themselves with the label "feminist," even though they live and understand their lives in ways others would not hesitate to call feminist.

One of the most powerful insights of second-wave feminism can be summarized in a principle that early on provoked a vast array of contentious responses from various vantage points outside the rather narrow circle then considered to encompass feminism. That principle is, of course, "the personal is political." As someone who initially found it difficult to reconcile what appeared to be a tautological equation of two realms in which very different kinds of oppression seemed to be at work, I must admit that I readily agreed with the one-dimensional argument that since male domination within a white domestic relationship differed substantively from state sponsorship of racism and class exploitation, the former was of secondary importance. Of course, differences *do* exist here; but, as Audre Lorde so consistently has declared, the terms of difference are not mutually exclusive. I find myself wishing that when I was her age, I had possessed Rebecca Walker's insight, as expressed in her introduction: "We fear that the identity will dictate and regulate our lives, instantaneously pitting us against someone, forcing us to choose inflexible and unchanging sides, female against male, black against white, oppressed against oppressor, good against bad." But I also find myself wishing that it were possible to apply her insight about "contradiction and ambiguity," about "using *and* much more than we use *either/or*," to our appreciation of historical feminism, as, for example, Gina Dent does in her stunning analysis of confessional, missionary feminism.

Some of us older folks discovered feminist possibilities while traveling down circuitous political roads that initially led us to declare ideological war against what we called "white middle-class feminism." Feminism became a possibility for us not because we decided to seek the comfort of a sisterhood without racial or class or sexual boundaries, but rather because we decided to stop playing the *either/or* game. At the same time, the emergence of new feminisms—Black feminism, women of color feminism (which, it must be noted, are not themselves monolithic)—often constructed the feminisms they railed against as the caricatures and stereotypes that we often use to represent adversaries. Of course, a retrospective vision facilitates such insights much more readily than a vision anchored in the quicksands of the present. And many of the stories in this anthology understandably are primarily concerned with the intersections of the immediacies of everyday consciousness and ideological representations of feminism: how to grapple with persisting patriarchal naming practices, with weddings and bachelor parties, sexual roles, musical preferences, career choices, and maternal desire.

What, in 1995, does it *mean* to be a feminist, anyway? With this anthology Rebecca Walker seeks to break the mold in which were forged many of the ideas about traditional feminism that prevail today. *To Be Real* . . . is a daring effort. Walker and many of her contributors recognize that anytime we challenge the "old school," we run the risk of treading dangerous turf. That is why those of us who strike out in search of change are so often subjected to harsh criticisms; it is understood that, whether we ultimately succeed or fail, something— quite possibly the future—is riding on the work we do.

Contributor Biographies

Allison Abner is a freelance writer, television producer, and the author of *Finding Our Way: The Teen Girls' Survival Guide.* She lives in New York City with her partner in parenthood and their son, Miles.

Jennifer Allyn received her master's in public policy from the Kennedy School of Government in 1994, and is now the Director of Development for The Coalition to Stop Gun Violence. **David Allyn** is a Ph.D. candidate in American history at Harvard University. He has contributed articles to *Tikkun* magazine and the *Washington Post.*

Anna Bondoc is a Filipina-American born in Manila in 1969, and raised in Cincinnati, Ohio. She makes her home in New York City where she has raised money for a young women's reproductive rights organization and served as fiction editor of the *Asian/Pacific American Journal.* In addition to working at the Children's Television Workshop, she pursues essay writing, baking without butter, and her fascination with all things Japanese.

Angela Y. Davis is a professor of History of Consciousness and recently was appointed Presidential Chair in African-American and Feminist Studies at the University of California, Santa Cruz. She is a member of the Board of Directors of the National Black Women's Health Project, and the author of numerous essays and articles. Her five books include *Women, Race & Class* and her forthcoming volume on Black women's music and social consciousness. Her next book project will focus on the criminal justice system.

Eisa Davis is a Berkeley, California, native whose articles, interviews, and reviews have appeared in hip-hop journals such as *Rap Sheet, Urb,* and *The Source.* She is currently studying acting and playwriting at the New School in the Actors Studio MFA Program, and dreaming on the subway in New York City.

Jeannine DeLombard is a cultural critic who lives in Philadelphia with her girlfriend, Laura. She is a graduate fellow at the Center for the Study of Black Literature and Culture at University of Pennsylvania, where she is also a doctoral candidate in English. Her work has appeared in the *New York Times Book Review, OUT, Girlfriends,* and *Lambda Book Report.*

Gina Dent is Assistant Professor of English and Afro-American Studies at Princeton University. She is the editor of *Black Popular Culture,* and speaks and writes on issues of contemporary culture, visual art, and feminist theory.

mocha jean herrup received a master's degree in media studies from the new school for social research, and is currently pursuing a ph.d. in american studies at the university of minnesota. she is also working on a video about the transgender movement. mocha jean can be reached on-line at herrup@echonyc.com.

bell hooks is a writer and professor who speaks widely on issues of race, class, and gender. Her books include *Outlaw Culture; Teaching to Transgress; Black Looks; Sisters of the Yam;* and, with Cornel West, *Breaking Bread: Insurgent Black Intellectual Life.* She is Distinguished Professor of English at City College in New York.

Lisa Jones is the author of a collection of essays, *Bulletproof Diva: Tales of Race, Sex, and Hair* (Doubleday/Anchor). She is a staff writer for the *Village Voice* and coauthor of three books with filmmaker Spike Lee. Jones's radio and stage plays have been produced nationally. A graduate of Yale University and New York University's Graduate School of Film and Television, she lives in Brooklyn, New York.

Min Jin Lee was born in Seoul, South Korea. She is a corporate attorney at the New York law firm of Haythe and Curley. Min Jin lives in New York City with her husband, Christopher.

Donna Minkowitz has been a writer for the *Village Voice, The Advocate,* and *Poz.* Her favorite topics are the gay movement, the religious right, and the emotional subtext of politics.

Elizabeth Mitchell is a Senior Editor at the political magazine *George.* She is married and lives in Brooklyn, New York.

Jason Schultz is the former coordinator of the Duke Men's Project, a national resource for college men working on issues of gender and sexuality. He is currently the Director of Special Projects for Stir Fry Productions, a company which specializes in diversity training and racial conflict resolution.

Danzy Senna has worked as a journalist for *Newsweek* and *SPIN* magazines. She is currently living in Los Angeles, where she is pursuing her MFA in Creative Writing at University of California at Irvine and writing a novel which explores race and gender passing in contemporary America.

Amruta Slee was born in Bombay, grew up in Sydney, and now lives in New York. She has worked in television and print journalism for ten years. One day she hopes to write a bestselling novel.

Gloria Steinem is one of the most influential writers, editors, and activists of our time. She travels in the United States and abroad as a lecturer and feminist organizer, and is a frequent media interviewer and spokeswoman on issues of equality. Among the many institutions/organizations she has cofounded are *Ms.* magazine, the Ms. Foundation for Women and Girls, the National Women's Caucus, the Women's Action

Alliance, and Voters for Choice. Her bestselling writings include *Outrageous Acts and Everyday Rebellions, Revolution from Within: A Book of Self-Esteem,* and *Moving Beyond Words.*

Veena Cabreros-Sud is a journalist, writer, and award-winning videomaker. She is a cofounder of Students Organizing Students (S.O.S.), a national student and youth-based reproductive rights organization, and is currently the Distribution Director at Third World Newsreel, a film production company based in New York City. She lives in New Jersey with her husband, Wesley Macawili, and their three-year-old son, Kumar Araw Kalayaan.

Greg Tate has been a staff writer at the *Village Voice* since 1986. He contributes two monthly columns to *Vibe* magazine and is currently featured as the Music Assignment Editor of *NetNoir,* "the cybergateway to Afrocentric culture" on America Online. In addition to being a cultural critic and playwright, Tate founded and is chief songwriter of the band Women in Love, whose independent CD, *The Sound of Falling Bodies at Rest,* was released in December 1994.

Jocelyn Taylor is a video artist from Washington, D.C., now living in New York. Her productions, *Father Knows Best, Looking for Labelle, 24 Hours A Day,* and *Frankie and Jocie* explore issues of coming out, sexuality, and eroticism and have been shown widely at national and international festivals. She is currently finishing *Bodily Functions,* a video about black female sexual evolution as a participant in the Whitney Museum Independent Study Program.

Veronica Webb was the first African-American woman to sign a major cosmetics contract, and is represented by the Ford Agency in New York. She is also a columnist for *Paper, Interview,* and the Italian weekly, *Panorama,* and has been a correspondent for national and international television programming such as "Front Page" (Fox), "Last Call" (CBS), and "The Sunday Show" (BBC).

Naomi Wolf is the author of *The Beauty Myth* (Anchor) and *Fire With Fire* (Ballantine). She is a frequent speaker on women's issues. She has a baby daughter and lives in Washington, D.C.

Acknowledgments

about the editor

Rebecca Walker is a contributing editor to *Ms.* magazine, and has written articles for *Harper's, Sassy, The Black Scholar,* and *Spin.* She is the cofounder of Third Wave, a national, multicultural membership organization devoted to facilitating and initiating young women's leadership and activism, and has been featured in many magazine articles and television programs about young feminists. For her work with Third Wave, she received the Feminist of the Year Award from the Fund for the Feminist Majority, the Champion of Choice Award from the California Abortion Rights Action League, and the Paz y Justicia Award from the Vanguard Public Foundation. Named by *Time* magazine as one of 50 Future Leaders of America, Rebecca lectures widely on young women and feminism and lives in Brooklyn, New York.